All-Maine Cooking

COMPLIED AND EDITED BY

Ruth Wiggin AND **Loana Shibles**

ISBN 0-89272-095-6

Cover design by Lurelle Cheverie

Printed and bound at Capital City Press, Inc., Montpelier, Vermont

30/14   29/13   28/12   27/11

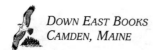

DOWN EAST BOOKS
CAMDEN, MAINE

All-Maine Cooking

Food, its preparation and its tastiness, is a favorite subject of the many fine cooks who live in the State of Maine, visit in the state or, from miles away, remember with nostalgia the recipes handed down in their own families for generations. When two Maine women, noted for their knowledge of Down East cooking, get together to compile a book of favorite recipes, everyone knows this is that special kind of cookbook which deserves a place of honor in any kitchen.

This entirely new edition of All-Maine Cooking was compiled from favorite recipes sent to Mrs. Ruth Wiggin and Mrs. Loana Shibles of Rockland by people as close as their neighbors and as far away as London, England. Maine's two Senators, Margaret Chase Smith and Edmund S. Muskie, are represented by recipes they particularly like. Many of the recipes in this book are those which have been used through generations of Maine families and never before made public. All are tested and approved Maine recipes. Many come from Colonial days and days when Maine was but a wilderness in the process of being settled by hardy pioneers.

Mrs. Wiggin and Mrs. Shibles have had long years of experience in Knox-Lincoln Extension in the homemaking and foods fields, and their work has also extended into the directing of 4-H Clubs in the Coastal area.

Among new sections in this edition of All-Maine Cooking are outdoor recipes, diabetic and sugar substitute foods, use of leftovers and preparation of game. This cookbook covers everything from soup to dessert (chowder to blueberry pie?) with many extras, seafoods, salads, breads, preserves, and main dishes to mention a few.

Altogether 326 fine cooks are represented by 523 recipes in this book. There is a page for the reader to jot down his or her own pet recipes, a handy index and a useful table of weights and measures. The recipes included were selected from the enormous quantity received from interested State of Mainers.

A friendly warning — recipes from the State of Maine are very habit forming. But — what a pleasant habit to acquire.

Zucchini Creole

6 medium-sized zucchini
3 tablespoons butter
3 tablespoons flour
3 large tomatoes
(or 2 cups canned)
1 small green pepper

1 small onion
1 teaspoon salt
1 tablespoon brown sugar
½ bay leaf
2 whole cloves

Slice zucchini thinly and place in a casserole. Melt the butter and add the flour, stir until blended. Peel, slice and chop the tomatoes, pepper and onion and add to the butter and flour. Also add salt, brown sugar, bay leaf and cloves. Cook for 5 minutes and pour over the squash. Cover with bread crumbs. Dot with butter and grated Parmesian cheese. Bake in moderate oven 350° until squash is done.

Submitted by Mrs. Andrew Olson, York Harbor, Maine

Parsnip Fritters

4 or 5 parsnips
1 teaspoon flour

1 egg, well beaten
Salt

Boil 4 or 5 parsnips until tender, remove skins and mash very fine. Add flour, salt and beaten egg. Make the mixture into small cakes and fry them on both sides in hot butter or beef drippings until golden brown. Serve very hot.

Submitted by Amy Hanscom, Newry, Maine

Stuffed Cabbage

1 large cabbage
1 pound hamburg
2 onions
½ cup bread crumbs

1 cup tomatoes
Salt and pepper
Slices of bacon or salt pork
1 cup water

Boil a large cabbage until nearly tender, in enough water to cover. Drain, cool; scoop out center very carefully. Fry 2 onions, add center taken from cabbage, chopped fine; cook for 3 minutes, and add hamburg, let sear a few minutes. Add the bread crumbs, tomatoes, salt and pepper. Fill cabbage with mixture and cover top with leaves of cabbage. Tie all firmly with a string. Bake with slices of bacon or pork; pour over all the water and bake 1 hour, basting often. Remove string and leaves and brown a little in the oven.

Submitted by Adah M. Carr, Bangor, Maine

1

Bacon and String Beans

1 can string beans (green)
2 medium potatoes, diced into
   ½ inch pieces
¼ pound bacon, diced

¼ teaspoon salt
1 small onion, chopped
1 cup hot water

Brown the bacon and combine with the other ingredients in frying pan. Cook about 30 minutes over medium heat or until potatoes are soft. Serve at once. Serves three.

Submitted by Mrs. Waldo Tyler, South Thomaston, Maine

Oven-Creamed Potatoes

Boil as many potatoes as you need. Cool, then peel. Slice into a shallow casserole. Sprinkle generously with flour and grated cheese. Turn potato slices lightly with a spoon to coat each slice. Add salt and pepper. Pour in enough milk to almost cover the potatoes. Top with grated cheese. Bake 45 minutes at 350 degrees.

Submitted by Marjorie Standish
"Cooking Down East", Portland Sunday Telegram

Lima Bean Dish

2 cups cooked macaroni
2 cups lima beans
4 hard boiled eggs
2 cups white sauce

1 cup grated cheese
1 pimiento cut in small pieces
1 slice of onion cut fine and
   cooked with macaroni

Make a white sauce and add grated cheese, remove from heat as soon as cheese is melted. Combine the macaroni and onion with the lima beans, eggs and pimiento. Place in serving dish and pour over it the white sauce. Serve hot. (No baking).

Submitted by Mrs. Clement B. Barter, Bath, Maine

Hulled Corn

1 quart corn (purchase
   grade A corn at grain store

¼ cup soda
1 tablespoon salt

Pick over the corn and wash. Let it swell overnight in a lot of cold water. Next morning add the ¼ cup soda, and cook in porcelain or iron dish, large enough so it won't boil over. Cook until tender, nearly all day. Drain liquid off and wash the corn under cold water to wash away the hulls (wash until all hulls are removed). Return the corn to cook awhile longer with clean hot water and 1 tablespoon salt; drain. Good served with milk

Submitted by Mrs. Flavilla Kennedy, Rockland, Maine

Gram Morey's Pork Stew

6 to 8 slices of salt pork
1 small turnip (cut in very small pieces)
2 quarts water

4 large potatoes (sliced)
2 large onions (sliced)
Salt and pepper

Fry out the pork slices in a kettle, add turnip and water. Cook until turnip is nearly done and add potatoes and onions. Salt and pepper to season and cook until done. This is good served with dumplings.

This recipe belonged to my grandmother, born in 1848 and lived on the sea coast in Castine all of her life.

Submitted by Mrs. Alice L. Mossler, Dover-Foxcroft, Maine

Poverty Stew

½ pound salt pork (cubed)
1 large onion (cut up)
1 quart sliced potatoes

Salt and pepper
Lump of butter

DUMPLINGS

1 cup flour
2 teaspoons baking powder
½ teaspoon salt

1 egg
Milk to make soft dough
(about ½ cup)

Fry salt pork in a kettle until lightly browned, fry onion in the fat until golden in color. Add sliced potatoes, cover with water and cook until done. Season with salt, pepper and butter. Combine flour, baking powder, salt, egg and milk to make a soft dough. Drop dumplings into the boiling soup, cover and cook 20 minutes.

Submitted by Mrs. Ella M. Webber, East Boothbay

Parsnip Stew

4 cups diced potatoes
4 cups diced parsnips
1½ quarts water
3 slices bread or 3 biscuits broken in large pieces or
10 soda crackers

1 can evaporated milk
1 quart fresh milk
2 tablespoons butter or thick cream
Pepper and salt to taste

Cook the potatoes and parsnips in the water until tender. Then add the evaporated milk, fresh milk, bread or crackers, butter, pepper and salt to taste.

Heat almost to boiling point or as for clam chowder.

Submitted by Mrs. Millard Bowden, Blue Hill, Maine

Carrot Loaf

1 teaspoon chopped onion	2 eggs, slightly beaten
3 tablespoons melted butter	1½ cups milk
1 cup bread crumbs	1 teaspoon salt
2 cups raw grated carrots	⅛ teaspoon pepper

Brown the onion in the butter and add to the bread crumbs. Add other ingredients and mix well. Put into buttered bread pan and bake in moderate oven until firm. Recommended: time 30 minutes, temperature 350°. Serves six. Your favorite cheese sauce adds much to the loaf.

Submitted by Mrs. Annie S. Porter, Skowhegan, Maine

Maine Baked Beans

3 cups beans (yellow-eyed or pea beans)	¼ teaspoon pepper
	½ teaspoon salt
¼ cup molasses	½ pound lean pork, scored
¼ cup brown sugar	(scant)
1 teaspoon dry mustard	1 whole small onion

Soak beans in water (to more than cover) overnight or parboil beans in the morning. It is not necessary to do both. If you parboil them, cover the beans well with water and bring to a boil; simmer for five minutes, drain, and rinse beans in colander under the hot water faucet.

Place whole onion and scored salt pork in the bottom of the bean pot; cover with parboiled beans. Mix molasses, brown sugar, dry mustard, pepper and salt with enough hot water to mix well. Add to beans with enough hot water to cover beans. Place cover on pot and bake in a hot oven, 400 degrees, until they begin to boil; lower temperature to 325 degrees until they are done. Add extra hot water as necessary. Keep cover on for 3 hours, then remove cover, and bake 3 hours longer. Remove onion and serve.

Submitted by Mrs. Cietta Whitmore, Rockland, Maine

Baked Beans

3 cups beans	⅛ teaspoon pepper
½ pound salt pork, scored	1 teaspoon dry mustard
1 teaspoon salt	3 tablespoons of molasses

Soak the beans overnight. In the morning add the salt, pepper, mustard and molasses and stir well. Place pork on top of beans, fill pot with hot water and bake in 325° oven for about 7-8 hours. Add water from time to time.

Submitted by Mrs. Vernon Libby, Bangor, Maine

4

Baked Beans
(Pressure Cooker Method)

2 pounds dry beans	½ teaspoon pepper
¾ pound salt pork	1 cup brown sugar (or
1 teaspoon ginger	white and 2 tablespoons
1 teaspoon mustard	molasses)

Wash beans, cover with boiling water (one inch over the beans), let set ½ hour. Drain. Place the salt pork cut in slices in bottom of pressure cooker and let fry until bottom is well covered with fat. Add the beans and cover with water about 1/3 inch over the top. Add ginger, mustard and pepper. Cook at 15 pounds pressure for 30 minutes. Take off pressure and pour immediately into an earthen bean pot and add the sugar. Cover with water and bake 2 hours at 350°

Submitted by Ruby MacDonald, Carmel, Maine

Potato Scouse

6-8 slices of salt pork	8 potatoes (sliced)
4 large onions (sliced)	Salt and pepper

Fry salt pork in iron Dutch oven or kettle. Add onions and potatoes, salt and pepper. Cover with water, stir occasionally. Cook until potatoes and onions are done and scouse has thickened. Use as little water as possible and no flour.

Fried cabbage may be made with above recipe substituting sliced cabbage for potatoes and onions.

Submitted by Mrs. Alice Mossler, Dover-Foxcroft, Maine

Corn Chowder

1 onion diced	1 can (2 cups) cream style
2 thin slices salt pork	corn
2 cups diced potatoes	2 cups evaporated milk
1 teaspoon salt	Dash pepper
2 cups boiling water	

Fry out salt pork and dice it. Add the diced onions and saute until almost transparent. Add the boiling water and diced raw potatoes and salt. When the potatoes are cooked about 10 minutes, add the corn and milk. Bring just to the scalding point. Do not boil. Serve piping hot with saltines. Serves 6. This recipe may also be used for clam chowder by substituting 1 cup minced clams for the 2 cups corn, or the flavor may be combined by 1 cup of each for a corn-clam chowder.

Submitted by Ruth H. Lamoreau, Presque Isle, Maine

Cabbage and Cheese Scallop

10 cups shredded cabbage
8 tablespoons flour
8 tablespoons fat
4 cups milk
1 cup buttered crumbs

Few grains pepper
2 teaspoons salt
2 cups finely cut cheese
2 tablespoons grated cheese

Melt the fat, in top of double boiler stir in the flour and milk gradually, stirring until thickened and smooth. Add the finely cut cheese and stir until melted. Cook the shredded cabbage in salted water 10 minutes and drain. Put in a greased baking dish a layer of cabbage and a layer of cheese sauce. Repeat until dish is full or ingredients are all used. Cover with buttered crumbs and grated cheese. Bake in a hot oven 450° for 20 minutes.

Submitted by Beatrice Harmon, Limington, Maine

Welsh Rarebit

2 cups milk
3 tablespoons flour
1 teaspoon mustard (scant)
Salt to season

2 cups grated cheese
2 egg yolks, beaten
Toasted crackers

Make a cream sauce of the milk, flour and mustard by adding a small amount of milk to the flour and mustard until it makes a thin paste; heat the remainder of the milk and add the flour paste to the hot milk, stirring until it thickens. Add salt to season; then, add the grated cheese. Cook until melted, then add the beaten egg yolks. Serve at once on toasted crackers.

Submitted by Miss Etta Beverage, North Haven

Cheese Custard

2 slices buttered bread
(cubed)
1 cup finely cut American
sharp cheese

2 eggs, beaten
2 cups milk

Place bread in a buttered casserole. Spread cheese over cubed bread. Combine eggs and milk. Pour over cheese and bread. Bake in moderate oven 350° for about ½ hour or until slightly browned.

Mrs. Pearl Norton sent in the same recipe, but substituting 4 slices of bread.

Submitted by S. Marjorie Hatch, Bar Harbor, Maine
and
Mrs. Pearl M. Norton, Limington, Maine

6

Lima Beans and Pork Chops

1 pound lima beans	½ teaspoon dry mustard
2 teaspoons salt	2 tablespoons sugar
2 tablespoons chopped onion	1 pound pork chops
½ cup ketchup	

Cook beans until almost tender. Season with salt, onion, ketchup, sugar and dry mustard. Pour into large flat baking dish. Add water to cover beans. Salt and pepper pork chops. Place on top of beans and cook one to one and a half hours at 350° or until pork chops are done.

Submitted by Mrs. Charles Tobin, St. Petersburg, Fla.

English Hot Pot

1 pound pork chops (cut up)	8 or 9 medium potatoes
3 or 4 medium onions	Salt and pepper

In a casserole, cut up or slice a layer of potatoes, a layer of onions, then a layer of the cut up pork. So on until all ingredients are used. Have the top layer potatoes, salt and pepper. Fill the dish with hot water. Bake in a moderate oven 350° for 2 or 3 hours. Cover until the last half hour. A delicious meal. Serves 4 or 5 people.

Submitted by Mrs. Langtry Smith, Vinalhaven, Maine

Chinese Spareribs With Sweet Sour Sauce

3 pounds meaty fresh pork spareribs	½ cup red wine vinegar
1 teaspoon salt	¾ cup water
1 tablespoon cornstarch	1 medium sized (or large) green pepper
1 cup dark brown sugar (firmly packed)	½ cup pineapple preserves

Arrange spareribs in large shallow pan. Sprinkle with salt. Roast in a slow oven, 325°, about 1¼ to 1½ hours or until browned. Turn once, about halfway through roasting period. Cut spareribs through every other bone so they will be in easy-to-handle pieces. In a sauce pan blend cornstarch and sugar. Gradually stir in vinegar and water until smooth. Remove stem and seeds from green pepper, cut in thin strips and add to the sauce. Cook over moderately low heat, stirring constantly until sauce is slightly thickened. Stir in pineapple preserves and heat thoroughly. Pour sauce over hot spareribs and serve at once over rice. Sauce with spareribs may be reheated. Serves 4.

Submitted by Mrs. Carol Howe, Bangor, Maine

One Dish Lamb Dinner

6 or 8 lamb chops
1 bunch carrots
1 bunch parsnips
2 green peppers (cut in rings)
4 onions (cut in slices)
8 potatoes (quartered)
1 large can whole tomatoes
1 teaspoon sugar (add to tomatoes)
1 tablespoon mint sauce

Partly fry lamb chops, brown on both sides. Cook vegetables 15 minutes, cook in as little water as possible. Save juices and add to tomatoes. Grease a large casserole or pan with butter, place chops on the bottom. Add all vegetables and juices. Add pepper rings, then the can of tomatoes with sugar and mint sauce. Bake 1 hour at 350° oven. (This can also be made with pork chops.)

Submitted by Mrs. John J. Shyne, Rockland, Maine

Pork Chops In Casserole

4½ cups potatoes sliced thinly
½ cup onions finely chopped
6 pork chops (cut ¾-in. thick)
1½ teaspoons salt
Pepper (a few grains)
1½ cans condensed tomato soup

In a large baking dish (about 2½ quart size) arrange alternate layers of potatoes and onions.

Brown pork chops in a skillet, with small amount of fat, season with salt and pepper and lay on top of potatoes and onions.

Pour tomato soup over potatoes and chops. Cover — put on lower oven rack. Cook for 1 hour at 375°.

Submitted by Mrs. L. T. Philbrick, North Leeds, Maine

Batter Sausage

1 pound of sausages
3 eggs
4 tablespoons flour
3 cups milk
Salt and pepper

Prick sausages and bake slowly in a deep dish, then pour off the fat. Make a batter of the eggs, flour, milk, salt and pepper to taste. Pour batter over sausages and bake 350° for about 45 minutes.

Submitted by Mrs. Donald O. Hanscom, South Paris, Maine

Raisin Sauce For Ham

½ cup brown sugar
½ tablespoon flour
½ tablespoon mustard
1½ cups water
½ cup vinegar
½ cup raisins

Mix all ingredients in a saucepan and cook to a syrup.

8

Stuffed Ham Slices

2 cups bread crumbs
2 tablespoons soft butter
½ cup chopped nuts
¼ cup chopped onion
¾ cup chopped celery

½ teaspoon poultry seasoning
⅛ teaspoon pepper
1 small can crushed pineapple
2 slices of ham

Mix all ingredients in order given. Put between 2 slices of ham and bake at 350° for 1 hour.

Submitted by Mrs. Mamie Ellis, Skowhegan, Maine

Baked Ham Supreme

Ham (size for your family)
2 tablespoons flour
1 tablespoon dry mustard
Cloves (whole cloves or ½
teaspoon ground)

Pineapple juice and slices
1 can whole cranberry sauce
or 1 jar of orange and
cranberry relish

Boil ham ¾ of an hour to remove excess fat and skin. Score like any ham. Make a paste of flour and mustard mixed with pineapple juice. Spread over the ham. Stud with cloves and spread over all 1 can of whole cranberry sauce or 1 jar of orange and cranberry relish (we like the relish better) (½ taspoon of ground cloves may be used in place of whole cloves, mix with flour mixture). Garnish with pineapple slices and pineapple juice. Bake in 350 oven 1 hour, basting while cooking.

Note: I have also found that whole cranberry sauce spread over baked stuffed chicken before baking is delicious. In my opinion it doesn't ruin the gravy, it makes a festive looking meal and adds variation to the meal.

Submitted by Mrs. Leo Russell, Bangor, Maine

Upside Down Ham Loaf

1/3 cup light brown sugar
1 cup drained crushed
pineapple
1 pound ground smoked ham
or shoulder

1 pound ground pork
1 cup dry bread crumbs
¼ teaspoon pepper
2 beaten eggs
1 cup milk

Sprinkle brown sugar over bottom of greased 5½ x 10½ inch loaf pan. Cover with crushed pineapple. Mix the ham and pork, bread crumbs, pepper, eggs and milk thoroughly and pack in the pan. Bake 1¼ hours at 375°. Turn upside down on a platter and serve.

Submitted by Miss Brenda Hemphill, Presque Isle, Maine

9

Use of Chicken Fat

(Method of Trying Out)

Those of you who use much chicken should try out your chicken fat and use it in cooking instead of butter and other fats. Try out by washing the fat and adding just enough water to cover until water has cooked away by simmering gently. Strain using fine strainer or cheesecloth. Pour into glass receptacle and use as needed for the following items. Keep in refrigerator.

WAFFLES WITH SAUSAGE

2 eggs

½ cup melted chicken fat

2 cups flour

2 cups milk

4 teaspoons baking powder

1 teaspoon salt

If sour cream is available, use ¼ cup and a pinch of soda. Mix above ingredients and bake in a waffle iron. Serve with maple syrup.

HOME-MADE SAUSAGE

10 pounds pork (half fat, half lean)

1 ounce pepper

4 ounces salt

½ ounce sage

Summer savory, if desired

Grind pork twice and add seasonings. Add hot water, a bit at a time and work in thoroughly. Stuff in cloth bags or double duty refrigerator foil in 1 pound packages. Store in cold place.

FARM GINGERBREAD

½ cup sugar

¼ cup chicken fat

1 egg

½ cup sour or buttermilk

½ cup molasses

1¾ cups flour

1 teaspoon soda

1 teaspoon cinnamon

1½ teaspoons ginger

¼ teaspoon salt

Mix in order given, mixing buttermilk and molasses together. Bake at 375 degrees for about 40 minutes or until it tests done.

Submitted by Mrs. Clemice B. Pease, Rockland, Maine

Pastry With Poultry Fat

Excellent pastry may be made from any poultry fat, such as goose, turkey or chicken. Use your regular pastry rule less one tablespoon of fat in measure. The fats must be cold and, in making the dough, handle quickly and lightly, so the fats do not become oily, but the crusts are light, tender and flaky. Render the poultry fat in a double boiler, strain and keep cold.

My regular pie rule is: One cup and one-half of flour (sifted measure), one-half a teaspoon of salt, one-half a cup shortening, one tablespoon of vinegar in five tablespoons of water (this is the proportion of the mixture, though I use as little liquid as possible. Lemon juice is fine but vinegar is cheaper).

Chicken Spaghetti Tetrazzini

½ pound spaghetti
1 medium chicken (4½ to 5 pounds)
⅛ pound butter
1 medium sized green pepper (cut in small pieces)
2½ cups diced celery

1 cup mushrooms (cut small)
2/3 stick butter
3 tablespoons flour
Chicken broth and rich milk to make 3 cups white sauce
2 tablespoons pimiento (cut fine)

Cook spaghetti in boiling salted water. Wash chicken in cold water, cook and dice. Saute in the ⅛ pound butter the green pepper, celery and mushrooms. Make 3 cups of rich white sauce using 2/3 stick of butter, the flour, chicken broth and rich milk. Combine chicken, spaghetti and vegetables, adding the pimiento. Pour the cream sauce over the chicken mixture and bake at 400° for 1 hour or until light brown.

Submitted by Mrs. Rita Ridgway, Lewiston, Maine

Chicken Pie

1 stewing chicken, cut up
12 small, whole onions
Salt and pepper to taste

4 tablespoons flour
1 cup milk

Cook the cut-up chicken, and onions, separately in salted water until tender. Remove the meat from the bones and place it in a buttered baking dish. Drain onions, being careful to keep them whole. Add to the chicken. Bring 4 cups of chicken broth to boil. Make thickening of milk and flour and stir into the boiling broth; add salt and pepper to taste. Stir until smooth and creamy. Pour, bubbling hot, over the chicken. Seal the top with rich biscuit or pastry crust.

BISCUIT CRUST

Sift together 2 cups flour, 2 teaspoons baking powder, 1 teaspoon salt. Cut in 2 tablespoons butter. Beat 1 egg in 1 cup milk and mix lightly into dry ingredients. Pat out on floured board. Cut hole to let steam escape, and fit over chicken pie. Bake at 450F. for 15-20 minutes until browned.

Submitted by Mrs. Sally K. Field, Bangor, Maine

Chinese Fried Chicken

1 broiler chicken   2 cups cream
  (cut up in pieces)   ½ teaspoon Worcestershire
1 teaspoon dry mustard   sauce
1 teaspoon salt   Flour, salt, pepper

Roll pieces of chicken in flour, salt and pepper. Pack these chicken pieces in a baking dish with straight sides. Fill the cracks between the chicken pieces with small pieces of bread. Dissolve 1 teaspoon of salt in the 2 cups of cream, add mustard and Worcestershire sauce. Pour this over the chicken. Let stand in refrigerator 4 to 6 hours. Bake at 400° for 1 hour. Take off cover and let brown.

Submitted by Mrs. Ernest Darling, Hampden, Maine

Potted Chicken
(An old-time church supper dish)

3 pound chicken, cut up   Dash white pepper
6 tablespoons flour   Crockery bean pot
1½ teaspoons salt

Cut up chicken as for fricassee. To each pound of meat allow 2 tablespoons of flour and season to taste. Mix flour and seasonings thoroughly. Roll each piece of meat in the mixture. Pack closely in a crockery bean pot and cover with boiling water. Bake in oven, about 350 degrees until it begins to boil, without the cover. After it starts to boil, cover, and let bake slowly at 325 degrees for 3½ hours.

Submitted by Mrs. Etta Anderson, Rockland, Maine

Savory Sausage Balls
(For Roast Turkey)

2 sticks celery   Salt
1 pound pork sausage meat Freshly ground black pepper
2 tablespoons crushed potato   to taste
  chips   Egg
½ teaspoon basil

Finely chop the washed celery. Mix with sausage meat, crushed chips, basil, salt and pepper to taste. Bind with beaten egg. Shape the mixture into balls. Thirty minutes before the end of cooking time, turn the oven up to 425°. Remove foil from the bird and place savory sausage balls around the bird to cook.

Submitted by Mrs. Dolores Naiva, So. Bristol, Maine

Baked Pickled Tripe

1½ pounds pickled tripe
Egg batter (beaten egg, about
2 eggs)

1 onion, cut up
3 green sweet peppers, sliced
1 can tomato soup

Put tripe on stove in water and let come to a boil. Take out, dry, cut in serving pieces, and dip tripe in egg batter and line baking dish with tripe. Pour over it sauce of onion and three peppers that have been cooked in butter with 1 can of tomato soup. Sprinkle top with cracker crumbs. Bake 1 hour (about 350°).

Submitted by Harold W. Libby, Easton, Maine

Busy Day Casserole

2 cups whipped potatoes
1 pound ground beef
1 medium sized onion
1 can cream style corn

1 10¾-oz. can tomato soup
½ teaspoon salt
¼ teaspoon pepper
Paprika

Break beef into small pieces in a fry pan and dice onion into it; fry until beef is cooked, then add tomato soup and can of corn, stir until mixed, also add salt and pepper.

Pour into a greased casserole dish and spread the whipped potatoes over the top. Bake 350° oven until the top of potatoes brown. Remove from oven and sprinkle with paprika. Serves 4-6.

Submitted by Mrs. Gertrude Goodrich, Skowhegan, Maine

Hawaiian Meat Balls

1 pound hamburg
1 teaspoon salt
¼ teaspoon ginger
1 egg
1 teaspoon water
½ cup flour
3 tablespoons of cooking oil

1 can chunk pineapple
¼ cup brown sugar
2 tablespoons cornstarch
¼ cup vinegar
1 tablespoon soy sauce
2 green peppers

Mix hamburg, salt and ginger well with the hands and shape into balls a little larger than a walnut.

Beat together egg and water, dip meat balls in egg mixture and roll in flour. Heat oil in an iron fry pan and brown meat. Remove from pan. Drain syrup from pineapple and add enough water to make 1 cup (reserve pineapple 'till later). Stir juice and water into pan of drippings, add brown sugar, cornstarch, vinegar and soy sauce. Cook 3 minutes, then add meat balls, peppers cut in strips and pineapple chunks. Stir well and simmer 15 minutes.

Submitted by Mrs. May Larkin, Howland, Maine

13

Italian Meat Balls In Tomato Sauce
SAUCE

1 onion, chopped
1½ tablespoons oil
1 can tomato paste
1 can water (paste can)
1 large can tomatoes

1 teaspoon sugar
¼ teaspoon basil
½ teaspoon parsley flakes
Salt and pepper to taste

MEAT BALLS

2 pounds hamburg
½ teaspoon minced garlic
2 onions, cut fine
3 cups bread crumbs
3 eggs

¼ cup grated parmesan
    cheese
1 teaspoon parsley flakes
Salt and pepper to taste

Fry the onion in the oil and add all the other sauce ingredients and cook slowly for 1 hour.

Mix the hamburg with all of the other ingredients for the balls. Roll in small balls and fry in vegetable oil. Keep turning until half cooked, then place meat balls in the sauce and continue cooking ½ hour, or until meat balls are as tender as you like.

Submitted by Mrs. Helen Spear, Rockland, Maine

Chinese Pepper Steak With Rice

1 pound slice of top round
steak (thin slice)
2 green peppers, thin strips
½ cup celery, thin crosswise
    slices
2 tablespoons minced onion
1 clove garlic
2 tablespoons salad oil

½ cup consomme (or hot
    water and bouillon cube)
Salt and pepper to taste
2 teaspoons cornstarch
2 tablespoons water
1 teaspoon soy sauce
Freshly boiled rice

Cut the top round diagonally against the grain in thin strips. Put the salad oil in a skillet. When it is good and hot put in beef slices. Stir quickly over high heat until beef is seared and brown. Add onion, garlic, green peppers and celery. Add the consomme or bouillon stock. Season with salt and pepper. Cover pan. Turn down heat to moderate and cook just five minutes. Thicken with the cornstarch blended with the cold water and soy sauce. Simmer five minutes more. Serve immediately with freshly boiled rice.

Submitted by Mrs. Stanley R. Tupper, Washington, D. C.

(Home Address, Boothbay Harbor, Maine)

Potted Beef

1½ pounds stew beef
6 carrots
1 green pepper
1 onion

1 can tomato paste
Salt and pepper
Crisco or salad oil

Simmer stew beef until tender. Salt and pepper. Cover bottom of fry pan with fat. Scrape carrots and slice, cut up green pepper and onion. Put vegetables in fry pan with fat and cook for a few minutes. Add tomato paste and 1 can of water. Add simmered beef and cook until carrots are tender. This is tender and delicious, cooked in this manner.

Serve with mashed potato, green beans and salad.

Submitted by Mrs. Raymond O'Brien, Rockland, Maine

Chinese Chop Suey

1 pound hamburg
1¼ cups of onions
1¼ cups celery

1 can bean sprouts
3 or 4 tablespoons soy sauce
Salt and pepper to taste

Fry hamburg in kettle with a little cooking oil or oleo. When brown add onions, cut in small pieces, also celery cut in small pieces and then soy sauce, salt and pepper. Cover with 3 cups of water and cook slowly until vegetables are done, adding water if needed. (Use water from bean sprouts). When cooked add one can of drained bean sprouts and heat well, add 2½ tablespoons of corn starch mixed with water for thickening. This is good for a main dish or served on toast for lunch.

Submitted by Mrs. Ada R. Reed, Millinocket, Maine

Nan's Skillet Spaghetti

1 pound hamburg
1 cup chopped onions
2 medium garlic cloves,
    chopped
1 can tomato paste
1 can tomato sauce
1 pint can tomato juice

1 cup water
2 teaspoons salt, little pepper
1 teaspoon sugar
1 teaspoon oregano
1 tablespoon chili powder
    (optional)

Cook hamburg, onions and garlic in small amount of fat. Then add the rest of the ingredients. Cook about 30 minutes. Serve on spaghetti.

Submitted by Mrs. Vernon Libby, Bangor, Maine

15

Casserole Of Beef

2 pounds round steak
1 carrot
1 turnip
4 onions
6 potatoes
1 tablespoon celery flakes
1 teaspoon salt
¼ teaspoon pepper

Cut the round steak in pieces and fry brown in a spider. Put the meat in a casserole with a little water and cook 1 hour at 325 degrees. Cut the vegetables in small pieces and fry in a generous amount of salt pork. After meat has cooked 1 hour add fried vegetables with pork fat, salt and pepper and enough water to make the whole moist. Cover and cook 2 to 3 hours at 325°.

Submitted by Mrs. Ruth E. Pratt, Farmington, Maine

Yorkshire Pudding

Roast beef or pork with
brown gravy
1 cup flour
1 teaspoon baking powder
¼ teaspoon salt
1 egg
1 pint milk

Combine above ingredients and beat well. Have ready 9" x 9" cake tin with about one half inch drippings from roast, *smoking hot.* Pour in the batter and place in hot oven 450°. Bake until done, about 20 minutes. (While thickening the gravy, taking up vegetables, etc.) Upon removing from oven cut in squares and serve piping hot immediately with brown gravy.

This recipe was given me by my husband's grandmother, Mrs. Fred Chase of Atkinson, Maine, in the winter of 1926.

Submitted by Inga J. Chase, Glen Cove, Maine

Hamburg Steak Pie

1 pound hamburg
2 medium size onions
2 tablespoons fat
4 potatoes (cubed)
3 carrots (diced)
1 or 2 teaspoons celery salt
¼ teaspoon salt
½ teaspoon pepper
2 tablespoons flour
2 cups water
Short biscuit crust
(or pie crust)

Place hamburg in frying pan, break up with fork, add onions and fat, brown slightly. Put in seasonings and water, simmer gently until potatoes and carrots are done. Add the flour smoothed to a paste in 3 tablespoons of cold water. Bring to boiling point. Pour into a deep casserole and cover with crust. Bake until crust is brown, about 25 minutes in 375° oven.

Submitted by Mrs. Agenard Bourret, Rumford, Maine

American Piece-A-Pie

1 cake yeast or dry yeast
¼ cup lukewarm water
1 unbeaten egg
¼ cup tomato sauce
   (¼ of 8 oz. can)
3 tablespoons melted veg.
   shortening

1 tablespoon sugar
1 teaspoon salt
½ teaspoon chili powder
2 cups sifted flour
2 tablespoons melted butter
   or oleo
2 cups shredded cheese

Soften yeast in the lukewarm water in a large bowl. Let stand 5 minutes. Add the unbeaten egg, tomato sauce, melted shortening, sugar, salt and chili powder. Blend thoroughly. Gradually add the sifted flour, blending thoroughly after each addition. Knead on well floured board until smooth, about 2 to 3 minutes. Cover, and let rise in a warm place until double in bulk, about 1 hour.

After dough is double in bulk, put on greased 15 x 11 inch baking sheet and pat or roll out until it is within ½ inch of the sheet. Brush with the melted butter and spread with the hamburger topping. Sprinkle with the shredded cheese (strong or mild). Bake in hot oven 425 degrees 15 to 18 minutes. Serve hot.

HAMBURGER TOPPING

½ pound ground beef
¼ cup chopped onion
¾ cup tomato sauce
   (remainder of can)

½ teaspoon chili powder
½ teaspoon salt
⅛ teaspoon pepper

Saute the ground beef and onion in skillet until partially cooked but not browned. Add the tomato sauce, chili powder, salt and pepper.

Submitted by Mrs. Mary Baum, Kittery, Maine

Meat Loaf

1 pound ground beef
1½ teaspoons salt
1 teaspoon poultry seasoning
2 cups bread crumbs
1½ cups milk

1 large carrot
1 large onion
2 stalks celery (trim off leaves)
2 large eggs, well beaten

Add salt and poultry seasoning to the meat, blend well. Mix the crumbs and milk with the meat. Put the vegetables, carrot, onion and celery, through the food chopper, and also add to the meat with the beaten eggs. Mix thoroughly. Pack into a well greased casserole (about 2 quart size). Cover and bake in a moderate oven 350° for 1 hour. Uncover and bake until top of meat loaf is browned.

Submitted by Miss Elsie Swanson, Bar Harbor, Maine

Grandmother's Meat Loaf

1 pound hamburg	1 teaspoon salt
½ pound ground veal	¼ teaspoon pepper
½ pound ground lamb	1 tablespoon butter
½ green pepper (chopped very fine)	2 eggs, slightly beaten
	½ cup water
1 onion (chopped fine)	1 can tomato soup
4 slices of white bread	

Soak the bread in warm water and drain well. Add bread to ground meat with the green pepper, onion, salt and pepper and eggs. Mix all together well. Form into loaf and place in a slightly greased baking pan. Pour the tomato soup over the top of the loaf. Dot with butter and lastly pour the ½ cup of water into the pan. Bake in a 350° oven for 1½ hours. Serve hot or cold. Garnish with parsley. In cooking, the soup will form a rich tomato colored gravy.

Submitted by Mrs. Shirley B. Grant, Brunswick, Maine

Smothered Meat Balls

½ cup milk	¾ pound ground beef
1 egg	1 cup onions, sliced
½ cup fine bread crumbs	4 medium potatoes
1 teaspoon salt	(cut in halves)
¼ teaspoon pepper	Salt
⅛ teaspoon nutmeg	

Combine the milk, egg, bread crumbs, salt and pepper, nutmeg and ground beef. Form into balls about 1 tablespoon each. Brown in hot fat in pressure cooker and add onions. Stir carefully to distribute onions in browned meat. Add the potatoes and sprinkle with a little salt. Cover and cook at 15 pounds pressure for 8 minutes. Reduce pressure quickly.

Submitted by Orilla Sampson, North Haven, Maine

Cooking Lean Beef

Salt pork	1 large onion, cut up
Lean beef	Salt and pepper to taste

Cut salt pork in small pieces and with a pointed knife insert the pieces of pork into the beef; using the amount of beef, according to the size of your family. Cut up the onion and place in an unbreakable bowl. Rub the beef with salt and pepper and place on the onion. Set the bowl in a kettle one-half full of boiling water; steam 4 hours. A rich gravy and tender meat results.

Submitted by Mrs. Maurice Glidden, Cooper's Mills, Maine

Oven Barbecued Steaks For 50

(A Church Supper Favorite)

15 pounds round steak (¾ inch thick)
(or chuck roast, cut in thick slabs)
½ cup salad oil
2 cups onions, thinly sliced
1 quart catsup
2 cups vinegar
½ cup brown sugar, packed
1½ quarts water
½ cup prepared mustard
¼ cup Worcestershire sauce
1 tablespoon salt
½ teaspoon pepper

Equipment needed: 2 large heavy skillets, 2 large roasting pans 12" x 15" x 5".

Cut steaks in 50 fairly equal portions or if you can get chuck roast on sale, have it cut for you in thick slabs. Pour ¼ cup saled oil into each skillet. Brown steaks on both sides, transfer to roasting pans. Pan fry onions in skillets. Add half of remaining ingredients to onions in each skillet. Stir and simmer 5 minutes. Pour one skilletful of sauce over steaks in each roasting pan. Cover pans. Bake in a moderate oven, 350 degrees for 2 to 2½ hours or until meat is tender.

Suggestions: Steaks may be kept in a slow oven (300 degrees) for an additional hour. It is well to move steaks around in sauce after first hour of baking to be sure each piece is covered with sauce.

Submitted by Mertie Sorensen, Port Clyde, Maine

Spanish Omelet

4 ounces bacon
1 small onion
1 medium sized tomato
5 mushrooms
Clove of garlic
6 eggs
½ teaspoon salt
Few grains pepper
1 teaspoon butter

Cut sliced bacon into half inch squares; fry gently till crisp, add the onion, tomato and mushrooms all chopped fine; rub a freshly cut clove of garlic on the spoon used to stir, while cooking 15 minutes. Break eggs into a bowl, season with salt and pepper. Give them a dozen or so strong strokes and turn into a frying pan, in which the butter has been melted and spread over the bottom and sides. Shake as usual, until nearly set. Spread the bacon and vegetables quickly over, fold, set it in the oven for one minute, turn it upon a heated platter and serve at once.

Submitted by Mrs. Christine MacDonald, Gardiner, Maine

Lobster Shortcake
(Mother's Recipe Since 1900)

4 cups lobster meat
2 cups cream
¼ pound butter or more (to fry lobster)
Pepper and salt to taste

1 tablespoon flour
¼ cup milk
Little sugar
Sprinkle of paprika

Melt butter in a large skillet. Add the lobster meat. Fry until red and dry and fat appears in the butter. Add cream, heat to boiling. Thicken slightly with the 1 tablespoon of flour wet-up-in the ¼ cup of cold milk. Add seasonings. Serve hot over light cream tartar biscuits split and buttered.

(Mother served this on special occasions.)

Submitted by Sue F. Bridges, Sedgwick, Maine

Lobster Stew

After boiling the number of lobsters you will require for your stew, remove the meat from the lobsters and place this in a cold dish. Save all the lobster shells except the back and head portion, after removing and throwing away the sac in the body shell of the lobsters.

Now take all the shells, body meat and small claws and place them in a large heavy kettle or bowl, and pound these thoroughly. Next place all this in a kettle and add two cups of hot water, cover and boil for about three minutes. Drain off a cupful of this liquid through a sieve and add it to your stew also any liquid left from the lobster meat that has been cooling. You may make your stew in your favorite way but the liquid from the shells should give it a real Down East flavor.

Submitted by James L. Burns, Rockland, Maine
(Skipper of "Looking Astern")

Lobster Stew

1 lobster (cooked)
1 quart milk

2 tablespoons butter
Salt and pepper to taste

Take out lobster meat. Save juice. Simmer lobster meat in butter. Season to taste. Add to milk. Add lobster juice. Heat below simmering point. Cream may be added to make a richer stew. Better if it sets for 4 or 5 hours in refrigerator. Do not cover hot stew until it is cold, then cover with a loose cover, like wax paper. Reheat below boiling point. Serve hot.

Submitted by Patricia Jones, Palermo, Maine

Lobster Casserole

Served often in the Blaine House

1¼ to 1½ pounds clear lobster meat
4 tablespoons butter
3 to 4 tablespoons flour
¾ teaspoon dry mustard

5 slices bread
1 pint all purpose cream
(medium cream)
F.g. salt
Paprika

Cut lobster meat into bite size and heat in small amount of butter until slightly warm. Make a sauce of the butter, flour, dry mustard, paprika, and part of the cream (about half). Combine with lobster meat. Break bread into small pieces and mix with sauce and lobster meat. (Do not use crust of bread). Add rest of cream or as much as needed to give a medium thickness to mixture. Finally, add 3 to 4 tablespoons of sherry. Put mixture in casserole dish.

TOPPING

When ready to heat, make a topping of cracker crumbs. Crush crackers very fine, warm in pan with butter until lightly browned. Spread this over casserole and bake in 325° oven for 20 minutes or until golden brown on top and bubbling. Serves 8 to 10.

Submitted by Mrs. John H. Reed, Fort Fairfield, Maine

Lobster Casserole

1½ cups lobster meat
1 cup milk
1 cup soft bread crumbs
1 egg well beaten

½ teaspoon dry mustard
2 tablespoons butter
1 tablespoon lemon juice
Crushed cornflakes

Combine all ingredients in a baking dish and top with crushed cornflakes. Bake at 350° for 1 hour.

Submitted by Mrs. Eleanor Conway, Vinalhaven, Maine

Fisherman's Cream Lobster

Use 2 ounces or more (according to the number you want to serve) of fresh lobster meat. Saute in plenty of butter until lobster starts to brown. Stir in enough evaporated milk until you can scoop it up with a spoon. Simmer and stir for 5 minutes or more to let the milk soak up the lobster flavor. Serve hot in a warm dish on toast. This will surprise you. It is delicious. If you should have any left, add some hot milk for a delicious stew.

Submitted by Capt. Ote Lewis, Ash Point, Maine

Baked Stuffed Maine Lobsters

8 lobsters (total about 12 lbs.)
12 egg yolks
1 pint heavy cream
½ cup rum or brandy
1 cup sherry wine

1 large can sliced mushrooms
6 green peppers (small)
6 tablespoons Parmesan cheese
2 tablespoons chopped parsley
Salt and pepper to taste

Boil lobsters about 7 minutes. Take all meat out of shells and claws. Cut in ½ inch square cubes. Reserve shell to stuff later. Warm heavy cream in double boiler and add egg yolks well beaten into paste. Add sherry, brandy, salt and pepper and Parmesan cheese. Saute mushrooms, green peppers and lobster meat separately. Combine all ingredients and stuff lobster shells. Garnish with bread crumbs and few thin strips of Swiss cheese. Bake at 375° for 15 minutes. Serve hot. Serves 8 persons. (May be made the day before.)

Submitted by Alice Kyros (Mrs. Peter), Portland, Maine

Maine Baked Stuffed Lobster

4 lobsters (alive)
1½ cups cracker crumbs
½ teaspoon salt

4 tablespoons butter (melted)
2 tablespoons hot water

Select 4 lobsters of one size. Split with a sharp pointed knife from head to tail. Open lobster flat. Remove intestinal vein, stomach and liver (tomalley). If you wish, save tomalley for adding to dressing. Crack claws. Prepare dressing by moistening crumbs with melted butter and hot water, add salt and liver.. Spread dressing generously in cavity and split of tail. Bake on cookie sheet in 450 degree oven for 20 minutes or until meat is loose in shell.

Submitted by Mrs. Edmund S. Muskie, Washington, D. C.
(Home address, Waterville, Maine)

Our Favorite Lobster

Raw lobster tails
2 eggs

Flour

Split in half raw tails, wash and dry on paper towels; then dip in beaten eggs, then roll in flour. Fry to golden brown in fat including some pork scraps. Season to taste. Lobster tails are shelled out easy when broken from main part of lobster, then pour boiling water over some and scoop out with a fork.

Submitted by Mrs. Bodine Ames, Matinicus, Maine

Lobster a la Newburg

½ pint of cream
1 tablespoon butter
1 tablespoon flour
Salt and cayenne pepper (few grains)

Yolks of 2 eggs
1 large lobster cooked, cut in pieces
Juice of half a lemon
Wine glass of sherry

Make a cream of the cream, butter, flour and egg yolks, season with salt and very little cayenne. Put the lobster meat in a double boiler and when hot, add the creamed mixture, allowing it to come just to a boil, then add the juice of half a lemon and a wine glass of sherry.

This was a recipe of Mrs. J. M. Wakefield, the wife of Warren's long time and much beloved physician.

Submitted by Marion C. Wood, Farmington, Maine

Cusk Custard

1 cup fresh fish, steamed
1 cup milk

1 egg
½ teaspoon salt, f. g. pepper

Bone and flake fish then beat egg, milk and seasoning and combine. Bake slowly 'till custard is set. One can of salmon can be used in place of fresh cusk.

Submitted by Hazel Hanscom, South Paris, Maine

Fish Crumb Pudding

6 tablespoons shortening
6 tablespoons flour
2 cups milk
¼ teaspoon salt

⅛ teaspoon pepper
¼ teaspoon celery salt
2 cups flaked haddock
1 cup buttered bread crumbs

Melt shortening, blend in flour. add milk, salt, pepper and celery salt, stirring until thickened. Add flaked fish. Place in a casserole, top with buttered crumbs and bake in hot oven 425° until browned. This also makes an excellent pie with crust as follows:

4 cups of soft bread crumbs
2 tablespoons minced onion
½ teaspoon celery salt
1 teaspoon salt

¼ teaspoon sage
1/3 teaspoon pepper
½ cup melted butter

Combine all ingredients. Press into well oiled 2 quart casserole and up sides of casserole. Bake at 375° for 25 minutes or until crust is brown. Pour in the filling, top with buttered crumbs and bake in hot oven 425° until browned.

Submitted by Mrs. Shirley Haraden, Bar Harbor

Mussel Ridge Fish Chowder
(To Serve 50 to 60)
Served Many Times at the Mussel Ridge Suppers

15 pounds fresh haddock fillets

2 tablespoons salt

1½ pounds salt pork, cut in
small cubes

3 pounds onions, sliced

1 peck potatoes, cubed

2 gallons milk

2 cans evaporated milk

1 pound butter

1 cup flour with water to
make paste

Cook fresh fish 10 minutes, drain, save water. Set fish to cool, as this is added last, just before serving to eliminate breaking up. Fry out salt pork, cut into small cubes; remove the cubes after they become brown and set aside to serve separately.

Slice onions and fry lightly in pork fat; add cubed potatoes to onion mixture and the remaining fish water, cooking until potatoes are tender. Add regular milk, evaporated milk and butter and let stand several hours, if possible, for flavor. This mixture may be divided in half at this time into two large double boilers so your chowder may be re-heated without scorching. At this time mix the flour and water to thicken slightly the chowder so that it is not a sloppy mixture; and the very last thing add the 15 pounds of fish (divided if you are using two double boilers). Stir as little as possible so that fish is not broken up. Four pounds of crackers or pilot bread will be needed to serve with this and of course nice dill or sour pickles.

My grandmother served this family style from a huge soup tureen and floated common round crackers on top until they looked like dumplings.

Submitted by Mrs. Clemice B. Pease, Rockland, Maine

Penobscot Bay Muddled Haddock
(Old Sea Coast Recipe)

Four slices of salt pork

1 haddock 3 to 4 pounds

Flour (to thicken)

Salt and pepper

Fry salt pork until crisp, crumble and leave in kettle with fat. Add haddock and water to cover. Cook until haddock leaves bones. Carefully remove haddock from water, remove bones and skin. Slightly thicken the liquid with flour. Add salt and pepper to taste. Then add chunks of haddock.

Submitted by Mrs. Alice Mossler, Dover-Foxcroft, Maine

Fillet Rollups

1½ pounds fish fillets (any kind)
1½ cups milk
1 teaspoon salt
Sprinkling of pepper

¼ pound Cheddar cheese
3 tablespoons butter or oleo
3 tablespoons flour
2 teaspoons Worcestershire sauce

Split fillets into 2 inch wide strips, roll up lengthways, secure with toothpicks and place in greased shallow pan, or casserole. Pour milk over and around fish rolls, add salt and pepper and cook uncovered in 350° oven around 30 minutes or until flaky. Melt butter or oleo in top of double boiler. Remove from heat, add flour and mix thoroughly. When fish are done, turn milk off into flour mixture stirring constantly. Now place milk and flour mixture over boiling water and stir until thickened. Add cheese (shredded) and stir until melted into smooth sauce. Add Worcestershire and mix thoroughly. Pour evenly over fish and return to oven for light browning.

Submitted by R. Waldo Tyler, South Thomaston, Maine

Baked Haddock With Stuffing

Four pound haddock
Salt and pepper to season
Salt pork (about ¼ pound)

3 tablespoons melted butter
Flour (about ½ cup)

STUFFING

½ cup cracker crumbs
1 cup bread crumbs
¼ cup melted butter
¼ teaspoon salt

⅛ teaspoon pepper
½ cup hot water
Onion juice (few drops)

Clean a four pound haddock, sprinkle with salt inside and out, stuff and sew. Cut gashes on each side of backbone and insert narrow strips of fat salt pork. Place on greased paper in a baking pan, sprinkle with pepper, brush over with melted butter; roll in flour. Place around the fish small pieces of fat pork. Bake one hour in hot oven (400°). Baste with the drippings in the pan. Stuffing—Mix ingredients in the order given and use as directed above. Serve with egg sauce.

EGG SAUCE

1/3 cup butter
3 tablespoons flour
1½ cups hot water
½ teaspoon salt

1/3 teaspoon pepper
2 egg yolks, beaten
1 teaspoon lemon juice

Mix the butter, flour, salt and pepper and add the hot water gradually. Boil about five minutes, then add beaten yolks of two eggs and the lemon juice and serve over the hot fish.

Submitted by Mrs. Ella M. Webber, East Boothbay

Shrimp And Onion Dinner

12 small white onions	3 cups warm milk
4½ tablespoons butter	2 egg yolks
4½ tablespoons flour	2½ cups cooked shrinp
¾ teaspoon salt	2½ cups hot mashed potatoes
⅛ teaspoon pepper	½ cup grated cheese
½ teaspoon celery salt	

Peel onions and cook rapidly until tender, but do not fall apart. Drain. Prepare a white sauce by melting the butter over direct heat. Combine flour with salt, pepper and celery salt and add to melted butter slowly, cooking and stirring until mixture is well blended and bubbling. Gradually add the milk stirring constantly. When smooth and thickened remove from heat. Add a little of the white sauce to slightly beaten egg yolks, and add to the white sauce, stir well then return to low heat and cook 2 minutes. Add shrimp and drained onions. Turn into greased heat-resistant serving dish. Arrange a narrow border of hot mashed potatoes around the edge of the dish, sprinkle grated cheese over all, slide under broiler until brown or in a hot oven. Serves 6.

Submitted by Josephine Seliger, Rockland, Maine

Hot Crab Sandwich

12 slices of white bread, 6 for bottom, 6 for top	½ teaspoon Accent
	½ pound cheddar cheese (grated)
2 cups of crabmeat (fresh or canned)	
	4 eggs
½ teaspoon salt	3 cups milk

Remove crusts from the 12 slices of bread and butter both sides. Place 6 slices in bottom of glass baking dish (about 9 x 13 size) Cover the buttered bread with crab meat. Add salt and Accent and cover with the grated cheese. Add the other 6 slices of buttered bread. Beat eggs and add milk Pour over the sandwiches, then cover with foil and refrigerate over night. Bake at 325° for 60 minutes. Serve sandwich on plate and have a hot sauce made as follows: 1 can undiluted mushroom soup, 1 cup button mushrooms and 2 or 3 tablespoons sherry, heated.

Submitted by Virginia P. Robbins, Maplewood, N. J.

Sea Food Chowder

2 pounds haddock fish sticks
1 can clam bouillon
1 pint chopped clams
1½ to 2 pounds lobster meat
   (cut coarsely)
1½ quarts of milk
2 quarts of potatoes (sliced thin)
1 onion
Small piece salt pork (diced)

Fry salt pork in kettle until well browned and saute onions in fat. Add clam bouillon, potatoes and cook until nearly done. Add fish sticks, clams and lobster meat. Cook until potatoes are done. Add milk and heat to boiling but do not boil. Serve hot. Serves 8 or 10.

Submitted by Mary E. Howard, Orrington, Maine

Sea Food Chowder
(Serves 12 to 15)

1½ pounds haddock fillets
1 pound fresh scallops
2 cans crab meat
2 cans minced clams
2 cans shrimp
Salt and pepper to taste
¼ pound butter
2 quarts hot milk or more

Cook haddock in water, salted to suit taste, until it can be flaked with a fork. Simmer scallops in just enough water to cook, about 5 minutes. Flake haddock, cut scallops in bite size pieces; put in a large kettle with water, in which fish and scallops were cooked. Add the clams, shrimp and crab meat; heat just long enough to blend. Add salt and pepper to taste. Add milk which has been heated just to the boiling point. Add the butter or margarine. Set aside to "ripen" until serving time. Then reheat to serve.

Submitted by Mellie P. Gillis, North Haven

Smoked Fish Chowder

1 small onion
2 tablespoons butter
2 cups fish water
1 pound finnan haddie
2 small carrots, diced
2 medium diced potatoes
4 cups milk
1 teaspoon salt
¼ teaspoon pepper

Simmer smoked fish until partially cooked, enough to remove the bones; set to one side, reserving 2 cups of the fish water. Cook diced carrots and potatoes in a small amount of water. Simmer chopped onion in butter until tender; add to cooked vegetables; then add fish water, finnan haddie and milk. Do not let boil. When hot, season to taste. This is an old recipe using smoked cod or haddock.

Submitted by Mrs. Frances Young, South Portland, Maine

Favorite Fisherman's Chowder

1½ pounds of fresh or frozen
   haddock fillets
12 medium white onions
   (whole)
4 or 5 potatoes thinly sliced
¼ cup of butter or margarine
3 tablespoons of butter

4 teaspoons salt
½ teaspoon pepper
1 ripe tomato (optional)
3 cups boiling water
1 quart milk scalded
1 cup evaporated milk

Cut fillets into 2 or 3 pieces. Saute whole onions with ¼ cup butter in Dutch oven or kettle until golden; then cook 10 minutes. Add the potatoes, salt, pepper and boiling water. Arrange fish fillets on top, cover, simmer 15 to 20 minutes, or until vegetables are tender. Add scalded milk, evaporated milk and 3 tablespoons of butter. Heat. Slice tomato and float on top of chowder. (Optional). Worcestershire sauce may be added but optional.

Submitted by Mrs. Arthur W. Briggs, Monticello, Maine

Mock Lobster Pie

1 can crabmeat
2 cups or 1 can shrimp
   (fresh or frozen)

1 cup or more chopped,
   cooked celery
1 cup mayonnaise

Mix above, put in shallow casserole.

TOPPING

Combine:
1/3 package prepared stuffing
   mix

1/3 stick of butter
   or margarine, melted
Spread evenly over top.

Bake in 350° oven for 30 minutes or until nicely browned.

Submitted by Mrs. Virgil Hills, Warren, Maine

Oyster Stew

1 quart oysters
2 blades of celery
2 slices crusty bread (toasted)
½ teaspoon salt
¼ teaspoon pepper

¼ teaspoon nutmeg
1 quart milk
3 tablespoone flour
3 tablespoons butter

Heat the oysters in liquid, do not boil. Let cool, save liquid. Grind oysters, celery and bread. Add the liquid (strained) and seasonings. Melt the butter in double boiler and stir in the flour. Add the milk gradually and stir until smooth. Combine the two mixtures. A cup of cream or extra lump of butter may be added.

Submitted by Mrs. Harold Dorgan, Ellsworth, Maine

Maine Clam Chowder

2 quarts sliced potatoes
1 pint clams, cut (or 2 or 3
    cans of minced clams

1 onion diced
1 pint top milk
⅛ pound butter or oleo

Cook the potatoes and onion in as little water as possible. If using canned clams use the broth instead of water. (A pressure cooker uses less water). When potatoes are soft add the clams, lower the heat, simmer 5 minutes and let set. For canned clams merely stir in and let set. When ready to serve, reheat, add top milk or add half and half to regular milk. Remove from heat, add butter according to richness of milk. Season to taste with salt and pepper.

Submitted by Olive Bonsey, Surry, Maine

Poor Man's Chowder

2 cups slack salted dry cod fish
1 quart water
2 cups diced potatoes
1 stalk celery
1 large onion
1 large carrot

1 pint can of tomatoes
1 tablespoon flour
2 tablespoons butter
Pepper and salt to season (a little
    sugar helps season)

Cook cod fish in the quart of water until tender. Flake and remove any bones. Remove fish from water and use all or part of the water fish was cooked in (if not too salt) to cook the vegetables. Add can of tomatoes and thicken slightly with the flour in a little water. Add cooked fish and seasonings salt, pepper, sugar and simmer to blend. Add the 2 tablespoons butter. Serve hot with dumplings.

I am now 78 years old. This chowder was often a supper dish in my childhood, made by my grandmother.

Submitted by Mrs. Sue F. Bridges, Sedgwick, Maine

Hollywood Chicken Pie
(Two Crust Pie)

1 can chicken and rice soup
1 can water (hot)
2 tablespoons flour

1 tablespoon butter
1 can water packed tuna fish

Melt butter and add the flour, then add the can of water gradually. Heat the chicken soup with the flour water mixture. Cook until thickened. Rinse the tuna fish with boiling water and drain. Break into small pieces and add to the thickened soup. Bake at 450 degrees for 15 minutes and then turn down oven to 350 and cook until bubbling hot. Serve with cranberry sauce.

Submitted by Mrs. Ruth Carlson, Rockland, Maine

Clam Fritters

4 eggs
4 tablespoons flour (heaping)
½ teaspoon baking powder

½ cup clam water
1 cup clams
Shortening for frying

In sifter put 4 heaping tablespoons of flour and ½ teaspoon baking powder. Sift into beaten eggs. Add clams (cut up, I cut necks and rims only). Mix thoroughly with clam water.

In a large fry pan place a little shortening (about 4 tablespoons) and fry.

When batter begins to thicken, cut in pie shapes and turn each, until done, it burns easily in center.

Submitted by Mrs. Ruby Hoffses, Rockland, Maine

Clam Biscuits

1 recipe of favorite biscuit
dough
1 pint chopped clams

2 tablespoons butter
Salt and pepper to taste

Make your favorite biscuit dough, roll and cut with large cutter. Dough should be about ½ inch thick. On one biscuit put an amount of chopped clams, either fresh or canned, season with salt and pepper to taste; top with a small piece of butter. Moisten edge of biscuit with water and place another biscuit on top. Press edges to seal. Bake in a hot oven, about 425° until they are golden brown (15 to 20 minutes). Serve either with butter or catsup. This is an an excellent Sunday night lunch. A biscuit recipe is given below for your convenience. You may want to use one-half of this recipe for the above amount of clams.

Submitted by Mrs. Marshall E. Reed, Wisconsin Rapids, Wis.

Old Fashioned Biscuits

4½ cups flour
2 teaspoons soda
5 teaspoons cream of tartar
1 teaspoon salt

1 tablespoon sugar
2 tablespoons shortening
2 cups milk (about)

Sift the dry ingredients together 4 times, then mix in the shortening. Make a soft dough with sweet milk. Knead quickly several times, roll to the desired thickness; cut with biscuit cutter, place on baking sheet and bake at 425° for 20 minutes. I put a pat of Crisco or butter on the top of each before baking.

Submitted by Mrs. Irving V. McNaughton, Sangerville, Maine

Mother Hubbard's Clam Pie

1 pint of clams	Salt and pepper
Small pieces of salt pork	Flour to thicken
1 small onion (chopped)	

Chop the necks of the clams not too fine. Fry small pieces of salt pork and remove pork from pan when done. Put the clams in the hot fat, add the onion, salt and pepper. Thicken with a little flour (so you can pour it) and bring to boil. Line a deep dish with a good pie or biscuit crust. Pour in the clams and cover with crust. Bake until crust is well done. Start at 400° for 10 minutes and 325° until crust is well done.

Recipe was given to my mother by her neighbor, Mother Hubbard, who was the wife of a clam digger. It differs from most clam pies as it has no potato or anything else that takes away flavor of clams.

Submitted by Flossie E. York, Kennebunk, Maine

Cranberry Island Clam Pie

1 pint clams chopped fine	Butter, pepper and salt to
1 egg, well beaten	taste
4 soda crackers, finely crushed	½ cup milk
½ cup clam water	

Make a rich pastry, put in pie tin with layer of clams and crumbs.

Beat egg, add clam water and milk and pour over clams. Have cracker crumbs on top. Cover with pastry and bake 1 hour at 350°.

Submitted by Mrs. Ada Lincoln, Ellsworth, Maine

Clam Puffs

(Maine Seafoods Festival Specialty Batter)

1 tablespoon melted butter	1 tablespoon baking powder
1 egg	1½ cups flour
1 cup milk	1 pint fresh shucked clams
½ teaspoon salt	

Beat egg and add melted butter and milk. Sift baking powder and salt with the flour, and add to egg and milk mixture. Squeeze out black area from clams, grind clams and mix with batter. Make in balls size of a walnut. Deep fat fry. Canned minced clams may be used.

This has been used for years by Maine Seafoods Festival.

Submitted by Capt. Ote Lewis, Ash Point, Maine

31

Maine Clam Patties

1 pint of Maine clams   1 egg beaten
   (chopped) $\frac{1}{2}$ to $\frac{3}{4}$ cup cracker crumbs

Combine above ingredients and make into patties. Fry in greased skillet until done.

Submitted by Muriel L. Polley, Machias, Maine

Downeast Scallops

1 pint Maine scallops $\frac{1}{2}$ can undiluted tomato soup
1 tablespoon butter   1 teaspoon dry mustard
3 tablespoons flour $\frac{1}{2}$ cup chopped stuffed olives
$\frac{1}{4}$ teaspoon pepper   1 tablespoon diced onion
$1\frac{1}{2}$ cups top milk   1 tablespoon diced green
1 cup grated American Cheese   pepper

Cut scallops in $\frac{1}{4}$'s. Put in saucepan, cover with cold water, bring to boil, cook slowly 5 minutes. Melt butter in fry pan. Cook green pepper and onion in this until tender. Add flour, pepper, mustard. Add top milk, slowly. Cook until thickened. Add cheese, soup, olives. Add drained scallops. Turn into buttered casserole. Top with buttered crumbs. Bake at 350° for 25 minutes. Serves 4.

Submitted by Mrs. John Compton, Rockland, Maine

Potted Mackerel or Herring

12-15 fish $\frac{1}{4}$ teaspoon powdered cloves
Vinegar to cover $\frac{1}{4}$ teaspoon allspice

Dress and trim fish, enough to loosely fill a large casserole or baking dish. Pour over them enough vinegar to cover completely. Then pour off vinegar into a sauce pan draining well. (This is an easy way to measure so as to have the right amount of vinegar). Add spices to vinegar and bring to a boil. Pour back on fish while hot. Cover and bake in 250 degrees to 300 degrees oven for 3 hours. Remove from oven and cool. Fish will have all bones dissolved and will keep indefinitely. A large quantity may be done, while mackerel are running in August, to last through the winter. Store in stone crocks. May be used as is for sandwiches, salads, etc.

This is an old "island" recipe. It came to me from my mother, Mrs. C. Elmer Joy of North Haven, Maine.

Submitted by Inga J. Chase, Glen Cove, Maine

Escalloped Oysters

1 pint oysters
1¼ cups rolled crackers
½ cup butter

1 cup milk
Pepper, salt

Clean and cook oysters in liquor, until edges curl. Take out of liquor. Cut up oysters. Add milk to liquor. Let it come to a boil. Add butter. Reserve some of butter to add to about ¼ cup crumbs, for topping. Use buttered casserole. Put oysters in casserole in layers with cracker crumbs. Pour in the milk, butter, etc. Salt and pepper. Put buttered crumbs on top. Bake at 400° for ½ hour. Serve 4. These are delicious.

Submitted by Marjorie Standish, Portland Sunday Telegram
"Cooking Down East"

Crab Shells

2 cans crab meat (large size)
2 hard boiled eggs
1 cup mayonnaise
1 tablespoon grated onion
1 teaspoon dry parsley flakes
2 teaspoons lemon juice

½ teaspoon Worcestershire
sauce
½ teaspoon prepared mustard
3 tablespoons sherry
1 cup coarse bread crumbs
(save ½ cup for the top)

Mix all ingredients together, put into scallop shells, or individual baking dishes, top with ½ cup buttered crumbs. Bake ½ hour at 325°.

Submitted by Virginia P. Robbins, Maplewood, N. J.

Shrimp, Crab and Scallop Casserole

1 can shrimp (can use fresh)
1 can crab meat (can use fresh)
¾ pound scallops
½ cup butter
¼ cup flour

1½ cups milk
2 tablespoons sherry
1 cup soft bread crumbs
¼ cup grated cheese
Salt and pepper and paprika

Cook sea foods in ¼ cup butter 4 or 5 minutes, stirring constantly. Add salt and pepper to taste. Blend in flour and gradually add milk stirring until thickened. Add sherry and more salt and pepper if needed. Pour in a shallow 1 quart baking dish. Melt the remaining ¼ cup of butter. Mix with bread crumbs and grated cheese. Sprinkle over top of cream mixture. Add paprika. Bake at 350° for 15 minutes or until light brown. Serves 4.

Submitted by Josephine Seliger, Rockland, Maine

Boothbay Harbor Crab Cakes

1½ cups crabmeat
3 eggs
1 cup cracker crumbs or soft
  bread crumbs
1/3 teaspoon salt
¼ cup melted butter or fat

drippings
2 teaspoons lemon juice
1 teaspoon minced green
  pepper
1 teaspoon minced celery
⅛ teaspoon pepper

Mix crabmeat, beaten egg yolks, crumbs and melted fat and all seasonings. Blend thoroughly. Fold in stiffly beaten egg whites and then turn into well greased pan of hot water and bake in a moderately hot oven 375 degrees for 25 minutes. Unmold and serve with the following lobster sauce:

LOBSTER SAUCE

1 cup milk
2 tablespoons flour
2 tablespoons butter

f. g. salt and pepper to taste
½ cup finely chopped cooked
  lobster

Make a hot medium white sauce by melting the butter, then adding the flour; cream to a smooth paste and add the one cup of milk. Cook until it has thickened. Add the chopped lobster meat. Serve over the hot crab cakes.

Submitted by Mrs. Leola Benner Peaslee, No. Edgecomb, Maine

Favorite Shrimp Dish

½ cup chopped onion
½ cup chopped green peppers
  (optional) good for color
1 tablespoon margarine or
  butter
1 can frozen condensed
  cream of shrimp soup or

cream of shrimp soup,
  canned
1 cup of dairy sour cream
¾ teaspoon curry powder
1 pound cooked cleaned
  shrimp

Cook onion in butter until tender, but do not brown. Add soup. Heat and stir until smooth. Stir in the sour cream and curry powder. Add the shrimp, heat slowly, stirring often, just 'til hot.

Serve over hot plain rice. Garnish with parsley, or can use chopped salted peanuts, or chopped hard boiled egg.

Makes approximately 4-6 servings.

Saffron rice may be substituted instead of the plain by adding a pinch of saffron powder to cooking water. Long grain rice is our favorite.

Submitted by Marguerite M. Pagurko, Bath, Maine

Pickled Salted Herring
(True "Swedish")

6 to 8 medium sized salted herring
3 large bay leaves
½ teaspoon ground allspice
2 teaspoons whole allspice

5 white onions, sliced thin
2 cups white vinegar
¼ cup water
1¾ cups sugar
¼ teaspoon salt, pepper

Skin, bone and soak herring in very cold water. Wipe dry with paper towels. Cut in 1 or 2 inch pieces; let set in pickle, made with above ingredients. This amount of pickle may cover 10 fish. Let set 24 to 36 hours. Cover bowl tightly.

Every Swedish family will have this made fresh as often as fish are obtainable. They eat this with baked beans or just crackers and of course at any Scandinavian smorgasbord. Keep in a cool place. Excellent.

Submitted by Mrs. Etta Anderson, Rockland, Maine

Mardi Gras Dinner
(With Cheese Sauce)

1½ cups minute rice
   (4⅝ ounce box)
1½ cups of water
2 teaspoons of salt
½ teaspoon oregano

1 can tomatoes
1 medium onion, thinly sliced
1 can tuna fish (packed in oil)
cheese sauce
Paprika

Place minute rice (right from the box) in a large baking dish (approximately 7½ x 11¾). Add water, salt, oregano and stir to moisten all of rice. Place tomatoes on top of rice (save a few pieces of tomato for garnish. Top with onion and tuna fish (use entire contents of can). Spread cheese sauce on top and garnish with tomato and sprinkle with paprika. Bake at 375 degrees for 25 minutes.

Cheese Sauce

3 tablespoons flour
¼ teaspoon salt
Dash of pepper
¼ cup of melted butter

2 cups of milk
2 cups of cheese (velveeta
   type) cut up.

Melt butter in top of double boiler and stir in flour, salt and pepper. Mix until smooth. Gradually add the milk stirring constantly. Cook and stir until sauce is thickened. Add cheese. Cook and stir until cheese melts.

Submitted by Mrs. Vernon Palmer, Caribou, Maine

Shrimp Delight

1 medium onion (minced)
2 tablespoons butter
1 cup thin cream or milk
1 can tomato soup
⅛ teaspoon soda

½ teaspoon Tobasco sauce (or
⅛ teaspoon Paprika)
1 cup cooked minute rice
1 can shrimp (cut coarsely)
Or fresh cooked shrimp

Combine all ingredients and cook in double boiler until thickened. Serve on crackers.

Submitted by Mrs. Thomas Nichols, Jackman, Maine

Salmon - Potato Pie

1 can salmon (1 lb.)
1 cup cooked peas
2 hard boiled eggs (sliced)
1 can cream of celery soup

1/3 cup milk
3 cups hot mashed potato
1/3 cup grated American
cheese

Drain salmon and flake into pieces. Put into 1½ quart greased casserole, add peas and eggs, pour in soup heated with milk.

Spoon potato around edges, sprinkle with cheese.

Bake at 375° 25 minutes, or until well heated and brown.

Submitted by Gertrude Moulton, Newport, Maine

Fish Casserole

2 pounds haddock fillets
3½ cups water
1½ teaspoons salt
½ teaspoon pepper
3 small onions (sliced)
3 tablespoons butter or substitute
3 tablespoons flour
1½ cups milk (scalded)

1/3 teaspoon salt (additional)
⅛ teaspoon pepper (additional)
⅛ teaspoon thyme
⅛ teaspoon sage
¾ teaspoon lemon juice
1/3 cup buttered crumbs
¼ cup grated American cheese

Simmer the fillets in the 3½ cups of water to which the salt, pepper and onions have been added, for 10 minutes. Flake the cooked fish, watching carefully for bones. Melt the butter, add the flour and when smoothly blended, add the milk gradually and bring to the boiling point, stirring constantly. Now add the salt, pepper, thyme and sage and again bring to boiling point. Arrange flaked fish and sauce in layers in a casserole, top with the blended crumbs and cheese. Bake in 350° oven 25 to 30 minutes. Serve immediately.

Submitted by Gloria C. Oliver, Dover-Foxcroft, Maine

Mother's Brown Bread
(Using Leftovers)

2 cups crumbs (bread, cake, cookies, etc.)
1 cup sour milk
2 teaspoons soda, dissolved in 1 cup hot water

¾ cup molasses
1 cup flour
1 cup corn meal
1 teaspoon salt

Pour the sour milk over 2 cups of your leftover crumbs; let these set over-night or until the mixture is soft. Put the mixture through a sieve. To this mixture, add the molasses, the soda and water mixture and then the flour, corn meal and salt. If more liquid is needed, add more hot water. Put in a greased tin and steam three hours.

As a little girl, I remember that all dried bread, doughnuts, cakes and cookies were put into a dish in the cupboard. On Friday night or early Saturday, my mother covered the dried leftovers with sour milk. After soaking until soft, she put the mixture through a sieve. To the mixture, she added the other ingredients. She made the best brown bread I ever tasted and, of course, it never tasted the same two weeks in a row. Nothing was measured, but I have worked out the above recipe.

Submitted by Mary Lincoln, Solon, Maine

Lamb Croquettes

2 cups left-over lamb
1 small onion
¼ green pepper

1 egg
Salt and pepper to taste
Bread crumbs to roll

Grind left-over lamb with a small onion and about a quarter of a green pepper according to your taste. Mix this with an egg and shape into croquettes; roll in crumbs and fry slowly in buttered frying pan until brown. Turn often.

Submitted by Mrs. Nancy Lamb, Rockland, Maine

Chicken Casserole

2 cups cooked chicken (diced)
¼ teaspoon pepper
½ teaspoon salt
1 can cream of chicken soup
2 teaspoons onion chopped
1 cup diced celery

½ cup almonds (slivered)
1 tablespoon lemon juice
¼ cup mayonnaise
3 hard boiled eggs (sliced)
2 cups crushed potato chips

Combine all ingredients in a casserole or baking dish and cover with crushed potato chips.

Submitted by Mrs. George Gherardi, Camden, Maine

Island Style Ham And Sweet Potatoes

6 medium sweet potatoes
1 tablespoon butter or margarine
½ teaspoon salt
⅛ teaspoon pepper
Milk (to whip potatoes)
2 cups coarsely cut up cooked ham
2 tablespoons butter or margarine

½ cup green pepper or pimiento strips
Pinch nutmeg
1 No. 2 can pineapple chunks (drained)
2 tablespoons brown sugar
1 tablespoon cornstarch
¾ cup pineapple juice
2 tablespoons vinegar

Cook, then mash the potatoes. Add 1 tablespoon butter, salt, pepper, nutmeg and enough milk to whip. Heat oven to 400°. In a skillet saute the ham in 2 tablespoons butter stirring until golden. Add green pepper (or pimiento) and pineapple chunks. Cook 2 or 3 minutes. Stir in combined brown sugar, cornstarch, juice and vinegar. Cook, stirring until thickened and clear. Pour mixture into 9-inch pie plate or casserole dish. Drop spoonsful of potato on top. Bake until hot in 375° oven about 20 to 25 minutes. Serves 4 to 6.

Submitted by Mrs. Irene Yerxa, Bridgewater, Maine

Ham And Egg Casserole

12 hard cooked eggs, sliced
1 small jar pimiento (chopped)
1 med. green pepper (chopped)
1½ cups left-over cubed ham

1 tablespoon salad bouquet herbs
¼ cup butter
3 tablespoons flour
3½ cups milk
½ cup sherry

TOPPING

1 package Pepperidge Farm stuffing

¼ cup butter

Mix together the first five ingredients and add to the white sauce made by creaming together the butter and flour and then add the hot milk and cook until thick; then add the sherry. Place in a buttered casserole and cover with the topping, which has been made by adding the melted butter to the stuffing mix. Bake at 350° for 20 to 30 minutes or until brown and bubbly. Serves 8 to 10.

(Formerly Penobscot 4-H Club Agent)
Submitted by Mrs. Elbert Stallard, Hingham, Mass.

Sunday Supper Casserole

2 cups milk
¼ cup flour
¼ cup Crisco
½ cup chopped onion
1 cup shredded American
  cheese (¼ lb.)

1 tablespoon mustard
3 cups sliced potatoes (raw)
  or leftover cooked potatoes
½ pound frankforts or 1 can
  luncheon type meat (or
  leftover meat)

Saute onions in Crisco until tender. Make a paste of the flour with a small amount of the cold milk, mixing well until smooth. Heat the rest of the milk in the double boiler and when hot, add the flour-milk paste, stirring until smooth and thick. Add the onions (sauted), mustard and cheese. Remove from heat and stir until cheese melts.

In a 2 quart casserole, alternate layers of potatoes, meat and cheese sauce. Bake at 325 degrees for about 1½ hours until potatoes are tender. If you have leftover cooked potatoes, this may be used in place of the raw potatoes. Make it up ahead of time and warm up about ¾ hour before serving time in a 350° oven.

Submitted by Mrs. Athleen Damon, Waldoboro, Maine

Chinese Egg Casserole

1 pint milk
6 tablespoons flour
4 tablespoons butter
¼ pound American Cheese
  (cut fine)

¼ pound sharp cheese
  (cut fine)
1 cup bread crumbs
4 hard boiled eggs

Put milk in double-boiler, thicken with flour. Add remaining ingredients. Put in casserole. Bake 15 minutes at 400°.

Submitted by Martha Hatfield, Corinna, Maine

Lobster And Cheese Delight

1 teaspoon chopped onion
3 tablespoons chopped green
  pepper
3 tablespoons butter
3 tablespoons flour
½ tablespoon prepared mustard

¼ tablespoon salt
1 cup canned strained tomatoes
1 egg slightly beaten
¾ cup heated milk
1 cup fresh lobster, leftover
½ cup grated cheese

Cook the onion and green pepper in the butter, add flour and stir well. Add mustard, salt, tomatoes, beaten egg, cheese. Blend well and add to the hot milk. Cook and stir until smooth. Last stir in the lobster. Serve on toast or in patty shells.

Submitted by Mrs. Percy Van Note, St.-George, Maine

Salmon Newburg

2 tablespoons butter or oleo	1 cup of salmon
1½ tablespoons flour	1 egg beaten
1 cup of rich milk or thin cream	Salt and pepper to taste

Mix butter and flour in top of double boiler, add milk or cream. Cook until it begins to thicken, then add salmon broken in bits, salt and pepper. Then add the beaten egg. Cook 2 minutes.

Serve on crackers or toast.

Submitted by Mrs. Clarence J. Stone, North Haven, Maine

Salmon Loaf

1 cup flaked salmon	1 teaspoon salt
1 cup soft bread crumbs	1 tablespoon melted butter
1 cup scalded milk	1 teaspoon lemon juice
2 eggs (beaten separately)	

Soak bread crumbs in scalded milk. Mix 2 beaten egg yolks, 1 teaspoon salt, 1 tablespoon melted butter, 1 teaspoon lemon juice and add to the bread crumbs. Lastly, add 2 beaten egg whites. Fold in. Cook in moderate oven 350° until firm, about 45 minutes.

Submitted by Mrs. Leroy E. Ames, Vinalhaven, Maine

Salmon Loaf

3 eggs beaten	1 onion, minced fine
1½ cups milk	Salt to taste
1 can salmon	¼ teaspoon poultry seasoning
2 cups soft bread crumbs	Large piece butter

Mix in order given and bake 1 hour in loaf pan at 325°.

Submitted by Mrs. John Pratt, Castine, Maine

Fish Cakes

1 cup salt fish, left-over	½ teaspoon pepper
2 cups mashed potatoes	Salt to taste
1 beaten egg	

Use left-over salt fish or salt fish that has been soaked, drained and flaked. Mix all ingredients and beat with electric beater until creamy. Taste for saltiness as you may need to use more potato. Form into small balls or cakes and cook in frying pan or in deep fat.

Roll them in flour before frying and let stand a bit before cooking. When frying in fry pan use salt pork for a better flavor.

Submitted by Mrs. John Pratt, Castine, Maine

Turkey Pie

2 cups cooked potato (hot or cold) diced
2 cups peas (cooked)
2 cups carrots (cooked)

2 cups turkey or more
Salt and pepper to taste
2 cups turkey gravy, thickened

Put potatoes, peas, carrots, and turkey in layers in a 3 quart greased casserole or baking dish. Pour over above the thickened gravy (not too thick.)

ENGLISH PASTRY FOR TOPPING

2 cups flour
2 teaspoons baking powder
1 teaspoon salt
Sift together above

2/3 cup shortening
½ cup hot water
1 tablespoon lemon juice
1 egg yolk (unbeaten)

Mix shortening, water, lemon juice and unbeaten egg yolk. Mix well and stir into the flour mixture. Roll the dough out the size of the baking dish and lay it over the top, pressing the dough on to stick. Bake at 400° for 25 or 30 minutes, or until nicely brown. Beef or chicken can be used.

Submitted by Phoebe Harmon, Limington, Maine

Chicken Casserole

1 can cream of chicken soup
½ cup milk
1 tablespoon chopped parsley
2 tablespoons pimiento

1 cup diced cooked chicken
2 cups cooked macaroni
A little onion
¼ cup buttered crumbs

Blend the soup and milk, add chicken, macaroni, parsley and pimiento and onion. Put in a 1 quart casserole and sprinkle ¼ cup of buttered crumbs on top. Bake 25 minutes at 375°.

Submitted by Mrs. Isabelle Barbour, Stonington, Maine

Ham Souffle

1½ cups bread crumbs
1½ cups milk
4 tablespoons melted butter
¼ teaspoon salt
¼ teaspoon pepper

1 full cup diced ham (cooked)
½ teaspoon dry mustard
2 eggs (beat yolks and whites separately)

Soak the bread crumbs in the milk about 30 minutes. Add the remaining ingredients; (adding beaten egg whites last.)

Bake in quart size buttered casserole in a pan of water at 350° for one hour. Note: (If ham is salty, use little or no salt.)

Submitted by Mrs. Langtry Smith, Vinalhaven, Maine

Scouse and potato puffs are two leftover recipes taken from M. Abbie Miller's personal cook book, dated September 25, 1900. Mrs. Cynthia Packard of Rockland submitted the book for our use.

Scouse

Pare and slice very thin several raw potatoes. Slice thin cold roast beef and Spanish or large onions. In the bottom of a large baking dish put first a layer of potatoes, then a layer of meat, then a layer of onions. Again alternate until pan is full. Add plenty of salt and pepper between the layers. Fill the pan half full of water, adding any left over gravy that may be at hand. Sprinkle flour over the top and bake until potatoes are soft all the way through and brown on top. Eat while hot.

Beef And Potato Cakes

2½ cups ground leftover beef	1 teaspoon bottled thick meat
1½ cups cold seasoned mashed	sauce
potatoes	2 teaspoons minced onion
½ teaspoon salt	Flour
Speck pepper	2 tablespoons melted fat

Mix together all ingredients except flour and fat. Shape into 6 patties or cakes. Roll very lightly in flour and saute in hot fat until brown on all sides. Note: Bacon, ham or sausage drippings or other shortenings may be used for the melted fat. Roast veal, ham, lamb or pork may be substituted for the beef.

Submitted by Caroline Constantin, Skowhegan, Maine

Potato Puffs

Cut up leftover meat, chopping fine. Season with salt and pepper. Put aside for later use. Boil potatoes to mash or use leftover mashed potatoes, according to how much left over meat you have. Make a paste of them with a beaten egg (or eggs according to the amount used). Roll out on a floured board. Cut with a saucer; place the seasoned meat on the potato paste and fold up. Fry in butter or fat until light brown.

Haddock Or Halibut Hash

½ pound cooked left-over haddock or halibut	Butter and milk
	Salt and pepper
6 medium cooked potatoes	

Mash hot potatoes with enough milk to make them light, fluffy and quite moist. Add the flaked fish, salt and pepper and mix thoroughly. Spread in a shallow pan with melted butter on top and brown in a hot oven, 375-400 degrees.

New England Poverty Pie

Beef (lamb, fowl or pork)
1 or 2 onions sliced
Carrots

Potatoes
Salt, pepper, bay leaves
(to season)

BISCUIT DOUGH

2 cups flour
¼ cup butter or shortening
1/3 cup sugar
3 teaspoons baking powder

1 teaspoon salt
1 egg beaten
¾ cup milk, about

Take desired amounts of leftover meat; cut in small pieces. Add onions and any other vegetables on hand. Cover with water and season with salt, pepper and bay leaf. Simmer until done and rather thick (a good half of the forenoon). Turn into a baking dish and cover with a rich biscuit dough. Sift together flour, sugar, baking powder and salt. Cut in butter or other shortening. Mix with beaten egg and milk to handle (about 2/3 cup). Drop by spoonfuls on the meat and vegetable mixture and bake in 450° oven until done.

This is a grand way to use up "leftovers", and with dessert and beverage makes a complete meal. This recipe is "old as the hills" and has many variations. Depending on "what's in the ice box."

Submitted by Inga J. Chase, Glen Cove, Maine

Ham Savory

1 tablespoon butter
1 tablespoon flour
½ teaspoon salt
2 cups milk
1½ cups cooked ham, chopped

1½ cups cooked potatoes, sliced
½ cup cracker crumbs
1 to 2 tablespoons butter

Melt the 1 tablespoon butter, blend with the flour and salt. Heat milk and add, stirring constantly. Cook until smooth.

Arrange chopped ham and sliced potatoes in layers in a greased casserole. Cover each layer with the white sauce. Sprinkle cracker crumbs over the top and dot with butter. Bake in moderate oven (375°) about 30 minutes or until crumbs are brown and sauce bubbles.

Note: Other meats may be used in this way and leftover gravy may be used in place of part of the white sauce. Roast pork is especially good. A little onion or Accent may be added for extra flavor. I sometimes add leftover carrots and peas.

Submitted by Mrs. Ralph C. Goff, Hollis Center, Maine

Cottage Pie

1 to 1¼ pounds cold, cooked meat

3 ounces butter

1 to 2 small cloves garlic, crushed

1 large onion, finely chopped

3 tablespoons flour

1½ cups good stock

Salt and pepper to taste

Milk (about 1/3 cup)

Melt butter and cook onion and garlic until soft. Sprinkle in flour and cook untill golden brown. Gradually add stock and cook, stirring until smooth and thick. Stir in coarsely ground meat. Season mixture well and turn into buttered pie dish. Cover it with boiled, mashed (beaten up till light with butter and a little hot milk) potatoes; like the meat, the potatoes should be a little on the wet side, but not sticky. Ridge the top deeply with a fork and brush with melted butter. Bake in hot oven, 425° for about 20 minutes, until ridges of potato are golden brown and crisp. Variations: Use different meats such as pork, minced bacon, smoked or salted meats, spiced beef, etc. For lamb use a little (tablespoon) of sweetish chutney or some plumped raisins. Serve with a salad.

Submitted by Mrs. Dolores Naiva, South Bristol, Maine

Turkey Or Chicken Croquettes

1 cup milk

3 tablespoons flour

5 tablespoons fat

½ teaspoon salt

¼ teaspoon pepper

1 cup of chopped meat

1 cup of dry bread crumbs

1 egg

Make a thick sauce with milk (you may substitute ½ milk plus ½ meat stock), flour, fat, salt and pepper. Fold in the meat. Cool. Prepare crumbs in a shallow dish and beat egg in a small bowl, ready for coating. Divide the cooled mixture into 8 parts and form each in a ball. Coat with crumbs, then roll on a board to form a cylinder; egg and crumb again and fry in deep fat. Serve with a mushroom sauce.

Submitted by Mrs. Joyce Burnham, Limerick, Maine

Macaroni And Shrimp Salad

2 cups macaroni

2 cups cooked shrimp, left-over

1 medium cucumber (cut up)

1 cup fresh tomatoes (cut up)

1 cup lettuce (cut up)

Mayonnaise

Cook macaroni and drain. Stir in rest of ingredients and mix up with mayonnaise, using the amount to suit your taste.

Submitted by Mrs. Merle Hichborn, Bangor, Maine

Roasting Sea Birds, Pheasant, Partridge or Woodcock
(As Cooked for Knox County Fish and Game Association)

4 sea birds, or
2 to 3 pheasants or
2 to 3 partridges or
6 to 8 woodcock
1 pound salt pork
1 loaf bread

4 medium onions, chopped
1 teaspoon poultry seasoning
Salt and pepper to taste
Water to make a real moist
dressing

Skin and clean birds that you intend to roast. Soak in salt water several hours. Slice the salt pork in thin slices (bacon may be used but salt pork is better.) Tack two slices of salt pork on each side of the birds using tooth picks. Place birds close together breast side up in a roasting pan and cover with a large amount of dressing. The dressing flavors the birds and keeps them moist.

In a large bowl or kettle, break up a loaf of bread; add chopped onion, poultry seasoning, salt and pepper to taste. Add enough water to make a real moist dressing. Do not be afraid to use too much dressing; use your own judgment, according to the size of birds. Cover dressing over the top of all the birds, covering them well.

Pour enough water in the bottom of the roaster to make 1 inch and keep about an inch of water in the roaster all during cooking. Cover roaster with a tight cover or use heavy-type foil. Bake in a very slow oven, 275 degrees, for 4 hours; the lower the temperature, the better the birds. The water in the bottom maks a good rich, thick gravy that is delicious.

Submitted by Mrs. Barrett M. Jordan, Rockland, Maine

Bread Sauce
(For Game Birds)

1½ cups milk
1 peeled onion, studded with
6 cloves
1 bay leaf

3 ounces fresh white bread
crumbs
1 ounce butter
Salt and pepper to taste

Pour milk into saucepan. Add prepared onion and bay leaf and heat gently to simmering point. Remove from heat, cover and leave 1 to 2 hours to allow the milk to become perfumed with the clove and onion. Strain milk and return to saucepan. Add bread crumbs together with butter. Season to taste and heat slowly for about 15 minutes until thick and creamy. Add more milk if required.

This is also used with chicken and turkey.

Submitted by Mrs. Robert Naiva, London, England

Baked Wild Duck

1 wild duck

FIRST STUFFING

4 medium apples, chopped
1 medium onion, chopped
Bread, about ½ loaf

1 teaspoon salt
⅛ teaspoon pepper

SECOND STUFFING

4 medium apples, chopped
1 medium onion, chopped
Bread, about ½ loaf
1 teaspoon poultry dressing

¼ cup butter
1 teaspoon salt
⅛ teaspoon pepper

For those who object to the "gamey" flavor of wild duck, the following method of stuffing preparation will be a large help. Mix together the ingredients for the first stuffing and stuff the duck. Place in roaster, with a small amount of water, and bake, covered, at 300 degrees, until it is half-done, about 1½ hours, depending on size. Remove stuffing from duck and throw away or feed to your animals.

Stuff duck again, using the second stuffing. Return to clean roaster and finish baking with a little water in the bottom to keep duck moist. Continue baking at 300 degrees for 1½ hours or until duck is tender. If you want duck to be more brown, remove cover during the last half hour.

Submitted by Joe Robbins, Waldoboro, Maine

Baked Pheasant

Clean pheasant and soak overnight in salt and water. Cover pheasant, breast side up, heavily with strips of bacon until the entire bird is covered. Add a little water in the bottom of the roaster pan, keeping water in the pan during the cooking period. Cover roaster with a tight cover or heavy foil. Bake in a 300 degree oven for 2 or 3 hours.

Submitted by Mrs. Gladys Burgess, Rockland, Maine

Venison or Moose Casserole

2 pounds venison or moose
    stew meat

1 can mushroom soup
1 package dry onion soup mix

Put meat into casserole, spread the mushroom soup over meat; sprinkle dry onion soup mix over all. Cover tightly and bake at 325 degrees for two hours. This makes its own gravy and no other seasonings are necessary.

Submitted by Mrs. Clara Miller, Crescent Beach, Maine

Venison Casserole

2 pounds venison
Seasoned flour
2 onions, minced
2 tablespoons butter

2 cups canned tomatoes
2 tablespoons pimiento
½ teaspoon salt

Cut the venison in 1½ inch cubes, roll in flour, season to taste with salt, pepper, accent, etc. In a heavy skillet, saute the onions in butter until golden; add meat cubes and brown. Place meat and onions in casserole, pour tomatoes over all, add pimiento and salt. Bake in 350 degree oven for 1½ to 2 hours or until meat is tender.

Submitted by Mrs. Clara Miller, Crescent Beach, Maine

Venison Pot Roast

3 to 4 pound venison roast
Seasoned flour
1 onion sliced

1 green pepper
1 small can mushrooms
1 cup water

Dredge roast with flour seasoned with pepper and Lawry seasoning. Brown meat in butter with the onion, green pepper and mushrooms. Cook in pressure cooker with 1 cup of water at 10 pounds pressure for 35 to 50 minutes, according to size roast. Thicken gravy.

Use this same recipe for cubed venison meat, cooking it for a shorter time. Make gravy and serve it over wide noodles.

Submitted by Mrs. Gladys Burgess, Rockland, Maine

Squirrel Stew

2 squirrels
1 medium onion

3 to 4 potatoes
Salt and pepper to taste

Skin squirrels and clean good, removing all hairs. Put in sauce pan with small amount of water, season with salt and pepper and add onion sliced. Simmer, slowly, until half cooked, then add potatoes, cut up or whole as you desire, cooking until squirrels are tender. Other vegetables may be added, such as carrot, turnip, etc., according to your liking, adding at the same time as you do the potatoes.

Submitted by Mrs. Sally Shumway, Rockland, Maine

Striped Bass Rabbit

2 pounds bass fillets
1 can cheddar cheese soup

½ can milk
¼ teaspoon dry mustard

Place fish in casserole. Combine other ingredients and beat until sauce is smooth, pour over fish. Bake, uncovered, in 325 degree oven for 1 hour.

Submitted by Mrs. Clara Miller, Crescent Beach, Maine

Southern Fried Coon

1 raccoon	1 celery stick
1 carrot	Flour to coat coon pieces
1 large onion	

Remove all fat from raw coon, cut up in pieces for frying; be sure to remove any fat on all pieces as this is very important for a good flavor. Soak over-night covered with water and ½ cup of salt. Drain off salt water and parboil in fresh water for 2 minutes. Throw water out. Cover again with fresh water, add the carrot, onion and celery; simmer until done. Remove meat from pot and dip in flour, coating all pieces well. Brown on both sides in your favorite shortening. Season with salt and pepper to taste; cook until tender. The broth can be used as a soup base or gravy.

Submitted by Mrs. Sally Shumway, Rockland, Maine

Fried Raccoon

The proper preparation of a raccoon is a long, tedious job but well worth it in the end. Every speck of fat must be removed for it to really be edible. Cut the "coon" in serving size portions, remove all fat, place in kettle, cover with water, add a couple stalks of cut up celery, a good sized onion, cut up, salt to taste; cover and boil until tender. Remove meat from stock and drain well. Saute in frying pan in a combination of butter and cooking oil. Use low heat so the meat doesn't get hard and crusty. Delicious.

Submitted by Mrs. Clara Miller, Crescent Beach, Maine

Raccoon Roast

Soak cleaned racoon in salt and water over night. Remove every bit of the fat. Place raccoon in a roaster pan on a trivet to let excess fat drip to the bottom. Cover the entire raccoon with poultry dressing, having a moist dressing. Add water to cover the bottom of the pan. Bake in 300 to 325 degree oven for 4 or 5 hours.

Poultry Dressing

10 slices of bread	1 egg, beaten
1 small onion, cut fine	Salt and pepper to taste
1 tablespoon poultry seasoning	Hot water
1 tablespoon butter	

Brown bread slices in oven until it resembles melba toast; break up in small pieces. Add onion, poultry seasoning, butter, egg, salt, pepper and enough hot water to make a moist dressing.

Submitted by Mrs. Harold Burgess, Rockland, Maine

Rabbit Pie

1 2½ to 3 pound rabbit, cut up	1 bay leaf
2 cups hot water	1 teaspoon salt
1 onion	Few grains pepper
2 celery tops	¼ cup flour
1 small carrot	

After skinning your rabbit, you should refrigerate it for a couple of days before using it. Soak rabbit awhile in salt water, using 2 quarts water to ½ cup salt, for at least an hour. Wash and drain on absorbent paper. Cook rabbit in a covered kettle with all of the ingredients, using just enough water to make a good broth for gravy. Bring to simmering point and simmer slowly until rabbit is tender (about 2 hours). Remove from broth and place on wire rack to cool. Remove meat from bones. Cut up in size pieces as you desire. Drain rabbit broth and make gravy. For 2 cups of broth, make a paste of ¼ cup flour and ¼ cup water. Pour paste gradually into 2 cups of broth and cook until thickened. Put rabbit meat in uncooked pastry shell; pour thickened broth over rabbit. Season well with salt and pepper. If there isn't enough gravy to make rabbit good and moist, add a little cream until of right consistency. Cover with top crust and bake in oven at 400 degrees until crust is brown, about 35 minutes.

Rabbit And Onions

12 small white onions	1 rabbit (2 to 2½ lbs.)
2 cups cider	cut in serving pieces
1 tablespoon vinegar	½ cup butter
½ cup flour	¼ cup chopped green pepper
2½ teaspoons salt	⅛ teaspoon garlic powder
1 teaspoon celery salt	½ cup slivered ripe olives
2 teaspoons paprika	(optional)
½ teaspoon pepper	3 tablespoons flour

Cook onions in cider and vinegar 30 to 40 minutes or until tender. Combine ½ cup flour, salt, celery salt, paprika and pepper. Roll rabbit pieces in flour mixture. Brown well in butter. Remove to large saucepan or casserole. Cook green peppers and garlic powder in butter until tender. Add to rabbit with olives, onions and cider. Cover. Cook over low heat 40 minutes or until rabbit is tender. Remove rabbit pieces and keep hot. Combine 3 tablespoons flour and little cold water to form smooth paste. Blend into pan liquid. Heat and stir until boiling and thickened. Serve over rabbit.

Submitted by Mrs. Catherine Anderson, Rockland, Maine

Jugged Hare

5 pounds rabbit, cut up
½ pound bacon
1½ cups chopped onion
1 cup flour
1½ teaspoons salt

¾ teaspoon pepper
6 cups red wine
6 cups beef bouillon
Bay leaves, Thyme

Fry bacon until crisp; use bacon fat and cook onion until clear. Remove onion. Shake rabbit in mixture of flour, salt and pepper (2 pieces at a time). Brown in bacon fat. Remove browned rabbit and place in sauce pan. Pour over rabbit wine and bouillon. Simmer 1½ hours, remove rabbit.

Roux

1½ cups melted butter
1½ cups flour
¼ pound aleo

3 (8 oz.) or 6 (4 oz) cans
mushrooms

Make Roux with melted butter and flour; add a little hot liquid from sauce pan. Mix until thickened. Add to rest of hot liquid in pan and, stirring constantly 1 or 2 minutes, add rabbit. Heat the ¼ pound oleo in sauce pan until melted, add mushrooms and brown. Add to other mixture along with onions and bacon about 20 minutes before end of cooking time. Serve with rice. Serves about 20.

Submitted by Mrs. Sally Cross, Rockland, Maine

Baked Rabbit

1 or 2 rabbits
½ pound bacon, sliced
1 large onion

½ teaspoon paprika
1 tablespoon vinegar
Potatoes

Cut up one or two rabbits. Soak over-night in cold water with 3 tablespoons of salt. Put rabbit in roaster and lay bacon strips and sliced onion over meat. Sprinkle paprika and vinegar over the rabbit. Bake, slowly, with a cover on the roaster in a 300 degree oven. After the first hour, add 4 potatoes or more, according to the number to be served. Continue baking until the meat and potatoes are tender.

Submitted by Mrs. Sally Shumway, Rockland, Maine

Rabbit Cacciatore

2 rabbits
½ cup flour
1 teaspoon salt
3½ cups canned tomatoes
½ cup chopped onions

½ cup chopped celery
1 clove garlic, cut fine
1 tablespoon sugar
1 tablespoon Worcestershire
    sauce

Cut rabbits into serving portions. Combine flour and salt in a paper bag; shake pieces of rabbit in flour mixture, then brown in fat. Add tomatoes and rest of ingredients. Cover and simmer about 3 hours or until rabbit is tender. Stir occasionally.

Submitted by Mrs. Clara Miller, Crescent Beach, Maine

Tasty Rabbit

1 rabbit (tame or wild)	Flour
2 large onions	Salt and pepper
1 small clove of garlic	Cut up rabbit
Cracker crumbs	

If the rabbit is wild, soak about 2 hours in baking soda and water; then put in kettle and boil for ½ hour. Simmer, in a small amount of fat in a frying pan, the onions and garlic. Wipe rabbit pieces dry, roll in cracker crumbs and flour, lay on top of onions, add ½ cup of water, salt and pepper. Cover pan and simmer until done.

Submitted by Mrs. Myrtle Nord, Fairhaven, Mass.

Rabbit Mincemeat

6 bowls ground meat (takes about 3 rabbits, saddles and hind legs)	2 tablespoons nutmeg
	2 tablespoons cinnamon
16 bowls ground unpeeled apples and juice	2 tablespoons salt
	2 bowls strong coffee
8 bowls sugar	2 pounds seedless raisins
1 bowl vinegar	1 pound seeded raisins, ground
2 bowls molasses	Juice of 3 oranges
2 pounds salt pork, ground	1 orange peel, ground
1 pound citron	1 gallon apple cider or juice
Juice of 4 lemons	Mixed fruits and peel
2 tablespoons cloves	(optional)

Use big bowls for measuring. Oleo may be substituted for salt pork if you desire. Cook all of these ingredients together for 2 days, slowly on the back of the stove or very low heat. I use a huge canner and stir it real often. It is jarred hot and put in hot sterile jars and sealed immediately; with so much cooking it is not necessary to cook it in a hot water bath after filling jars. This recipe makes 16 to 17 quarts and keeps years. We think that rabbit makes the better mincemeat.

Submitted by Mrs. Joan Jasper, East Machias, Maine

Clear Camp Coffee

Measure one rounding tablespoon coffee and 1 cup cold water for each person. Put over fire and bring slowly to just a boil. Remove from fire, stir, and allow to set 2 or 3 minutes. Put on fire and again bring to just a boil. Add a little cold water to settle the grounds. Set near fire where it will keep warm until served.

Boiled Coffee
(Using Egg Shell)

Measure 2 level tablespoons coffee for each cup. Add a clean crushed egg shell and enough cold water to moisten the coffee grounds. Add ¾ of a measuring cup of freshly boiled water for each cup to be made. Bring to the boiling point. Remove from the fire, but keep hot for 5 minutes to allow the grounds to settle. A little cold water may be added to help settle grounds.

Quick Quantity Coffee

Use 1 teaspoon of instant powdered coffee to one cup of boiling water. Pour the water on the coffee. Set near fire where it will keep hot and improve the flavor by setting for a few minutes.

Camper's Hot Chocolate

1 tall can evaporated milk	5 marshmallows
1 small can chocolate syrup	Few grains salt
2 to 3 cans water (use milk can)	

Mix ingredients well. Heat, stirring frequently. This can be made over the fire using a large fruit can or a shortening can (3 pound size). Top hot chocolate with a marshmallow in each cup. Variations: This may be served cold for chocolate milk. Dry milk is always easy to carry on a camping trip. For the above recipe, substitute 1 2/3 cups of dry milk to 5 cups water for the evaporated milk and water.

Hiker's Chocolate Peppermint
13 CUPS

3 tall cans evaporated milk	1 pinch salt
4 chocolate bars (5-cent size)	2 quarts of water
1 chocolate peppermint patty (5-cent size)	

Using a 4 to 5 quart kettle bring water to a boil, add pinch of salt, milk, chocolate bars and peppermint patty. Stir over low heat until hot but not boiling. These ingredients are easy to carry and hiker's chocolate easy to make. Variation: Substitute three quarts of milk for canned milk and water.

Becky's Sloppy Hamburgers
(Teen-age Specialty)

1½ pounds hamburg	1½ teaspoons salt
½ cup chopped onion	½ bottle chili sauce
1 cup chopped celery	2 tablespoons vinegar
2 tablespoons butter	¼ cup chopped green pepper
2 tablespoons brown sugar	Hamburg buns

Mix brown sugar, salt, chili sauce, vinegar and green pepper together and place in a jar, for convenience, for out-door cooking.

In a heavy frypan placed on a grill over hot coals, brown the beef, onions and celery in the butter or margarine; when tender, add the ingredients already mixed in the jar. After it starts to simmer, place on outside of grill and cook slowly until the mixture becomes thick. Toast inside of hamburger buns on top of the grill and spoon mixture over the top. Most teen-agers like to top the mixture with the other half of bun and eat like a hamburger.

Submitted by Rebecca D. Wiers, St. Albans, Maine

Barbecued Venison

½ cup cider vinegar	½ cup Worcestershire sauce
1 cup water	2 sticks oleo
2½ cups catsup	1½ tablespoons prepared
1 teaspoon paprika	mustard
1 teaspoon pepper	2 teaspoons chili powder
½ cup brown sugar	

While deer is slowly cooking over outdoor fire, mix the above ingredients together and use for the sauce. Broil slowly 10 minutes and brush all sides of the venison several times during the last 30 minutes of cooking.

This same barbecue sauce is also excellent for chicken cooked on the outdoor grill.

Submitted by Willie Templeton, Rockland, Maine

Grilled Wieners

7 medium sized wieners	½ pound sharp cheese
2 tablespoons prepared mustard	7 strips bacon (about ½ pound)

Slit the wieners lengthwise to form pockets and spread the inside with the mustard. Insert strips of cheese in each wiener. Wrap the bacon strips around the wieners and fasten with toothpicks. When needed for the picnic, cook on a grill.

Submitted by Robert Wiggin, Rockland, Maine

Shish Kabobs

1 pound stew beef	Mushrooms and tomatoes
3 green peppers	(optional)
1 jar of small onions	French dressing

Cut beef into 1½ inch chunks. Let stand in French dressing for several hours or over night. Cut green pepper into quarters. On a skewer, string beef chunks, onion and green pepper, alternately. One may also add tomatoes and mushrooms. Lay over charcoal and keep turning until done.

Submitted by Charles McMahon, Rockland, Maine

Smothered Hamburg Patties

(Served to Jakes Rangers by Bentley Glidden)

Seasoned hamburg patties	Canned mushroom soup with
Sliced onions	½ can water to each can soup
Sliced green peppers	used

Panfry hamburg patties, sliced onions and green pepper. When almost done add canned mushroom soup with one half can water to each can soup. Heat and serve. Bentley Glidden of Damariscotta, is chief cook and serves excellent meals. These hamburg patties are served on our first night or the second which is one of our favorite dishes.

Submitted by Maurice "Jake" Day, Damariscotta, Maine

Hamburg Dinner In Foil

1 pound hamburg	4 carrots, cubed
1 onion, chopped	Butter
4 potatoes, cubed	Salt and pepper to taste

Divide hamburg into 4 portions. Cut 4 aluminum foil pieces, 12 inches each. Loosen hamburg apart and place each portion in the center of a piece of foil. Divide chopped vegetables and place on top of hamburg; then sprinkle each with a pat of butter and season with salt and pepper desired. Fold up foil with a double fold, sealing tight. Place on charcoal grill and cook about 30 to 45 minutes, turning after the first 15 minutes. Test for doneness.

Bannocks
Camp-fire Treat

1 cup flour	2 teaspoons baking powder
1 teaspoon salt	1 cup cold water

Put a good chunk of lard in the frying pan and let it get real hot.

While the lard is heating, mix dough. Sift together the flour, salt and baking powder. Mix well with the cold water. Make 2 small cakes; drop in hot fat. Brown on one side, then turn and brown on the other side. These are good with bacon and eggs, or yams, or sardines with tomatoes. They must be eaten while hot. This recipe can be doubled or make as many as one wishes. Our sports used to enjoy them real hot, after a hard day's hunting. Some enjoyed them with raw tripe from the brine. This is an old-time recipe.

Submitted by Mrs. Ada Pine, South Lincoln, Maine

Barbecue Sauce
(Serves 100)

6 bottles catsup
2 cups salad oil
2 bottles Worcestershire sauce
5 (6 oz.) jars horseradish
2 tablespoons garlic salt

7 tablespoons prepared mustard
1 cup cider vinegar
12 ounces fresh lemon juice
1 bottle (2 oz.) Tabasco sauce

Blend and stir thoroughly. Other ingredients of your choice may also be added. This is just perfect for beef to be charcoal broiled, basting often and especially at outings for groups. This keeps one year. Yields 5 quarts.

Barbecued Onions On Grill

Clean and peel required number of good sized onions, quartered; break open, but do not separate. Lay onions on good sized piece of heavy foil. Sprinkle with water. Sprinkle liberally with salt, sugar and pepper. Wrap onions with drug store wrap (so steam will not escape) and cook in or on the coals about 45 minutes.

Use same procedure for cooking in your oven 450 degrees 45 minutes.

Submitted by John R. Compton, Rockland, Maine

Roast Corn
(Without Husks)
Method I

Husk corn and place on double thick squares of aluminum foil. Season. Wrap and seal edges with a fold. Place on grill and cook about 6 minutes. Turn once or twice.

Method II

Husk corn and place several ears between a wire hinged toaster. Place on charcoal grill or outdoor fire, turning until they are speckled brown or to suit your taste. Brush on melted butter and season.

Roast Corn
(With Husks On)

Leave husks on corn with some of the long butt to use for a handle. Clean off some of the silk and examine for corn worms. Soak in salted water while you prepare the fire. Place corn on hot grill, turn frequently and cook until the kernels change color or to suit your tasts. Brush on butter and season to taste.

Togue Fish Chowder

Mr. Maurice "Jake" Day relates about one memorable fish chowder he made the "Jake's Rangers" that the boys remember as follows:

"I fried onions in fat until soft, added diced potatoes, water, salt and pepper; cooked until potatoes were almost done, cooked togue in water, strained fish water into potatoes and added the boned and skinned togue. Milk and a can of evaporated milk came next. Last I added a pint of whiskey. Needless to say, it was a large chowder, enough to serve ten men generously, and the 'Rangers' agreed it was a delicious one on that cold rainy day."

Submitted by Maurice "Jake" Day, Damariscotta, Maine

Grilled Lake Trout

2 pounds lake trout split or fillets
¼ cup French dressing
1 tablespoon lemon juice
1 tablespoon grated onion
2 teaspoons salt
Dash pepper

Combine ingredients to make basting sauce. Baste fish with sauce. Place fish in well-greased, hinged wire grill or toaster. Cook on a barbecue grill about 4 inches from moderately hot coals for 8 minutes. Baste with remaining sauce. Turn and cook for 7 to 10 minutes longer or until fish flakes easily when tested with a fork.

Fresh Boiled Shrimp
(With Cocktail Sauce)

5 pounds fresh shrimp
1 onion
1 lemon, sliced (optional)
½ cup salt
4 cups water

Place water in large kettle, add onion, sliced lemon and salt. Cover and bring to a boil over hot charcoal fire. Add shrimp and bring to a boil; then cover and cook for 5 minutes. Do not cook too long or shrimp will be tough. Drain. Serve with cocktail sauce. Serves 6.

Cocktail Sauce

1 cup catsup	2 drops tabasco sauce
1 cup chili sauce	1 ½ teaspoons Worcestershire
1 tablespoon horseradish	sauce
1 tablespoon vinegar	Paprika
	Few grains salt

Simmer all ingredients together for 20 minutes. Use hot or cold. Makes approximately 2 cups sauce.

Campfire Smelts

3 pounds whole smelts or other small fish	1/3 cup chopped parsley
	2 teaspoons salt
1/3 cup chopped onion	Dash pepper
3 strips bacon, cut in half	

Clean fish, wash and drain on paper towels. Cut 6 squares of heavy-duty foil, 12 inches each. Grease lightly. Divide fish into 6 portions. Place each portion of fish on one half of each square of foil. Sprinkle each serving with onion, parsley, salt and pepper. Place bacon on top. Fold other half of foil over fish and seal edges by making double folds in the foil. Place packages of fish in a bed of hot coals. Cook for 15 minutes, turning twice. Serve by cutting a big crisscross in the top of each package. Serves 6.

Shrimp Cooked In Foil

3 pounds fresh shrimp	½ cup chopped parsley
2/3 cup butter	2 tablespoons lemon juice
1 small onion, chopped	1 teaspoon salt
2 tablespoons chili sauce	Dash Worcestershire sauce
½ teaspoon garlic salt	Dash tabasco
2 cans (4 oz. each) sliced mushroom, drained	

Remove shells, clean and wash shrimp, drain and pat dry on paper towels. Cut 6 squares of heavy-duty foil, 12 inches each. Divide shrimp into six portions. Place each portion of shrimp on ½ of each square of foil. Place mushrooms on top of shrimp. Combine remaining ingredients. Pour sauce over shrimp (about 3 tbsps. for each portion). Fold other half of foil over shrimp and seal edges by making double folds in the foil. Place packages of shrimp on a barbecue grill about 4 inches from moderately hot coals. Cook for about 20 minutes or until done. Serve by cutting crisscross opening in foil.

Fish Fry

2 pounds haddock fillets or	1½ teaspoons salt
other fish fillets or	Dash pepper
6 pan-dressed rainbow trout,	½ cup flour
etc.	¼ cup yellow cornmeal
12 slices bacon	1 teaspoon paprika
¼ cup evaporated milk	Lemon wedges or tarter sauce

Cut fillets into serving pieces. Fry bacon until crisp. Remove bacon, reserving bacon fat for frying. Combine flour, cornmeal and paprika. Dip fish in milk mixture and roll in flour mixture. Place fat in heavy frying pan. Place on a barbecue grill about 4 inches from hot coals and heat until fat is hot, but not smoking. Add fish and fry 4 minutes. Turn carefully and fry for 4 more minutes or until fish is brown and flakes easily when tested with a fork. Drain on absorbent paper. Serve with lemon wedges or tartar sauce.

TARTAR SAUCE FOR FISH

1 cup mayonnaise or salad	2 tablespoons chopped onion
dressing	2 tablespoons chopped parsley
2 tablespoons chopped pickles	2 tablespoons chopped olives

Combine all ingredients and chill. Makes approximately 1½ cups sauce. Serves 6.

Lobster and Mushrooms On Grill

Boil a lobster which weighs about two pounds. Drain, cool and remove meat. Cut the meat into pieces and arrange alternately with mushrooms, lightly sauted on six skewers. Dust with salt and paprika. Turn the skewers in a plate on which has been placed two tablespoonfuls of lemon juice mixed with a teaspoonful of minced parsley. Dip in oil, roll in fine, bread crumbs and broil over a hot charcoal fire, turning frequently, until golden brown, 5 to 10 minutes. Serve with Maitre d' Hotel Butter.

MAITRE d'HOTEL BUTTER

¼ cup butter	1 teaspoon finely minced
½ teaspoon salt	parsley
⅛ teaspoon pepper	1 tablespoon lemon juice

Cream butter, add salt, pepper, minced parsley, and then add very slowly, one tablespoon of lemon juice.

Charcoal-Broiled Live Lobster

Live lobsters	Salt and Pepper to taste
Melted butter	Lemon sauce (optional)

Split live lobsters with a sharp pointed knife from head to tail.

Open up lobster and remove intestinal vein and stomach. If you like tomalley and coral, leave them in the lobster. Crack large claws slightly. Place lobsters, shell-side down, and broil over coals, brushing melted butter before and during cooking. Cook on shell-side for 10 to 15 minutes; then broil on meat side just to a light brown, but try to keep moist and juicy. Serve with melted butter or lemon sauce.

Lemon sauce is made by adding a teaspoonful of lemon juice to $\frac{1}{4}$ cup butter and a little pepper.

Barbecued Halibut Steaks

2 pounds halibut steaks or other fish steaks
1 clove garlic, finely chopped
1 can (8 oz.) tomato sauce
2 tablespoons lemon juice
1 tablespoon Worcestershire sauce
$\frac{1}{4}$ cup chopped onion
2 tablespoons chopped green pepper
2 tablespoons butter
1 tablespoon sugar
2 teaspoons salt
$\frac{1}{4}$ teaspoon pepper
Lemon wedges

Cook onion, green pepper and garlic in butter until tender. Add remaining ingredients and simmer for five minutes, stirring occasionally. Cool. Cut steaks into serving-size portions. Pour sauce over fish and let stand 30 minutes, turning once. Remove fish, reserving sauce for basting. Place fish in well-greased, hinged wire toaster. Cook on a barbecue grill about 4 inches from moderately hot coals for 8 minutes. Baste with remaining sauce. Turn and cook for 7 to 10 minutes longer or until fish flakes easily when tested with a fork. Serve 6.

New England Clam Bake

1 peck of clams (in shell)
1 bushel or more of seaweed
4 gallons ocean salt water
Sheet metal or heavy foil
Fireplace
Cloth bag
Newspapers

Have a good hot fire and cover with sheet metal or if just a grate use heavy tinfoil to hold seaweed and keep from flames. Put clams in cloth bag and place between layers of seaweed. Cover seaweed with newspaper and keep wet with salt water. Fresh water can be used if necessary. This helps steam clams and keeps paper from getting afire. Lobsters and corn in husks can be cooked at same time between layers of seaweed. Cook about 40 minutes or until clams start to open slightly. Dip in melted butter and eat. A few clams boiled in water will give clam liquor if desired.

Submitted by Mrs. Nancy Lamb, Rockland, Maine

Caesar Salad

1 cucumber
Radishes, as many as needed
Green pepper, cut into tiny bits
    probably a half pepper
1 red onion, sliced thinly
3 or 4 tomatoes, depending on
    size

Olives, ripe ones are preferable
    (small can) or small bottle
    of stuffed olives
Roquefort cheese, small
    amount
Lettuce

Slice cucumbers, radishes, onion, add bits of green pepper, tomatoes cut in wedges, olives sliced thinly, keep in refrigerator until ready to serve, then drain, and add cheese broken into small pieces, lettuce or other greens cut into small pieces; add French dressing and one whole egg and mix, tossing gently. Have prepared in advance one slice of bread cut into cubes and fried in butter and a small amount of garlic. Before serving scatter these on top with a few olive slices for color and decoration. This serves ten.

Submitted by John Egerton, Thomaston, Maine

Bean Salad

1 can Frenched green beans
1 can Frenched yellow beans
1 can kidney beans (in brine)
2 medium onions sliced
1 cup green pepper sliced
1 small can mushrooms sliced

½ cup salad oil
½ cup vinegar
½ cup sugar
1 teaspoon salt
½ teaspoon pepper

Put kidney beans in colander and rinse well. (Can use baked kidney beans if well rinsed.)

Combine salad oil, vinegar, salt and pepper to make dressing.

Combine all vegetables and mushrooms. Let ripen in above dressing for at least 12 hours before serving.

Submitted by Eleanor Jones, East Hampton, Conn.

Pickled Red Cabbage

(M. Abbie Miller's Cook Book, September, 1900)

Take a sound red cabbage, shave off, sprinkle each layer with salt, let remain over night. In the morning wash off salt, have vinegar enough to cover; take handful of whole cloves and allspice, coffee cup of brown sugar, scald well, throw over cabbage through strainer. It is fine.—A. H.

Submitted by Mrs. Cynthia Packard, Rockland, Maine

Molded Beet Salad

1 envelope unflavored gelatine
½ cup cold water
1½ cups pickled beet juice and water
½ teaspoon salt
½ teaspoon grated onion
1 teaspoon prepared horse-radish
1 cup chopped pickled beets
1 cup finely shredded cabbage
1 cup chopped celery

Soak gelatine in cold water; use ¾ cup of pickled beet liquid and ¾ cup of water to make the 1½ cups. Add the salt, grated onion and horseradish and dissolved gelatin. Mix well. Chill until partially set. Stir in the beets and cabbage (celery if you like). Pour into a mold and let set until firm. Unmold on lettuce.

Submitted by Mrs. Edna Dyer, North Haven, Maine

Tuna Party Salad

2 envelopes plain gelatine
½ cup cold water
1 cup chili sauce
3 tablespoons lemon juice
1 cup mayonnaise
1 cup heavy cream, whipped
2 cans (6½ or 7 oz.) tuna fish
1 cup ripe olives quartered
1 cup finely chopped celery

Soften gelatine in cold water. Heat chili sauce to boiling. Remove from heat and add softened gelatine, stir until dissolved. Add lemon juice and chill until partly set. Fold in mayonnaise, whipped cream, olives, celery and flaked tuna. Pour into 2 quart mold. No dressing necessary.

Submitted by Mrs. Sally Cross, Rockland, Maine

Fish Salad

1½ pounds haddock fillet
2 small carrots
1 stalk celery
1 small onion
½ green pepper

Cook the haddock fillet and flake it being careful to remove any small bones. Cut up fine the carrots, celery, onion and green pepper. Add to the flaked haddock.

Mix the haddock and vegetable mixture with the following dressing. Let it set for several hours. Serve on lettuce.

DRESSING

¾ cup mayonnaise
¼ cup catsup (scant)
Salt and pepper to taste
2 or 3 sweet pickles, cut up
2 tablespoons pickle juice

Mix all ingredients together in the order given.

Submitted by Mrs. Christine McMahon, Rockland

Tasty Cole Slaw

1 small cabbage	Few sprigs of chives
3 small carrots	Paprika
1 cup mayonnaise or salad dressing	Salt and pepper to taste

Put the cabbage, carrots and chives through food grinder. Add enough mayonnaise to hold ingredients together. Mix together well and put into a round mold. Sprinkle paprika over the top. Let mold set until firm, then slide out on to a plate.

Submitted by Mrs. Myrtle Nord, Fairhaven, Mass.
(formerly of Friendship, Maine)

Cabbage Salad

4 cups shredded cabbage	Dash pepper
½ cup green pepper	2 tablespoons vinegar
2 tablespoons sugar	1 teaspoon French mustard
1 teaspoon salt	½ cup salad dressing
1 teaspoon celery seed	

Mix salad ingredients in order given and pour over shredded cabbage and chopped or thinly sliced green pepper. Chill before serving.

Submitted by Mrs. Douglas McMahon, Rockland, Maine

Sillsalad
(From Sweden)

8 cold boiled potatoes	3 large apples, peeled and cut up
4 cold boiled beets	
1 pound cold boiled beef, small pieces	3 medium salted herring, skinned, boned and cut up (soaked in cold water)
2 large dill pickles, diced	

Dry herring with paper towels. Mix all of the salad ingredients and combine with the following dressing.

DRESSING

1 cup heavy cream, whipped	¼ teaspoon white pepper
2 tablespoons vinegar	Lettuce
2 teaspoons sugar	Sliced beets for garnish
½ teaspoon salt	

Mix heavy cream with vinegar, sugar, salt and pepper. Arrange salad on lettuce leaves with sliced beets for a garnish. Most delicious.

This is my mother-in-law's recipe, straight from Gottenborg Sweden, 100 years ago and more.

Submitted by Mrs. Raymond Anderson, Rockland, Maine

Jellied Salad

1 package lime jello	½ cup shredded carrots
1 cup boiling water	1 cup stuffed olives, sliced
1 cup shredded pineapple	1 cup of cold liquid (fruit
1 cup celery, cut very fine	juice and water)

Mix a package of jello with the boiling water and cold liquid. Cool and add the pineapple, celery, carrots and olives. Put in the refrigerator to set. Serve on lettuce with salad dressing.

Submitted by Evelyn Comey, Shapleigh, Maine

Corned Beef Salad

1 can corned beef	½ teaspoon salt
3 hard boiled eggs (cut)	1 cup Miracle Whip
1 small onion cut fine	1 package lemon jello
2 cups celery cut or chopped	1 cup hot water

Mix jello with hot water, cool, add Miracle Whip. Beat, add all other ingredients and place in salad mold.

Submitted by Gladys S. Mooers, Milo, Maine

Cabbage Salad

1 cup vinegar	Salt and pepper to taste
½ cup sugar	1 tablespoon butter
1 teaspoon mustard	1 teaspoon celery seed salt
1 teaspoon cornstarch	1 head of cabbage, shredded
1 egg, beaten	

Mix all the ingredients together, except the cabbage and celery seed salt. Cook until it thickens, then add celery seed salt. Pour over shredded cabbage; use dressing over cabbage while it is still warm.

Submitted by Mrs. Alice N. Pike, Springvale, Maine

Potato Salad

1 cup cream	1 small onion chopped
2/3 cup salad dressing	1 small can peas or left over
1 heaping teaspoon French's	peas
mustard	Salt and pepper to taste
3 tablespoons vinegar	1 hard cooked egg sliced (for
Sugar to taste	garnish)
5 or 6 boiled potatoes	Dash of paprika

Whip the cream and add the salad dressing, mustard, vinegar and sugar to taste. Dice the cooked potatoes and add the chopped onion, peas and seasonings. Garnish with sliced eggs and dash of paprika.

Submitted by Miss Mary C. Taylor, Lubec, Maine

Potato Salad

5 or 6 large potatoes	¼ cup sugar
2 or 3 tablespoons mayonnaise	1 small onion
	2 eggs
1 tablespoon mustard	½ teaspoon salt
1 tablespoon vinegar	Paprika

Peel and cook the potatoes, let cool; then cut up into a bowl. Add mayonnaise, mustard, vinegar, salt and sugar, mixing thoroughly. Boil and mash eggs and add to the salad. Slice raw onion and add.

Submitted by Mrs. Natalie Sylvester, Rockland, Maine

Fruit Salad

1 large can sliced pineapple	Few grains salt
½ cup sugar	½ cup whipping cream (added
2 eggs	to dressing)
2 tablespoons flour	

Cut up in cubes the following fruit: 2 bananas, 2 oranges, 2 pears, 1 large bunch of grapes, 2 cups melon cubes, 2 cups watermelon cubes, 2 cups marshmallows (miniature), and sliced pineapple, cut up or tidbits. This amount will make 8 good servings. Heat the pineapple juice (from the can of pineapple, about 2 cups). Mix sugar, flour, salt, yolks of eggs and add to hot juice. Cook until thick. Add beaten egg whites and cook 2 minutes. Cool in refrigerator. Prepare fruit and cut in desired size pieces. Add whipped cream to dressing just before putting on the fruit.

Submitted by Mrs. Charles McMahon, Rockland, Maine

Speedy Salad

1 package instant vanilla pudding	1 cup whipped cream
	1 jar maraschino cherries (4 oz.)
1 can drained fruit cocktail (1 lb. 14 oz.)	6 ounces miniature marshmallows
1 can mandarin oranges (11 oz.)	2 medium bananas, sliced

Prepare one package of instant vanilla pudding according to the directions. Fold in one cup whipped cream. Drain the fruit cocktail, mandarin oranges and the cherries well and fold into pudding. Add the miniature marshmallows and sliced bananas. Chill thoroughly. Makes 8 to 10 servings. This is very good. Note: Sour cream may be substituted for sweet cream by adding 1 teaspoon vanilla and 2 teaspoons sugar.

Submitted by Mrs. Burt Hazelton, Winslow, Maine

Whipped Lime Jello Salad

1 package jello
1 small can crushed pineapple, drained
1 small package cream cheese

Water plus pineapple juice to make 1 cup
½ cup cream

Mix the jello with boiling hot water, pineapple juice mixture until it is dissolved. Let it set until it starts to jell. Whip the cream and cream cheese and add the pineapple. Whip the chilled jello that is partly jelled; then add the cream cheese mixture. Pour into a mold and set in the refrigerator until firm.

Submitted by Mrs. Donald Coffin, Machias, Maine

Thanksgiving Or Christmas Salad

2 cups cranberries
1 orange (not peeled)
1 cup sugar

1 package lemon jello
2 cups hot water
1 cup chopped celery

Grind the cranberries and the orange and add the sugar. Let stand until the sugar is dissolved. Dissolve the jello in the hot water. Let stand until cool. Then mix with the first mixture and add the celery. Chill until firm.

Submitted by Mrs. Herman Robinson, Dixfield, Maine

Cinnamon Swirl Salad

3 cups boiling water
½ cup red cinnamon candies
1 6-oz. or 2 3-oz. packages lemon jello
2 cups sweetened applesauce
1 teaspoon lemon juice

Dash of salt
½ cup chopped nuts
2 3-oz. package cream cheese (soft)
¼ cup milk
2 tablespoons salad dressing

Put boiling water in sauce pan, add the red cinnamon candies and stir until nearly dissolved, then add the lemon jello; stir until dissolved. Remove from stove and add the applesauce, lemon juice and salt. Let set until it starts to jell and add the nuts.

While this is jelling more, mix the cream cheese with the milk and salad dressing using the electric mixer, if possible.

Turn the jello mixture into about an 8" x 8" pan; spoon cheese topping on and swirl in with a fork. Put in the refrigerator until firmly set. This makes a good salad, dessert or just good lunching.

If you are in a hurry for this to jell, use one cup of boiling water then add 2 cups of cold water after you add the applesauce.

Submitted by Frances Bartlett, Bangor, Maine

Spring Garden Salad

2 packages apple or lemon jello
3 cups boiling water
1 can pineapple chunks, drained (13½ oz.) plus syrup
½ cup chopped walnuts

10 Maraschino cherries, cut in half
1 cup shredded carrots
¼ cup chopped green peppers
Walnut halves

Dissolve jello in boiling water. Add syrup from pineapple. When the gelatin begins to thicken divide in half. To one part add pineapple chunks, cherries and ½ of the chopped walnuts. Pour into 6 cup mold. Chill.

Add remaining ingredients to the rest of the gelatin. Pour over the first layer. Chill until ready to serve. Unmold on lettuce; garnish with mayonnaise. Crown with walnut halves. Serves 6.

Submitted by Mrs. Leon Beal, Waterboro, Maine

My Favorite Christmas Molded Salad

1 large package cherry or raspberry jello
1½ cups boiling water
1 can whole cranberry sauce
1 small can crushed pineapple

2 peeled and chopped oranges
1 cup fresh grapes
½ cup dates, cut up
½ cup chopped nuts

Dissolve the large pkg. of jello (or 2 3-oz. pkgs.) in the boiling water; add the whole cranberry sauce, break up and mix well. Add the crushed pineapple, chopped oranges, grapes, dates and nuts. Mix well and put in an 8" x 12" pyrex pan to chill. When chilled cut in squares to serve.

Submitted by Mrs. Effie T. McKusick, Dexter, Maine

King Salad

1 package lemon jello
1 package lime jello
2 cups boiling water
8 ounce package cream cheese
1 large can evaporated milk

¾ cup mayonnaise
½ cup chopped nuts
¼ cup stuffed olives
Few Maraschino cherries, cut up

Mix the lemon and lime jello with the boiling water until dissolved. Let cool slightly. Add the cream cheese, evaporated milk and mayonnaise. Beat well; then fold in the nuts, olives, cut up, and few cherries.

Put in oblong pan and refrigerate. Garnish with half cream and half mayonnaise. This will serve 12 to 16 persons.

Submitted by Eleanor Boothby, Limington, Maine

Crushed Pineapple Carrot Mold

1 can pineapple, drained (#2)	¼ teaspoon salt
Pineapple juice added to water	2 tablespoons lemon juice
to make 1½ cups	1 cup grated carrots
1 package lemon jello	1 cup cream, whipped
½ cup sugar	

Drain the can of pineapple, using the juice to make 1½ cups of liquid. Heat to boiling and add the jello; stir until dissolved. Add the sugar, salt and the lemon juice. Chill until slightly thickened and add the pineapple and carrots. Whip the cream stiff and fold into the gelatin mixture.

Pour into an 8 inch ring, mold (that equals 1½ qts.) Chill.

Submitted by Mrs. Marion Goodwin, North Berwick, Maine

Grapefruit Lime Salad

1 can unsweetened grapefruit	1 large package lime jello
sections (#2)	2 cups Fresca
2 oranges, cut up	1½ cups boiling water plus
¼ cup cherries, cut up	Fruit juice to make 2 cups

Dissolve jello in the boiling water, then add the Fresca and let partly jell. Add fruit and let set in the refrigerator until well jelled.

Submitted by Mrs. Ruth Carlson, Rockland, Maine

Tomato Avocado Salad

1 can tomato soup and water	1 package orange jello
to make 16 ounces	½ avocado—cut in small
Grapefruit sections (½ grape-	pieces
fruit)	

Heat tomato soup and water to boiling; add the orange jello and dissolve. Add fruit, put into a mold and chill.

Submitted by Mrs. Betty Wildes, Sanford, Maine

Rhubarb Salad

2 cups rhubarb	Few drops of red coloring
2/3 cup sugar	¾ cup nuts
1 tablespoon plain gelatin	1 cup diced celery
½ cup cold water	1 tablespoon lemon juice

Dissolve the gelatin in the cold water and add to hot rhubarb and sugar and stir to melt the gelatin mixture. Add the red food coloring. When cool add the other ingredients, then pour in mold and jell in the refrigerator.

Submitted by Dorothy Ridlon, Kennebunkport, Maine

Quick and Easy Jellied Salad

1 package strawberry jello
1 cup boiling water
1 small can crushed pineapple

1 small can whole cranberry
sauce
Few walnuts for garnish

Mix the jello and boiling water; cool, then add the pineapple and whole cranberry sauce. Fold together and sprinkle a few cut-up walnuts on top. This is delicious served with chicken.

Submitted by Mrs. Erla Kierstead, Caribou, Maine

French Salad Dressing

½ cup salad oil
1/3 cup ketchup
⅛ cup vinegar
¼ cup sugar

½ teaspoon salt
Dash of pepper
Juice of one lemon
1 peeled onion (keep whole)

Mix all of the above ingredients together and float the one peeled, whole onion in the jar of the mixture.

Submitted by Mrs. Carol Howe, Bangor, Maine

Salad Dressing

2 eggs
½ cup vinegar
½ cup sugar
1 teaspoon salt

1 teaspoon dry mustard
2 tablespoons flour (heaping)
1 tablespoon butter (large)
1 cup milk or cream

Beat eggs. Add to vinegar and heat on stove. Mix together with sugar, salt, flour and mustard and make a paste with the milk or cream. Add to the heated eggs and vinegar and stir constantly. Add the butter at last. This is especially good with salmon.

Submitted by Miss Mertie Cahoon, Madawaska, Maine

Dressing For Cabbage Slaw

2 eggs
2 tablespoons sugar
¼ cup water
¼ teaspoon salt

¼ cup vinegar
¼ teaspoon mustard
1/16 teaspoon celery salt
2 tablespoons fat

Beat the eggs and add all of the other ingredients except the fat. Cook in double boiler until thick stirring constantly. Add the fat just before removing from fire. Cool and use as dressing for cabbage slaw.

Submitted by Mrs. L. A. Philbrick, No. Leeds, Maine

Uncooked Salad Dressing

Beat all together with the egg beater. This makes about 1 pint.

1 can condensed milk
2 well beaten eggs
1 teaspoon salt

1 teaspoon mustard
½ cup vinegar

Submitted by Miss Effie Nye, Skowhegan, Maine

Sour Blueberries

Place a quart of fresh blueberries in a two quart jar. Cover with cold water and ½ cup sugar. Cover with cheese cloth and keep in a cool place until fall when it is time for the making. The cellar is best for keeping the berries.

Very good, and makes the mincemeat very dark and tasty.

Submitted by Mrs. Christie Hardison, Cherryfield, Maine

Real Maine Mincemeat

1 quart cooked ground venison or beef	1 package raisins
2 quarts chopped pie apples	1 teaspoon cinnamon
2 cups suet	1 teaspoon cloves
½ cup vinegar	1 teaspoon salt
½ cup meat liquid	1 cup sugar
	1 cup molasses

Mix all ingredients together well. Cook mixture slowly over low heat, stirring often to keep from sticking, until it thickens and the apples are done (don't let it cook until dry). Store in canning jars if desired.

Submitted by Mrs. John Cakouros, Woolwich, Maine

Venison Mincemeat

6 cups ground venison liberally moistened with stock	1 package currants
12 to 14 cups chopped or coarsely ground Baldwin apples	1 jar grape jelly
3 cups ground beef suet	1 jar red jelly (chokecherry, crabapple or currant)
3 ground oranges, 1 with skin	1 pint molasses
1 package ground seeded raisins	1 pint sweet cider
1 package seedless raisins	2 cups sugar
1 package golden raisins	5 teaspoons salt
1 pint canned citron (include liquid)	3 teaspoons cinnamon
	2 teaspoons powdered cloves
	2 teaspoons nutmeg
	2 cups water

Cook piece of venison (neck meat is fine) in salted water until very tender. Cool in liquid.

Mix well and cook slowly (uncovered) in very large heavy kettle (pressure canner is ideal) about 3 hours or until "rich" looking. Stir occasionally to prevent sticking. Taste during cooking for sweetness and seasoning. Put hot into jars and seal. Makes 7 or 8 quarts.

Submitted by Mary Thomes Carlson, Harrison, Maine

Grandmother's Pear Mincemeat

7 pounds ripe pears	1 cup vinegar
1 lemon	1 tablespoon cinnamon
2 packages of seedless raisins	1 tablespoon allspice
6¾ cups sugar	1 teaspoon ginger

Core and quarter pears. (Do not peel). Cut lemon into quarters, remove seeds.

Put through the food chopper pears, lemon and raisins.

Combine all ingredients. Bring to a boil. Simmer 40 minutes, pack in hot jars and process in hot water bath 25 minutes.

Submitted by Mrs. Marilyn M. Wiers, St. Albans, Maine

Nan's Apple Chutney

12 large apples	1 cup chopped raisins
4 large onions	1 tablespoon cloves
2 sweet peppers	2 cups sugar
6 green tomatoes	1 quart vinegar
1 tablespoon salt	1 tablespoon celery seed
1 tablespoon cinnamon	1 tablespoon dry mustard

Chop fine, apples, onions, peppers, tomatoes and raisins. Add the remaining ingredients and cook very slowly for one hour. Place in sterilized jars and seal.

Submitted by Mrs. Eleanor Keene, Medomak, Maine

Honey

5 pounds sugar	10 roses
1½ pints water	40 red clovers
Alum (size of a bean)	20 white clovers

Combine all ingredients and boil three minutes. Set 15 minutes. Strain and pour into jars.

Submitted by Mrs. Elsie Pennell, Machias, Maine

Old Fashioned Cucumber Pickles

Cucumbers	Rock salt

When cucumbers are gathered from the vine wash and put in a firkin or ½ barrel. Arrange a layer of cucumbers and a layer of rock salt. Alternately use enough salt to make sufficient brine to cover pickles. No water. They form their own brine. Keep under a heavy weight. When the weight is removed to add more cucumbers, rinse the weight off, as a scum will gather and settle on it. To prepare pickles for use, soak over night in hot water until fresh. Let stand in spiced vinegar and serve.

Submitted by Mrs. Leo Russell, Bangor, Maine

Mother's Mustard Pickles

1 quart small cucumbers
1 quart large cucumbers
(cut up)
1 quart button onions
1 quart green tomatoes
(cut up)

2 cauliflowers, cut up
2 red peppers, cut up
2 green peppers, cut up
4 quarts cold water
½ cup salt

Let vegetables stand in the water and salt. (Use ½ cup of salt or until water tastes salty). Let stand overnight.

In the morning, drain well and rinse with cold water if vegetables are too salty.

Cook in water to cover until almost tender. Do not overcook. Drain well.

Add the following hot sauce to the drained vegetables.

MUSTARD SAUCE

6 cups vinegar
3 cups sugar
1 cup flour

2½ tablespoons mustard
2½ teaspoons turmeric

Mix dry ingredients together and make a thin smooth paste by adding some of the cold vinegar slowly. Bring the remainder of the vinegar to a boil and add slowly to the paste.

Cook slowly until of right consistency. Sauce should be a little thicker than you want as it will become thinner when the drained vegetables are added. (Taste for sweetness).

Add thick sauce to the drained vegetables and simmer slowly until all ingredients are thoroughly hot. Seal in clean sterile jars.

Submitted by Mrs. William Stevens, Rockland, Maine

Tomato Pickles

2 pecks tomatoes
3 bags onions (3 lbs. bags)
1 cup salt
2 quarts vinegar
2 quarts water

3 pounds brown sugar
2 pounds white sugar
1 box mixed spice (make into
bag)

Slice tomatoes and onions in a large kettle—a layer of tomatoes, layer of onions sprinkle with salt, until you have used up tomatoes and onions and salt. Let set over night. The next morning, drain well the tomato and onions. Combine vinegar, water, sugar and spice bag. Add the tomato mixture and cook until tender. Seal in hot jars.

Submitted by Mrs. Henry Hutchinson, Rockland, Maine

Watermelon Pickles

1 quart vinegar
5 pounds sugar
¼ pound stick cinnamon
¼ pound whole cloves
Rind of large melon

Peel and cut melon rind in small pieces. Put in large kettle, cover with cold water and let come to a boil. Drain and cover again, let boil ten minutes.

Make a syrup of vinegar, sugar and spices and add melon. Let cook until soft and tender.

Submitted by Gladys Mooers, Milo, Maine

Ripe Cucumbers

25 ripe cucumbers (about)
2 cups brown sugar
¼ teaspoon salt
2 cups water
2 cups vinegar
1 teaspoon mustard seed
2 teaspoons mixed pickling spice
1 teaspoon celery seed
½ teaspoon turmeric
½ teaspoon cinnamon

Put whole spices in cloth bag. This makes enough liquid for 25 average size ripe cucumbers peeled and cut up after seeds are removed.

Simmer until tender to a fork. Bottle and seal while boiling hot.

Submitted by Mrs. Althena Brown, Morrill, Maine

Piccalilli

2 dozen green tomatoes
1 head cabbage
1 dozen large cucumbers
1 dozen onions
6 large green peppers
2 dozen small cucumbers
Salt
1 quart water
1 quart vinegar
1 gallon vinegar
3 pounds sugar
½ pound white mustard seed
2 tablespoons ground mustard
3 tablespoons cinnamon
1 tablespoon cloves
1 tablespoon black pepper
1 tablespoon allspice
1 tablespoon ginger

Chop fine, tomatoes, cabbage, cucumbers, onions and small cucumbers and put all together in a large jar. Stir in a handful of salt and let set overnight. Drain. Add 1 quart of water and 1 quart of vinegar, cook 10 minutes. Drain again and put back into jar.

Scald 1 gallon of vinegar with sugar and spices.

Pour on the vegetables in the jar and stir well.

This does not need to be sealed.

Submitted by Bertha Hoyt, North Anson, Maine

Spiced Relish

1 unpeeled, seedless orange

2 cups washed, drained
  cranberries

1 cup sugar

¼ cup orange juice

1 tablespoon prepared mustard

⅛ teaspoon allspice

Cut oranges in pieces and put through food grinder with cranberries. Add sugar, orange juice, mustard and allspice. Let stand 24 hours stirring occasionally. Makes 2 cups.

Submitted by Mrs. Leon Beal, Waterboro, Maine

Golden Glow Pickles

2 quarts cucumbers

3 tablespoons salt

5 onions

2 red peppers

2 cups vinegar

1½ cups sugar

1½ teaspoons turmeric
  powder

Cut cucumbers up fine and cover with salt and hot water. Let stand.

Cut onions and peppers up fine and mix with sugar, vinegar and turmeric powder.

Drain cucumbers well and add the rest of the ingredients. Cook slowly until done. Seal hot.

Submitted by Mrs. Stella Hollister, Hartland, Maine

Carrot Marmalade

Carrots (peeled to make
  two cups)

1 lemon

½ cup sugar

Put through the meat grinder 1 lemon with rind (but not seeds), and carrots, peeled to make 2 cups. Add ½ cup sugar. Let stand several hours before serving. Very good with meat, etc.

Submitted by Etta Beverage, North Haven, Maine

Linderberry Treat

2 medium cabbages

8 medium carrots

8 sweet red & green peppers

12 onions

½ cup salt

3 pints vinegar

6 cups sugar

1 teaspoon mustard seed

1 teaspoon celery seed

Grind the vegetables and add the salt. Let stand 2 hours. Drain. Mix vinegar, sugar and spices. Add to the vegetables. Mix thoroughly. Do not cook. Put in tight jars.

Submitted by Mrs. Dorothy Robbins, Ellsworth, Maine

Dried Fruit Conserve

1 cup dried apricots
1½ cups dried peaches
1—1/3 cups orange juice
4 tablespoons grated orange
rind

6 cups seedless raisins
1 or 2 tablespoons lemon
juice
6 cups sugar

Pour boiling water over peaches, then pour off immediately. Put 4 cups of water on peaches and boil 10 minutes or until skins slip; cool, remove skins from each peach and return to water. (If preferred peaches may be soaked overnight and then skins removed before cooking.)

With the peaches combine the apricots which have been washed and soaked in 2 cups boiling water. Cook fruit until tender. Crush with a potato masher or chop fine with a sharp knife. It is not necessary to put through a sieve if the skins have been removed. Add the remaining ingredients and a cup of water if the mixture seems too dry.

Cook slowly and stir until of the consistency of jam. Pour into hot glasses and seal at once with paraffin.

Submitted by Carrie C. Libby, Easton, Maine

Spiced Rhubarb Sauce

6 cups rhubarb
5 cups sugar
¾ teaspoon cloves

¾ teaspoon cinnamon
¾ cup vinegar (I use cider
vinegar)

Cut rhubarb in 1 inch pieces, mix with other ingredients and boil until thick. Put in clean sterilized jars and wax to seal. (I have used jars with rubbers and clamped immediately).

Submitted by Mrs. Richard Lovell, Sanford, Maine

Apple Sauce

6 to 8 tart apples pared and
sliced
½ cup water

½ cup sugar (or to suit taste)
Cinnamon (if desired)

Put apples and water into a saucepan, cover tightly, and cook over moderate heat without stirring until apples are mushy (about 20 minutes). Add sugar stir just to mix, and cook for a minute or two longer. Remove from heat and whip with spoon to a smooth stiff sauce. A little ground cinnamon may be added to give sauce a darker color and spicy flavor.

Cherried Cranberries

4 cups cranberries

2 cups sugar

1 cup water

¼ teaspoon soda

¼ teaspoon salt

Mix ingredients together and boil slowly for 15 minutes and set aside until cool.

Makes two pints. Will keep quite awhile in refrigerator.

Submitted by Virginia G. Smith, Limington, Maine

Cranberry Fluff Relish

1 package cranberries ground (raw)

1½ cups finely cut marshmallows

1 cup diced celery

2 cups sugar

1 cup chopped nuts

1½ cups cream, whipped

Mix and let stand overnight in the refrigerator the cranberries, marshmallows, celery and sugar.

Before serving fold in the 1 cup chopped nuts and 1½ cups cream, whipped.

It is a relish but we sometimes use it as a light dessert.

Submitted by Mrs. Robert Dall, Orono, Maine

Cranberry Jelly

1 quart cranberries

2 cups water

2 cups sugar

Pick over and wash 1 quart cranberries. Cook with 2 cups water until tender. In the meantime heat 2 cups sugar in a low oven. (Do not scorch the sugar). Then work the berries through a sieve, press all the juice out, return the juice to the stove to a boil. Remove it off the heat. Stir the hot sugar into the hot juice. Stir well. Pour at once into a hot glass or earthen dish. Do not boil the juice while adding the sugar.

Submitted by Mrs. Flavilla Kennedy, Rockland, Maine

Pineapple and Rhubarb Jam

5 cups diced rhubarb

1 cup crushed pineapple, drained

4 cups sugar

1 package strawberry jello

Mix the rhubarb, pineapple and sugar and let stand 30 minutas. Then slowly bring to a boil and simmer 12 minutes.

Remove from heat and add the package of strawberry jello and stir until dissolved. Put in jelly glasses and cover with melted wax. Let cool and cover.

Submitted by Miss Lura York, Skowhegan, Maine

Popovers

1 teaspoon melted fat
2 eggs
1½ cups milk

1 cup flour
¼ teaspoon salt

Sift flour and measure 1 full cup; add the salt. Beat the eggs until frothy and add the milk; beat until all blended and add melted butter. Turn, slowly, into the dry ingredients. Beat until smooth. Turn into greased pyrex cups. Place in a cold oven and set temperature at 375 degrees and bake for 50 to 55 minutes. These can be mixed the night before and used for breakfast. (Do not open oven while baking).

Mr. Barter says, "These are real good."

Submitted by Mrs. Clement B. Barter, Bath, Maine

Coffee Ring

½ cup shortening
1 cup sugar
2 eggs
1 cup sour milk

2 cups flour
1 teaspoon baking powder
1 teaspoon soda
1 teaspoon vanilla

TOPPING

½ cup chopped nuts
1 teaspoon cinnamon

¼ cup brown sugar

Cream shortening and sugar, add eggs and rest of ingredients. Put half of batter in greased tube pan. Sprinkle half of topping over this batter; add rest of batter and sprinkle the remainder of the topping over the top. Bake at 350 degrees for 45 minutes.

Submitted by Mrs. Ruth Thompson, Rockland, Maine

French Breakfast Puffs

1/3 cup shortening
½ cup sugar
1 egg
½ cup milk

1½ cups flour
1½ teaspoons baking powder
½ teaspoon salt
¼ teaspoon nutmeg

Mix together first 3 ingredients, add flour mixture, alternately with milk. Fill greased muffin tins 2/3 full. Bake 350 degrees for 20 minutes. Remove from tins and roll in the following topping:

TOPPING

2 tablespoons melted butter
½ cup sugar

1 teaspoon cinnamon

After rolling puffs in topping, serve hot.

Submitted by Mrs. Burt Hazelton, Winslow, Maine

76

Numshedooles

(An Old Family Recipe)

2 cups flour
1 teaspoon cream of tartar
½ teaspoon soda

Few grains of salt
Milk (about ¾ to 1 cup)

BOILING SYRUP

1 cup molasses
¼ cup sugar

2 tablespoons butter

Sift together the flour, cream of tartar, soda and salt, twice. Add the milk to make a dough like biscuits, roll thin and cut out the same as biscuits and fry in deep fat as you would doughnuts. Boil the molasses, butter and sugar together for two or three minutes and as soon as the dough is removed from the hot fat, drop into the boiling molasses; just boil until well coated. Serve at once for a supper treat on Sunday night or for a good breakfast dish.

The original recipe states that a goodly portion of the fat should be either bear grease, deer tallow or both. Doubt if we would enjoy that today and it might also be a problem to get usually. Here on the farm, this is often served for breakfast. Sticky, but good!

Submitted by Mrs. Muriel M. Patten, Levant, Maine

Grandmother Shibles' Molasses Biscuits

½ cup molasses
¼ cup sugar
½ cup thick sour milk
1/3 cup shortening (bacon fat, butter or lard)

2½ cups flour, sifted
½ teaspoon soda (heaping)
¼ teaspoon ginger
½ teaspoon salt

Beat the molasses, sugar and shortening together until well mixed. Sift 2 cups of the flour with the dry ingredients. Add the sour milk to the creamed ingredients until well mixed; add the sifted dry ingredients and lightly mix. Add the rest of the flour, if necessary, to make a soft biscuit dough. Knead lightly and roll out to ¾ inch thickness. Cut with a biscuit cutter, place on a cookie sheet. Bake at 375 degrees for 15 to 20 minutes or until done.

Submitted by Mrs. Loana Shibles, Rockland, Maine

Baking Cream Biscuits

3 cups flour, sifted
1 teaspoon soda
2 teaspoons sugar
1 teaspoon salt

2 heaping teaspoons baking cream (bake-well cream)
1 heaping tablespoon shortening
1¼ cups milk (about)

Sift together the flour, soda, sugar, salt and baking cream. Cut in the shortening, add milk until dough is soft. Place on floured board, knead quickly, roll out and cut. Place on baking sheet, dot with butter and bake in a 400 degree oven for 15 minutes or until golden brown.

Submitted by Mrs. Mabel McMahon, Rockland, Maine

Rye Biscuits

3 cups flour

1 cup rye flour

2 teaspoons salt

6 teaspoons baking powder

½ cup shortening

1½ cups milk

Sift together the flours, salt and baking powder. Cut in the shortening and add the milk until it becomes a soft dough, easy to handle on the bread board. Knead lightly and quickly on board and roll out and cut with biscuit cutter. Top biscuits with a little milk or bits of butter. Let set awhile before baking and they will lighten up. Bake in a 450 degree oven for about 12 minutes.

Submitted by Mrs. Carl Carlson, Rockland, Maine

Buttermilk Biscuits

4 cups flour

½ cup shortening

1 teaspoon soda

2 teaspoons baking powder

1½ teaspoons salt

2 tablespoons sugar

2 cups buttermilk (about)

Sift together the flour, soda, baking powder, salt and sugar. Cut in the shortening and add the buttermilk, about 1½ cups, and then the amount extra to make a nice soft dough easy to handle on the floured board. Knead quickly and lightly; roll out and cut to desired size. Place on baking sheet, top each biscuit with butter, and bake at 450 degrees for about 15 minutes.

Submitted by Mrs. Elmer Williams, Topsham, Maine

Corn Oysters

2 eggs, well beaten

1 tablespoon sugar

1 can cut corn
   (drained mostly)

2 teaspoons baking powder

Salt to taste

Flour to make a drop batter

Mix together the eggs, sugar and corn. Next add some flour with the baking powder and salt and mix thoroughly with the egg mixture. Add more flour until you have a drop batter. Fry in deep fat, and serve with maple syrup. This is extra good with chicken.

Submitted by Miss Etta Beverage, North Haven, Maine

Corn Meal Griddle Cakes

(No Eggs)

1-1/3 cups corn meal	1 teaspoon salt
2/3 cup flour	1 tablespoon shortening
¾ cup milk	1 tablespoon molasses
1½ cups boiling water	4 teaspoons baking powder

Scald corn meal in bowl with boiling water, add milk, melted shortening and molasses, add flour, salt and baking powder which have been sifted together. Mix well. Bake on hot griddle until brown. Serve with molasses or maple syrup.

Submitted by Mrs. Ruth Bowden, Blue Hill, Maine

Griddle Cakes

(A Very Old Recipe)

2 eggs, well beaten	1 teaspoon salt
2 tablespoons sugar	Flour to make a soft drop
2 cups buttermilk	batter
1 heaping teaspoon soda	

Mix together the eggs, sugar, buttermilk, soda and salt. Add enough flour to make a soft drop batter. I use a piece of bacon on a fork to grease my griddle or frying pan. Drop by tablespoon, turning over once. Serve at once, with maple syrup.

Note: Neither sweet milk nor sour milk will make griddles to taste like these. Buttermilk must be used for flavor.

HOME MADE SYRUP FOR GRIDDLE CAKES

1 cup white sugar	1 cup hot water
2 cups brown sugar	1 teaspoon vanilla

Boil together the white sugar, brown sugar and hot water for five minutes. When cool add the vanilla.

If you have a "little" maple syrup, this may be added and no one will know it if the "cook keeps still." I have done it many times in "my day at The Haven's Inn".

Submitted by Miss Etta Beverage, North Haven, Maine

Quick Cranberry Muffins

1½ cups fresh cranberries	1 egg, beaten
3 tablespoons sugar	1 cup milk
2 cups Bisquick	

Chop the fresh cranberries and add the sugar; then add to Bisquick, beaten egg and milk. Bake in oven at 400 degrees for about 20 minutes. This makes 12 muffins.

Submitted by Mrs. Clarence J. Stone, North Haven, Maine

Blueberry Muffins

1½ cups fresh blueberries
(washed)
1½ cups flour
½ teaspoon salt
3 tablespoons sugar

3 teaspoons baking powder
1 egg
¾ cup fresh milk
3 tablespoons melted shortening

Wash the fresh blueberries, drain thoroughly. Mix and sift the flour with salt, sugar and baking powder. Beat the egg and mix with the fresh milk. Stir the egg and milk into the flour mixture, then add the berries and melted shortening. Mix well and pour into greased muffin pans, filling each one ¾ full. Bake in a hot oven — 400 degrees — for 20 minutes. Makes nine to twelve muffins, depending on size.

Submitted by Margaret Chase Smith,
United States Senator, Washington, D. C.

Blueberry Muffins
(Sour Milk)

½ cup sugar
4 tablespoons shortening
1 cup sour milk
2¼ cups flour

1 teaspoon soda
1 teaspoon baking powder
½ teaspoon salt
1 cup blueberries

Cream shortening, sugar together, stir in the sour milk. Sift flour, soda, baking powder and salt together, mix lightly with the liquids and add blueberries. Bake in 400 degree oven, in muffin tins, which have been greased, for about 25 minutes or until done.

Submitted by Annie Timberlake, Livermore Falls, Maine

Squash Muffins

Beat 1 egg. Add
2 tablespoons sugar
1 cup milk. Add
2 cups flour
2 tablespoons baking powder

½ teaspoon salt
Stir in
2/3 cup squash
3 tablespoons melted
shortening.

Beat well. Bake 25 minutes at 375 degrees.

(You will think I have made two mistakes — the amount of baking powder IS 2 tablespoons and you do beat them quite well. They are rich yellow, light and absolutely delicious. I used them one year on Christmas cards and still get calls from all over the country for a copy).

Submitted by Peg Rogers, Solon, Maine

Holiday Muffins

¼ cup   soft butter or
   substitute
½ cup sugar
1 large egg
1½ cups sifted flour
2½ teaspoons baking powder

½ teaspoon salt
½ cup whole milk
¾ to 1 cup fresh blueberries,
   sliced strawberries or whole
   raspberries (about ½ and
   ½ for best results)

Cream the butter (better flavor) and sugar together and then add the well beaten egg, beat well. Sift together 1¼ cups of the all-purpose flour (superb results obtained with ¼ cup cake flour and the rest all-purpose flour), baking powder and salt. Add dry ingredients alternately with the milk. Do not beat — mix gently only until flour is mixed. Mix ¼ cup of flour, remaining, with the berries and then add to the mixture, barely mixing, to produce a muffin of fine grain and tenderness. Bake on middle shelf of 400 degree temperature, using tins of your choice that have been lightly greased with Crisco and dusted with flour. Fill tins 2/3 full. Bake for about 12 to 20 minutes depending on size.

Combination of colored berries was used for novelty for many years at a small coast inn on July 4. The same basic proportions are fine for using chopped dates, apricots, cranberries, sliced, chopped, fresh, ripe, but firm peaches and other choices.

Submitted by Mrs. Katharine Savage, Northeast Harbor, Maine

Oatmeal Muffins

1 cup sifted flour
2 tablespoons sugar
2 teaspoons baking powder
½ teaspoon soda
1 scant teaspoon salt

¾ cup quick cooking
   rolled oats
¼ cup vegetable shortening
1 egg
1 cup buttermilk

Sift flour, sugar, baking powder, soda, and salt together; add oats. Cut in shortening. Add eggs and buttermilk and mix only until dry ingredients are dampened. Bake in 420 oven about 25 minutes. Makes a dozen muffins.

Submitted by Barbara Farren, Addison, Maine

Whopovers

1 egg, beaten (put in cup
   and fill with milk)
1 large teaspoon soda

1 teaspoon salt
2 teaspoons cream of tartar
Flour (about 2 cups)

Beat one egg in a cup, fill the cup with new milk; put it in a mixing bowl. Sift flour, soda, salt and cream of tartar together. Add

81

the egg-milk mixture to the dry ingredients and mix like biscuits. Knead quickly and roll out; then cut with biscuit cutter. Fry in hot lard and eat with syrup. They are delicious.

These will roll over in the fat themselves. If a little hard on taking from the fat, put in covered dish for a few minutes.

Submitted by Eula N. Goodwin, Anson, Maine

Fried Corn Bread

1¼ cups corn meal	1 teaspoon salt
¾ cup sifted flour	2 eggs, beaten
1 tablespoon sugar	1 cup evaporated milk
4 teaspoons baking powder	Hot fat for frying

Sift corn meal, flour, sugar, baking powder and salt into mixing bowl. Add beaten eggs and milk. Stir until blended.

Drop by tablespoonfuls into shallow hot fat in skillet or into greased griddle; when bread becomes bubbly on top, turn and brown on other side. Yield, about 30 rounds. These are delicious with maple syrup, and are good buttered while hot.

Submitted by Mrs. Paul Sawyer, Ellsworth, Maine

Johnny Cake

¼ cup melted shortening	1 cup corn meal
¼ cup sugar	2 teaspoons cream of tartar
1 egg	1 teaspoon soda
1 cup sweet milk	1 teaspoon salt
1 cup flour	

Sift together all of the dry ingredients. Combine the milk, egg and melted shortening. Add these liquid ingredients all at once to the dry ingredients and beat only until they are moistened.

Bake in a greased 8 x 8 inch pan at 400 degrees for 30 minutes. Cut in squares.

Submitted by Amy Wathen, R. N., Augusta, Maine

Johnny Cake

½ cup molasses	1 cup sour milk
1 cup corn meal	1 teaspoon soda
1 cup flour	1 egg

Beat egg and add molasses, unsifted corn meal, and sour milk, in which the soda has been added. Stir well, then put in the sifted flour and stir again. Do not over-stir. Bake in a greased pan, 400 degree oven.

Submitted by Mrs. Eleanor C. Duran, East Corinth, Maine

Grandmother's Brown Bread

2 cups graham flour	1 cup molasses
1 cup white flour	1½ teaspoons soda
1 cup sweet milk	1 teaspoon salt
1 cup sour milk	

Sift the flours, but use the coarse part of the graham, also. Add the soda to the sour milk and dissolve. Add the liquids, all at once, to the dry ingredients; stir, just enough to mix. Put in a pail and set in a kettle of water and steam for 3 hours.

The pail I use is a lard pail, but if you do not have one, you can divide the batter equally into 2 or 3 pound Crisco cans.

Submitted by Mrs. Harley Stevens, South Paris, Maine

Martha Russell Yates' "Togus Loaf"

1 cup corn meal	½ cup molasses
1 cup flour	1 teaspoon soda, rounding
1 cup sweet milk	1 teaspoon salt
1 cup sour milk	

Combine the ingredients as given, adding the wet ingredients to the well mixed flour, cornmeal, soda and salt. Steam for 2½ hours in a brown bread tin, greased thoroughly to avoid sticking. This recipe has a different texture and taste than regular brown bread. I am 82 years old, and this is my mother's recipe.

Submitted by Mrs. R. Gregory Wilson, Newcastle, Maine

Brown Bread

1½ cups hot water	1 cup corn meal
1 cup quick rolled oats	1 cup flour, sifted
2 tablespoons shortening	1 teaspoon soda
2/3 cup molasses	1 teaspoon salt

Pour the hot water over the rolled oats; add the shortening, molasses, corn meal and the flour, sifted with the soda and salt. Pour into a greased container and steam for 3 hours.

Submitted by Mrs. Maggie Gray, Boothbay Harbor, Maine

Graham Brown Bread

2 cups unsifted graham flour	1 teaspoon salt
½ cup molasses	2 cups sweet milk
1 egg	2 teaspoons soda
2 tablespoons sugar	

Dissolve the soda in the milk. Combine the dry ingredients with the molasses, egg and milk. Steam in a double boiler three hours.

Submitted by Mrs. Heloise Ward, Solon, Maine

Cranberry Nut Bread

2 cups flour
1 teaspoon baking soda
1 teaspoon salt
¾ cup sugar
1 egg, slightly beaten

2/3 cup milk
¼ cup melted oleo
1 cup whole cranberry sauce
1 cup chopped nuts

Sift dry ingredients in large bowl. Add rest of ingredients and mix only to moisten. Bake in greased loaf pan at 350 degrees, about one hour. This is the best cranberry bread I have ever found.

Submitted by Mrs. Earle A. Hodgkins, Jefferson, Maine

Apple Bread

¼ cup shortening
1 cup sugar
2 eggs, beaten
1½ to 2 tablespoons sour
   milk, with
½ teaspoon soda
2 cups flour

1 teaspoon salt
2 teaspoons baking powder
1 teaspoon vanilla
1 cup unpeeled red apples,
   chopped
¼ cup nut meats

Cream together the shortening and sugar, add the beaten eggs and beat well. Sift and measure the flour, salt and baking powder together. Mix the sour milk and soda together; add to the creamed mixture and then add the sifted dry ingredients, vanilla, chopped apple and nuts. Bake in a greased loaf pan for 1 hour at 350 degrees.

Submitted by Mrs. Edith Clough, Fairfield, Maine

Irish Soda Bread

4 cups sifted flour
¼ cup sugar
1 teaspoon salt
1½ teaspoons baking powder
2 tablespoons caraway seeds
   if desired

¼ cup shortening
2 cups raisins
1-1/3 cups buttermilk
1 egg
1 teaspoon soda

Sift the flour, measure and add the sugar, salt and baking powder. Blend in the shortening. Add soda to the buttermilk, then the beaten egg and add to the dry ingredients, quickly. Knead gently to form a round loaf. Cut cross in the top and place in a casserole. Bake in a 360 degree oven for about 50 minutes. Cool in the pan for 10 minutes, before turning out.

Submitted by Mrs. Ada Lincoln, Ellsworth, Maine

Lemon Bread

6 tablespoons Crisco	¼ teaspoon salt
2 eggs	Rind of 1 lemon
1 cup sugar	½ cup milk
1½ cups flour	Juice of 1 lemon
1½ teaspoons baking powder	¼ cup sugar

Blend the Crisco, eggs and sugar together until fluffy. Sift the flour and measure, then add the baking powder and salt, sift again; add alternately to the creamed mixture with the milk and finally, add the grated lemon rind. Pour into a greased loaf pan and bake for one hour in a 325 degree oven. When removed from the oven, pour the juice of one lemon mixed with ¼ cup of sugar over the top. Cool in the pan.

Submitted by Virginia Smith, Limington, Maine

Jiffy Graham Bread

½ cup brown sugar	1 cup flour
¾ cup cold water	1 teaspoon salt
½ cup vegetable oil	1 teaspoon soda
¾ cup milk	2 cups graham flour, unsifted

Mix together in a small bowl, the brown sugar and water, then add, oil and milk. Sift together the flour, salt and soda and add to the liquid ingredients. At last, add the graham flour. Mix well and put in greased bread pan and bake in a slow oven at 275 degrees F. for two hours.

Submitted by Lauraine M. Smith, Madison, Maine

Buttermilk Bran Pan Bread

2 tablespoons shortening	1 cup buttermilk
¼ cup sugar	1¼ cups flour
1 egg	1 teaspoon salt
1 cup all bran	2 teaspoons baking powder
½ teaspoon soda	

Blend shortening and sugar thoroughly; add egg and beat until creamy. Add bran and buttermilk; let soak until most of moisture is taken up. Sift flour with salt, baking powder and soda, and add to first mixture, stirring only until flour disappears. Pour into greased pan and bake in moderately hot oven, 425 degrees, about 25 minutes. Cut into squares and serve while hot. Raisins may be added; use ¼ cup raisins to each cup of flour. Yields nine three-inch squares.

Submitted by Mrs. S. L. Banton, Newport, Maine

Plain Doughnuts

3 tablespoons melted butter
1½ cups sugar
2 eggs
1 cup buttermilk
4 cups flour

3 teaspoons baking powder
½ teaspoon baking soda
1 teaspoon salt
1 teaspoon nutmeg
½ teaspoon cinnamon

Combine first four ingredients and beat until light. Sift dry ingredients and add to first. Stir in well, refrigerate for several hours or overnight. Pour on floured board and knead until smooth. Roll ¼ inch thick and cut out. Fry at 380 degrees using thermometer. Turn once. Makes 36.

Submitted by Virginia Wardwell, Rockland, Maine

Sugar Doughnuts

1 cup sugar
1 egg
3 tablespoons butter, melted
1 cup sweet milk
4 cups flour (about)
1 teaspoon soda

2 teaspoons cream of tartar, heaping
2 teaspoons vanilla or
2 teaspoons lemon and
¼ teaspoon nutmeg

Beat the egg well and add the sugar and the melted butter. Sift about 3 cups of flour with the cream of tartar, soda and salt; add to the doughnut mixture with the sweet milk. Add remaining flour, if necessary, to make a soft dough, easy to roll. Add vanilla for flavoring or if you prefer, use the lemon flavoring with a little nutmeg. Roll out on floured board and cut. Fry in hot fat and cook until golden brown. Roll in sugar, if desired.

Submitted by Emily Sadler, West Jonesport, Maine

Spud Doughnuts

1 cup sugar
2 eggs, beaten
2 tablespoons salad oil
1 cup mashed potato
1 cup sour milk
1 teaspoon soda

4½ cups flour
4 teaspoons baking powder
1 teaspoon salt
1 teaspoon nutmeg
1 teaspoon lemon extract

Beat eggs and sugar until light, add salad oil, potato and milk, to which soda has been added. Beat until smooth. Add flour and other dry ingredients and the flavorings. Fry in deep fat.

Submitted by Mrs. Edgar Treffey, Presque Isle, Maine

Raised Doughnuts

1 cup scalded milk	1 cup brown sugar
1 yeast cake	3 beaten eggs
½ cup lukewarm water	1 teaspoon nutmeg
1 teaspoon salt	4 cups flour (divide in two
½ cup butter	parts)

Dissolve yeast in the lukewarm water. Cool the scalded milk to lukewarm and add the yeast that has been dissolved; add the salt and 2 cups of flour to make a stiff batter. Let rise four or five hours or overnight in refrigerator.

Add melted butter, sugar, beaten eggs, nutmeg and 2 more cups of flour. Roll out one inch thick, cut and let rise for one hour. You may use a biscuit cutter and make jelly doughnuts. Fry in deep fat until brown on both sides. Cover with sugar, if desired.

Submitted by Mrs. Helen Reynolds, Pittsfield, Maine

Applesauce Doughnuts

1½ tablespoons butter	½ teaspoon salt
1½ cups brown sugar	½ teaspoon soda (scant)
2 eggs	½ teaspoon nutmeg
1 cup applesauce	½ teaspoon cinnamon
4 cups flour	4 teaspoons baking powder

Cream butter and add sugar, beating constantly; add beaten eggs, applesauce and other ingredients. Fry in deep fat from 3 to 5 minutes at 375 degrees.

Submitted by Muriel Polley, Machias, Maine

Chocolate Doughnuts

2½ squares chocolate	2 teaspoons vanilla
2 tablespoons oleo	3 cups flour
2 eggs	1¼ teaspoons soda
1¼ cups sugar	1 teaspoon salt
1¼ cups buttermilk	¼ teaspoon cinnamon

Melt the chocolate and oleo in top of the double boiler; beat together the eggs and sugar and add the melted chocolate mixture. Blend in the buttermilk and vanilla.

Sift together flour, soda, salt and cinnamon; add to the liquid mixture. Mix well and chill a long time (over-night). Roll, cut and fry in deep fat, temperature of 360 to 370 degrees.

Submitted by Louise Fleming, Howland, Maine

Molasses Doughnuts

(War Recipe)

2 eggs
1 cup molasses
1 cup buttermilk
4½ to 5½ cups flour
1½ teaspoons soda
½ teaspoon salt

½ teaspoon ginger
1 teaspoon cinnamon
1 teaspoon vanilla
3 tablespoons melted shortening

Beat eggs in bowl first, then add molasses and buttermilk; add the rest of the ingredients in the order given. using spices of your choice and enough flour to make a soft dough easy to roll. I use a big white coffee cup for measuring to get my 3 dozen and I also cut them a pretty good size.

This recipe is also good using ½ cup of sugar and ½ cup of molasses, in place of all molasses. This recipe was used during the war when sugar was scarce. Fry in deep fat, 375 degrees, until done.

Submitted by Edith Hermon, Athens, Maine

Raised Doughnuts

1 cup sugar
¼ teaspoon salt
2 cups scalding milk
½ cup shortening
1 yeast cake

1/3 cup warm water
2 eggs
8 cups flour (about)
¼ teaspoon soda

Dissolve yeast in warm water. Add sugar, salt and shortening to the scalding milk; let cool to lukewarm, then add beaten eggs and dissolved yeast. Sift flour and measure out 6 cups; add the soda to this and sift together, then add to the liquid ingredients, beating until smooth. Add enough of the other 2 cups of flour to make a dough with the consistency of bread (a soft dough). Place in a greased bowl, grease top of dough and cover.

Rise once to about double in bulk. Roll out on floured board and cut with doughnut cutter, rise until light. Fry in deep fat. Variation: Dip in thin confectionary frosting and place on cake rack over wax paper to drip. When cool, cover doughnuts with a towel to keep doughnuts from becoming sticky.

Submitted by Mrs. Albert Morton, Newry, Maine

Grandmother's Yeast Muffins

1 yeast cake	2 tablespoons sugar
¼ cup warm water	1 teaspoon salt
2 tablespoons shortening or oil	1 egg, well beaten
1 cup scalded milk	3 cups flour

Combine and let stand 5 minutes the yeast cake and warm water. Combine the shortening, scalded milk, sugar and salt. Let cool until warm. Stir in the dissolved yeast. Add the well beaten egg; stir in 3 cups sifted flour, about a cup at a time. Mix well. Brush with melted shortening and cover. Let rise until double in size. Punch down, and spoon in greased muffin tins, half full. Let rise about 1 hour. Bake in 400 degree oven for 15 minutes.

Submitted by Mrs. Julia Poirier, Dexter, Maine

Dark Yeast Rolls

½ cup shortening	1½ cups boiling water and
½ cup rolled oats	milk combined
½ cup all-bran	2 packages dry yeast
1 teaspoon salt	½ cup lukewarm water
3 tablespoons molasses	4 cups flour
2 tablespoons brown sugar	

Mix shortening, oats, all-bran, salt, molasses and sugar together and pour the boiling water and milk over them. Cool until lukewarm and add the yeast dissolved in the ½ cup of lukewarm water. Add the flour and mix well. Let rise until double in bulk. Knead dough and form into rolls. Place on greased baking sheet and let rise until double in bulk. Bake, 425 degrees, about 20 minutes.

Submitted by Mrs. Howard Nevells, Brooklin, Maine

Sixty Minute Rolls

2 yeast cakes	¾ teaspoon salt
¼ cup lukewarm water	¼ cup butter
1¼ cups milk	3 tablespoons sugar
3½ to 4½ cups sifted flour	

Dissolve yeast in lukewarm water. Put milk, sugar, salt and half the butter into a saucepan and heat until lukewarm. Add yeast and flour; cover and put in a warm place for 15 minutes. Turn out on floured board and pat to ½ inch thickness. Cut with 2 inch biscuit cutter. Brush with remaining butter and fold dough over. Let rise on greased baking sheet in warm place for 15 minutes. Bake in 450° oven for 10 minutes.

Submitted by Ethel H. Poland, Athens, Maine

Grace's Refrigerator Butter Rolls

1 yeast cake
1 tablespoon sugar
2 tablespoons warm water
½ cup milk
½ cup Crisco

2 eggs, beaten well
¼ cup sugar
1 teaspoon salt
3 cups all-purpose flour

Dissolve the yeast and sugar in the 2 tablespoons of warm water. Heat the milk and Crisco, and then cool to lukewarm. Beat the eggs until light and add the ¼ cup sugar and salt. Combine the egg-sugar mixture and the dissolved yeast. Stir in alternately the warm milk-Crisco mixture with the all-purpose flour. In the bowl, knead enough to make dough smooth. Cover, and place in refrigerator 24 hours or more. Three hours before using, remove from refrigerator and divide into 4 parts. Roll out each part in a round like pie-crust. Spread with softened butter; cut in 8 wedges as a pie, and roll up each wedge. Let rise on buttered cookie sheet for 3 hours. Bake at 375°, for about 10 minutes.

Submitted by Mrs. Inza Hilyard, Cushing, Maine

No-Knead Sweet Rolls

½ cup milk
3 tablespoons shortening
3 tablespoons sugar
1½ teaspoons salt

½ cup cold water
1 dry yeast
1 egg, beaten
3¼ cups flour

Scald milk, add shortening, sugar and salt. Cool to lukewarm by adding ½ cup cold water. Add the dry yeast dissolved in part of the liquid. Blend the beaten egg. Add 3¼ cups flour and mix until blended. Cover and let stand 15 minutes. Roll out in an 18 x 12 inch rectangle. Spread dough with the following:

¼ cup melted butter
¼ cup brown sugar

2 teaspoons cinnamon
Nuts or raisins, if desired

Roll as for jelly roll, cut in 1 inch slices or make a ring. Place in a greased pan. Let rise until double, about 1 hour. Bake 375 degrees for 20 to 25 minutes.

Submitted by Mrs. Christine McMahon, Rockland, Maine

All-Bran Refrigerator Bread

2/3 cup shortening
1 cup all-bran
1 cup boiling water
½ cup sugar
2 eggs, well beaten

2 yeast cakes
1 cup warm water
1½ teaspoons salt
6½ cups sifted flour or more

Mix together the shortening, all-bran and boiling water. Let cool; then add the sugar, 2 well beaten eggs, the yeast, that has been dissolved in the warm water, salt and the flour to make a stiff dough. You can mix and put in the refrigerator for 2 or 3 days, covering tight or you can mix, knead for 5 minutes or more until it is smooth, let rise and then knock down and shape into loaves; let rise again and bake in oven 425 degrees for 25 minutes. This can also be used for rolls.

Submitted by Mrs. Anna Gould, Union, Maine

Oatmeal Bread

2 cups slow-cooking oatmeal	½ cup warm water
1 tablespoon salt	½ teaspoon sugar
1/3 cup shortening	2 dry yeast
3½ cups boiling water	7 to 8 cups flour (including
½ cup molasses	kneading)

Mix together the oatmeal, salt, shortening and the boiling water. Stir and let it cool. Add the molasses. In the warm water, add the sugar and the yeast. Stir and let stand a few minutes; then add to the cooled oatmeal mixture. Add flour until you have a stiff dough. Let rise in a greased bowl until it is double in bulk; punch down and let rise again for a finer grain of bread. Knead dough until it is smooth and then shape into loaves and place in greased loaf pans. Let rise until double and rounded slightly over the pan. Bake at 400 degrees about 40 minutes.

Submitted by Mrs. Norman Hilyard, Cushing, Maine

Anadama Bread

½ cup corn meal	1 tablespoon salt
2 cups boiling water	2 packages dry yeast
2 tablespoons shortening	½ cup warm water
½ cup molasses	7 or 8 cups white flour

In large bowl, combine corn meal and boiling water. Add next three ingredients. Cool to lukewarm. Sprinkle yeast into warm water, let stand until dissolved, about 10 minutes. Stir into cornmeal mixture. Add flour to make a stiff dough. Knead until smooth and elastic. Place in greased bowl and cover with a towel. Let rise until double in bulk. Punch down, turn, and let rise again, about 45 minutes. Divide dough in half and knead into two loaves. Use 10 x 5 x 3 pans. Brush with salad oil and let rise until dough is barely above top of pan. Bake at 425° for 15 minutes. Reduce heat to 375° and bake 30 minutes longer. Remove and rub top with butter.

Submitted by Mrs. Esther Graves, Rockland, Maine

Nissua

(One of The Best Finnish Bread Recipes)

1 cup sugar (heaping)
1 teaspoon salt (heaping)
1 can evaporated milk, scalded
2 dry yeast
¾ cup warm water

4 eggs, beaten
½ cup melted butter
10 cardamon seeds, crushed or
1 teaspoon ground cardamon
7 cups flour (about)

Into a large bowl, measure the sugar and salt; over this, pour the scalded evaporated milk. Cool to lukewarm. Dissolve the yeast in the warm water and add to the cooled evaporated milk mixture. Beat the eggs and add; also add the melted butter and cardamon seeds, crushed. Last add enough flour to make a very soft dough, about 7 cups.

Knead the dough on a floured board until the dough becomes smooth, elastic and does not stick to the board or hands. Place in greased bowl, grease top of dough, cover and let rise until double in bulk; punch down in bowl, turn over and let rise until double in bulk again. Divide dough into three parts to make three good size braids. Place braids on greased cookie sheet. Brush with melted butter, let rise until double in bulk. Bake at 350° for 40 minutes. Remove from oven. Baste with a syrup; made by boiling together ¼ cup water and ¼ cup sugar until sugar is dissolved. Return to oven for a few minutes to dry syrup.

Instead of the syrup coating, you can decorate top with confectionery frosting, sprinkled with nuts, cherries, etc.

Submitted by Mrs. Helmi Ranta, Rockland, Maine

Raisin Bread

1 cup milk, scalded
2 tablespoons shortening
¾ cup sugar
2 eggs, beaten
1 yeast cake

1 cup lukewarm water
1 cup seeded raisins
6 cups flour
1 teaspoon salt

Dissolve yeast cake, part of sugar and salt in the lukewarm water. Add the lukewarm milk, shortening and 2 cups of flour. Let rise 1 or 1½ hours, then add beaten eggs, rest of sugar, raisins and rest of flour. Rise again and put in pans. Rise in pans until they are light and doubled in bulk. Bake at 375 degrees for about 40 minutes.

Submitted by Mrs. Doris Adams Andrews, Berlin, Mass.

War Bread

1 cup rolled oats	¾ teaspoon salt (scant)
1 cup corn meal	4 cups boiling water
1 cup graham flour	1 yeast cake
1 tablespoon lard	¼ cup warm water
½ cup molasses	

Mix together the rolled oats, corn meal, graham flour, lard, molasses, salt and boiling water. Stir until nice and smooth. Set away, until it gets lukewarm. Dissolve the yeast cake in the warm water and add to above mixture, when it is lukewarm. Stir in white flour until it becomes a stiff dough. Place in a greased bowl, grease top, cover, and let rise all night in refrigerator. In the morning, mix in just enough flour to mould into loaves. Let rise in greased baking pan. Bake in 350 degree oven for 1 hour.

Submitted by Mrs. Florence Barrett, Eastport, Maine

Prune Bread

½ pound dried prunes	½ teaspoon salt
¾ cup boiling water	1 egg
1¾ cups flour	2 tablespoons melted
¾ cup sugar	shortening
1 teaspoon baking soda	

Soak prunes in cold water for 2 hours; drain, pit prunes and chop. Add boiling water, let stand for 5 minutes. Sift together flour, sugar, soda and salt. Add prune mixture. Beat egg and add, then add shortening, mix well. Pour into a greased loaf pan 8½" x 4½" x 2½". Bake at 325 degrees, for 1 hour. Remove from pan and cool on a wire rack.

Submitted by Mrs. J. Raymond Watts, Farmington, Maine

Easy Yeast Bread

1½ cups luke warm water	1 egg
1/3 cup sugar	1/3 cup shortening
½ yeast cake	Flour (about 4½ cups)
1 teaspoon salt	

Place water, sugar and yeast in mixing bowl or kettle and stir thoroughly. Add salt and 1½ cups flour and mix well. Add egg and shortening and flour enough to make a stiff dough. Let rise to about double. Make into 1 large loaf and approximately 12 rolls (depending on the size). Let rise to double again and bake in a moderate oven, 375 degrees, for about 40 minutes.

Submitted by Miss Effie Nye, Skowhegan, Maine

Potato Rolls

1½ cups lukewarm milk
¼ cup sugar
1 cup mashed potatoes
   (sieved)
2 teaspoons salt

2 packages dry yeast
¼ cup warm water
¾ cup soft shortening
4 to 4½ cups sifted flour

Mix together the lukewarm milk, sugar, mashed potatoes (can use dry potato mix) and salt. Dissolve the 2 dry yeast in the warm water and add to the potato mixture. Then add the soft shortening. Mix well. Gradually, add the flour until you have a stiff dough. Turn dough on a floured board and knead until smooth and elastic. Cover over on board and let stand for 10 minutes, to lighten up. Roll ¼ inch thick. Cut with a 2½ inch cookie cutter. Brush with melted butter and fold in half. Place on a greased cookie sheet, grease tops, and cover. Let rise about 1 hour. Bake for 15 minutes in a 400 degree oven. Brush with melted butter for a soft crust after baking.

Submitted by Mrs. Mary Baum, Kittery, Maine

Bread Starter Or Emptyings
(The Old Time Method)

The "starter" or "emptyings", as it is called in this recipe, is made by putting a large mixing spoonful of flour with sugar and salt added, into a one and a half quart pitcher. To this add one quart of warm, fresh milk. Put the pitcher on a warm shelf until the lactic fermentation has nearly filled the pitcher.

Measure out one and a half quarts of flour after sifting; sift one and a half teaspoons of soda through the flour three times; use "emptyings" enough to make a fairly soft dough. Roll out and cut. Bake in a hot oven.

Save a piece of the dough to put back in the pitcher, as well as the scrapings from the mixing bowl. More new milk or buttermilk may be added as needed. The original recipe says it didn't smell good in preparing, but made wonderful biscuits. So much home-made bread and biscuits were made in those days, this "starter" pitcher did not have a chance to get too old. I have never made it myself, but my husband says his mother used to and it was delicious.

Submitted by Mrs. Ernest Myrick, Brewer, Maine

Potato Yeast

Grate 3 potatoes (medium); pour on boiling water until it looks like thick starch, add 1 heaping tablespoon salt, 3 heaping tablespoons sugar and cool. When cool, add one cake of yeast; let rise in warm place stirring now and then, store in cool dry place. When making a batch of bread use 1 cup of potato yeast to each batch of bread. This makes 3 to 4 loaves. When yeast is down to 1 cup, make more by using the remaining cup, in place of yeast cake used in original batch.

Submitted by Mrs. Leo Russell, Bangor, Maine

Home-Made Yeast

6 large potatoes

3 pints water

Handful of hops

1 cup flour (about)

½ cup sugar

1½ teaspoons ginger

2 tablespoons salt

1 cup yeast (made before) or

½ yeast cake

2 tablespoons water

Boil 6 large potatoes in the 3 pints of water. Tie a handful of hops in a small muslin bag and boil with potatoes. When thoroughly cooked, drain the water over enough flour to make a thin batter (about 1 cup). Heat enough to cook the flour; this makes the yeast keep longer, set aside to cool. When just warm, add the potatoes (mashed), sugar, ginger, salt and 1 cup yeast from the last time or ½ yeast cake dissolved in 2 tablespoons of warm water. Let stand in warm place, until it has risen, then put in large mouthed jug and cork tightly; set away in cool place. Two-thirds cup of this yeast will make 4 loaves.

Salt-Rising Bread
YEAST

11/3 cups water (hot to touch)

1 teaspoon salt

½ teaspoon brown sugar

1 cup coarse flour

1 teaspoon flour, added twice

Combine water, salt, brown sugar and enough coarse flour to make a thin batter (about 1 cup). Set aside to rise over a double boiler of moderately hot water, covered. Keep temperature even to promote fermentation; add a teaspoon of flour twice during this process. The yeast should reach top of bowl in about 5 hours.

Bread

6 cups flour

Yeast (made above)

1 quart of warm milk

Sift the flour into a bowl; make an opening in center, add yeast. Add warm milk (not hot) and stir into pulpy mass with spoon. Cover and let rise 1 hour. Knead into loaves, adding flour to make proper consistency. This will make 4 loaves. This was considered prize bread 100 years ago.

Submitted by Mrs. Gertrude Hupper, Tenants Harbor, Maine

Mother's Baked Indian Pudding

1 cup yellow corn meal
¾ cup of ground suet
1 teaspoon ginger
¼ teaspoon cloves
1 teaspoon salt

1 cup molasses
½ cup brown sugar
2 quarts milk
3 eggs
1 cup raisins

Mix corn meal, suet, spices, salt, molasses and brown sugar together.

Bring 1 quart of milk to boil and add slowly, over the above mixture. Cook over low heat until meal does not sink to bottom.

Add the eggs, beaten, to the meal mixture and turn into a buttered crock (about 4 quart size).

Cook at 300°. Bake for 8 hours. After first hour, 1 cup of raisins may be added and also add 1 more quart of cold milk, 1 cup at a time. Do not stir. This makes the whey.

Serve with scoop of vanilla ice cream on top.

NOTE! Makes a large pudding, that keeps well or to use for a large gathering such as an Extension Meeting.

Submitted by Sue F. Bridges, Sedgwick, Maine

Old Fashioned Indian Pudding

1 pint of milk (scalded)
3 handfuls corn meal (about ¾ cup)
¾ cup molasses
½ teaspoon salt
½ teaspoon cinnamon

½ teaspoon ginger
1 apple (peeled and cored, coarsely chopped)
1 handful of raisins
1 pint cold milk

Scald 1 pint of milk in double boiler. Put 3 handfuls of corn meal, wet with a little cold milk, into the scalded milk. Boil for an hour or more. Cool and add molasses, salt, cinnamon, ginger, apple, raisins and 1 pint of cold milk.

Bake all day, about 6 hours, in a very slow oven 250°.
Top each serving with whipped cream.

Submitted by Mrs. Mildred M. Allen, Fryeburg, Maine

Raspberry Roll

1 cup fresh raspberries	4 teaspoons baking powder
½ cup sugar	2 large tablespoons shortening
2 cups sifted all-purpose flour	2 tablespoons sugar
1 teaspoon salt	7/8 cup milk

Sift flour, salt, baking powder, and sugar into a large bowl. Cut in shortening. Add the milk slowly. Mix like biscuit dough. Roll out this dough to ½ inch thickness. Dot the dough with butter and then cover with fresh berries. Sprinkle the berries with ½ cup sugar.

Roll as a jelly roll and cut into ½ inch slices. This makes from 10 to 12 slices. Butter a large oblong glass baking dish. Place the slices in the pan with cut side down. Then pour the following syrup over the slices.

1 cup sugar	1 tablespoon butter
1 tablespoon flour	1 cup water
Salt	1 teaspoon vanilla

Measure sugar, flour and salt into a saucepan. Add water slowly. Add butter and bring to a boil. Boil three minutes. Add vanilla and pour over the slices.

Bake at 425 degrees for ten minutes, then reduce heat to 350 degrees and bake 20 minutes longer. Serve warm, topped with whipped cream or ice cream.

Submitted by Mrs. Rosine Stowell, Paris, Maine

Blackberry Pudding

1 cup molasses	½ cup soft oleo
1 pint blackberries	1 egg yolk
Pinch of salt	2 teaspoons hot water
2 cups flour	Egg white beaten stiff
1 teaspoon soda	1 teaspoon vanilla
1 cup powdered sugar	

Combine flour, soda, salt, molasses and blackberries. Steam for 2½ hours.

For sauce beat together sugar, oleo, egg yolk and hot water. Beat well after adding each ingredient. Add egg white beaten stiff and vanilla. Refrigerate.

When blackberries are out of season, canned boysenberries partially drained, work well as a substitute.

Submitted by Mrs. Beverly Oliver, Farmington, Maine

Blueberry Toast

1 quart blueberries (canned or fresh)

½ cup sugar

½ cup water (add to fresh blueberries)

Combine above ingredients and bring to a boil.

Let simmer while you make toast.

Butter toast generously and spoon blueberries over it.

Serve hot with a generous chunk of cheese, or with cottage cheese. Good lunch or supper dish.

My father-in-law liked split toasted biscuits with the hot blueberries. No doubt English muffins would be very good also.

Submitted by Mrs. Mildred M. Allen, Fryeburg

Blueberry Pudding

1 quart of blueberries

1/6 cup of sugar

1 tablespoon flour

½ teaspoon grated orange rind

12 almond paste macaroons

½ cup vanilla cookie crumbs

2 eggs

¼ cup sugar

1½ teaspoons grated orange rind

½ teaspoon almond extract

Mix 1/6 cup of sugar, flour and ½ teaspoon of orange rind and toss with blueberries. Combine the other ingredients with the eggs beaten lightly and spread over the blueberries. Bake at 350° for 25 minutes or until delicate crust forms. Serve warm with plain or whipped cream. (This freezes well too.)

Submitted by Virginia Robbins, Maplewood, N. J.
(Summer Resident of East Machias)

Fruit Pudding

½ cup sugar

1 tablespoon butter

1 egg

½ cup flour

½ teaspoon salt

Either apples, rhubarb or blueberries can be used. Fill baking dish ¾ full of fruit, cover with ½ cup sugar and sprinkle with nutmeg.

Cream sugar and butter, break egg in side of bowl, beat and add to sugar and butter. Add flour and salt. Cover apples with mixture. Bake at least 1½ hours at 300°.

Submitted by Mrs. Richard Johnson, Stockholm, Maine

Crumb Pudding

1 pint of sweet crumbs (cake, cookies, doughnuts or mixture of crumbs)
¼ cup molasses
½ teaspoon salt
2 heaping tablespoons flour

1 heaping teaspoon soda
1 egg
1 cup milk
1 cup raisins, dates or ½ cup of each
½ cup chopped nut meats

Mix all ingredients together, put into well greased can and steam 2 hours.

Candied fruits, left over jam, jelly, in any amounts may be added. The more fruit the richer the pudding. Serve warm with whipped cream, ice cream, hard sauce or favorite hot sauce.

Submitted by Mrs. Frank Lydic, Princeton, Maine

Steamed Pineapple-Date Pudding

1 beaten egg
½ cup sugar
½ teaspoon salt
3 tablespoons melted butter
1 cup pineapple juice (unsweetened)
1 cup chopped dates
¼ cup chopped raisins

½ cup chopped nuts
1 teaspoon vanilla
1½ cups flour
¼ teaspoon salt
1 teaspoon baking powder
¾ teaspoon soda
1 teaspoon cinnamon
¼ teaspoon nutmeg

Beat egg and sugar, add salt, melted butter and pineapple juice. Stir in fruits and nuts and vanilla. Add sifted dry ingredients, beat thoroughly. Fill greased molds two-thirds full, cover tightly and steam 2 hours.

Serve hot with favorite sauce. My favorite sauce follows:

ANGEL SAUCE

¼ cup butter or margarine
2 cups sifted confectioners sugar
¼ teaspoon nutmeg
3 tablespoons boiling water

1 egg white, unbeaten
Brandy, rum or sherry to taste
½ cup heavy cream, whipped

Put butter, sugar and nutmeg in bowl and pour boiling water over to soften. Add egg white and beat well until fluffy. Fold in whipped cream and flavor to taste. Store in refrigerator until ready to serve.

Submitted by Mrs. Frank S. Wright, Clermont, Florida

Caramel Dumplings

1¼ cups flour	2 tablespoons butter
1½ teaspoons baking powder	1/3 cup milk
1/3 cup sugar	½ teaspoon vanilla
⅛ teaspoon salt	

Sift dry ingredients, cut in butter and add milk and vanilla. Drop by rounded teaspoons into boiling caramel syrup. Cover and cook gently for 20 minutes without removing cover.

CARAMEL SAUCE

2 tablespoons butter	¼ teaspoon salt
1½ cups brown sugar	1½ cups boiling water

Simmer together for 5 minutes. Drop in dumpling batter.

Submitted by Mrs. Millard Bowden, Blue Hill, Maine

Caramel Custard

¾ cup of sugar caramelized	1 tablespoon sugar
1 quart milk heated	Pinch salt
3 eggs	

Caramelize sugar in iron frying pan. Stir constantly until melted. Do not let it get hot enough to smoke or it will be bitter.

Pour quart of heated milk very slowly onto the melted sugar. Simmer until the sugared mass is melted. Cool and pour onto 3 eggs, beaten slightly, with 1 tablespoon sugar and pinch of salt.

Set in water and bake slowly until firm, 350° about 45 to 50 minutes.

CARAMEL SAUCE

1½ cups of sugar, caramelized	1 cup hot water

Pour hot water over caramelized sugar and simmer to syrup.

Submitted by Mrs. Gladys Babb, Farmington, Maine

Pudding Delight

3 slices of bread, well buttered	1 teaspoon cinnamon
1 egg	¼ teaspoon salt
1/3 cup molasses	1 quart milk heated
1/3 cup sugar	

Place the bread in bottom of casserole. In separate bowl, beat egg and add molasses, sugar, cinnamon and salt. Pour this mixture over the bread and add the heated milk.

Bake 2½ hours in 325° oven stirring occasionally. Serve warm with whipped cream or ice cream.

Submitted by Polly Hutchinson, Rockland, Maine

Grammie B's Snow Pudding

1 envelope plain gelatine   3/4 cup sugar
1/4 cup cold **water**   Juice of 1 1/2 lemons, strained
1 cup hot water   1 egg white

Soak the plain gelatine in the cold water five minutes. Add the hot water and sugar. Stir until dissolved. Add the strained lemon juice. Chill until it begins to harden. Meanwhile, beat egg whites to a stiff froth and add to partly set mixture.

Beat everything together until it is high and frothy; then chill until it sets. Serve with the following custard sauce:

SAUCE

1 egg yolk   1 cup milk
1/4 cup sugar   Pinch of salt
1/2 teaspoon cornstarch   1/2 teaspoon vanilla

Beat together the egg yolk, sugar and cornstarch. Scald the milk and pour slowly into egg yolk mixture in the top of the double boiler. Cook until it thickens, stirring all the time.

Submitted by Sally K. Field, Bangor, Maine

Coffee Souffle

1 1/2 cups leftover coffee   2 eggs (separated)
1 1/2 cups milk   Pinch salt
2/3 cup sugar   1/2 teaspoon vanilla
1 tablespoon gelatin

Place in double boiler the coffee, milk, sugar, gelatin, salt and egg yolks and heat until gelatin is dissolved.

When cool add the stiffly beaten egg whites and vanilla. Mould and when ready, serve with whipped cream.

Submitted by Mrs. Warren E. Dutton, Denmark, Maine

Orange Pudding

5 oranges   1/8 teaspoon salt
1/2 cup sugar   1 quart milk (boiling)
1 cup sugar   2 eggs
1 tablespoon cornstarch

Peel oranges, cut up and cover with 1/2 cup sugar and let stand. Mix 1 cup sugar, cornstarch and salt with enough water to make a paste. Pour the boiling milk on this, stirring until blended. Cook until thickened and add two beaten egg yolks, stirring constantly.

When thickened add the oranges and use the egg whites for meringue.

Submitted by Mrs. John Pratt, Castine, Maine

Tutti Frutti Dessert

1 cup sugar	1 well-beaten egg
1 cup flour	1 can fruit cocktail
½ teaspoon salt	(fruit and juice)
1 teaspoon soda	

TOPPING

½ cup brown sugar   ½ cup broken nut meats

Mix together the dry ingredients, sugar, flour, salt and soda and add the beaten egg and fruit cocktail.

Spread in a greased eight inch pan; sprinkle on topping. Bake in oven, 350 degrees for 45 minutes. Cool, cut in squares. Serve with whipped cream. Delicious.

Submitted by Louise Winslow, Newport, Maine

Apple Crisp

1 quart of apples	¾ cup flour
¾ cup water	1 teaspoon cinnamon
1 cup sugar	4 tablespoons butter

Pare and slice apples in baking dish. Add water.

Mix flour, sugar and cinnamon; work in the butter. Spread over apples and bake until apples are cooked and top brown.

Submitted by Rena Perkins, Guilford, Maine

Chocolate Steam Pudding
(My Grandmother's)

3 tablespoons butter	1 cup sweet milk
1 cup sugar	2 cups sifted flour
1 egg (beaten)	6 teaspoons baking powder
2½ squares bitter chocolate	Pinch salt

Melt butter and chocolate together; beat egg, add sugar. Combine chocolate mixture with egg and sugar. Add milk and dry ingredients. Put in greased angel cake pan and steam for 2½ to 3 hours. Keep warm until ready to serve.

SAUCE

1 pint all purpose cream	¼ pound of butter or oleo
1 cup sugar	1 teaspoon pure vanilla

Mash the sugar and vanilla into the softened butter with a table fork. Leave it grainy, not creamed. Before serving, whip cream and fold sugar-butter mixture into the cream.

Submitted by Mrs. Tressa A. Stowell, Bryant Pond, Maine

Steamed Pudding

¼ cup butter	1 teaspoon salt
½ cup molasses	1 teaspoon nutmeg
½ teaspoon soda	1 teaspoon cinnamon
½ cup sweet milk	1 teaspoon cloves
1¾ cups sifted flour	½ cup raisins

Dissolve the soda in the molasses and add all the other ingredients. Pour into greased dish and steam 1½ to 2 hours. For a holiday dessert I use golden raisins and small jar of candied cherries cut up or serve with vanilla sauce, hard sauce or molasses sauce.

VANILLA SAUCE

1 cup sugar	2 cups boiling water
3 tablespoons flour	2 tablespoons butter
½ teaspoon salt	1 teaspoon vanilla

Mix well sugar, flour and salt in saucepan and gradually add 2 cups boiling water. Boil 5 minutes, stirring constantly. Remove from heat and add butter and vanilla. Serve hot.

MOLASSES SAUCE

1/3 cup butter	1 tablespoon milk
2¼ cups confectioner's sugar (sifted)	2 tablespoons molasses

Cream butter well and add confectioner's sugar, milk and molasses. Place in a bowl or drop by tablespoon onto greased pan and chill.

Submitted by Mrs. Fred Duren, Richmond, Maine

Spokane Pudding

2 tablespoons butter	1 teaspoon soda
2 tablespoons sugar	1 teaspoon vanilla
½ cup molasses	f.g. salt
½ cup hot water	2 egg whites beaten stiff
1½ cups flour	

Mix together all ingredients except egg whites, which you fold in last. Steam one hour in a tight steamer. Serve hot with the following sauce.

SAUCE

2 egg yolks	1 cup heavy cream
1 cup confectioners sugar	1 teaspoon vanilla

Beat egg yolks and add confectioners sugar, one fourth cup at a time, and beat hard. Fold in whipped cream and vanilla. Serves eight.

Submitted by Susan Brown, Fairfield, Maine

Christmas Pudding

½ cup butter (melted)
1 cup molasses
1 cup milk
2½ cups flour
1 teaspoon soda

1 teaspoon cloves
1 teaspoon cinnamon
¼ teaspoon nutmeg
½ teaspoon salt

Mix molasses, melted butter and milk. Sift dry ingredients together and stir into the molasses mixture. Grease 1 large mold or two small ones and put pudding mixture in. Steam 3 hours. (I put a greased paper in bottom of mold and pudding comes out easily to be sliced. Serve with foamy sauce.

FOAMY SAUCE

3 eggs
2 cups sugar

2/3 cup of hot water.
2/3 cup butter

Melt butter, add sugar, beat in the eggs. Add hot water and beat all together.

This recipe has been used in my mother's and my family for 60 years. I have never missed having it for Christmas or Thanksgiving for 50 years.

Submitted by Mrs. Eleanor Furbush, Oakland, Maine

Plum Pudding

1¾ cups sifted flour
½ teaspoon salt
1 teaspoon ginger
1 teaspoon cinnamon
½ teaspoon cloves
1 cup chopped dates
1 cup seedless raisins

½ cup chopped walnuts
1 egg
1 tablespoon butter
2/3 cup boiling water
1 cup molasses mixed with 1
    teaspoon soda.

Sift the dry ingredients into a bowl, mix in dates, raisins and nuts. Beat the egg until thick and lemon colored, then stir in butter, water, and molasses mixed with soda.

Add the flour mixture to the egg mixture and blend thoroughly. Place in a well greased 1½ quart mold or clear glass casserole. Tie wax paper over top of mold. Steam 1¾ hours. Serve hot with a pudding sauce.

Note: If pressure sauce pan is used (4 quart or larger) put pudding on rack, place cover on sauce pan in position to cook without pressure control. Steam without pressure 25 minutes. Adjust pressure control and cook at 15 pounds pressure for 1 hour.

Submitted by Mrs. Barbara Cox, Charlotte, Maine

Molasses Pudding

(Served for 3 generations)

½ cup sugar
½ cup molasses
½ teaspoon soda
½ teaspoon salt

2 cups blueberries, blackberries
or chopped tart apples
1 cup flour (or more)

Measure sugar into mixing bowl; stir soda into molasses and mix thoroughly until it foams. Add this to sugar with the salt. Stir until well blended. Wash berries or apples, and lift from the water into the sugar molasses mixture. Fold in carefully so as not to crush the fruit. Then add the flour until of the right consistency; the batter should be fairly stiff. It does not want to run from the spoon—just so it falls in a lump when dropped from the spoon. Flours differ in the amount of liquid needed, so the exact amount is difficult to give.

Bake in a greased 9 inch pie plate in a 350 degree oven, about 30 minutes. Serve hot with pudding sauce.

PUDDING SAUCE

½ cup sugar
2 tablespoons cornstarch
2 cups hot water
1 tablespoon butter

Pinch of salt
½ teaspoon vanilla
1 teaspoon lemon extract

Mix sugar, salt and cornstarch together. Add hot water and butter to the dry ingredients and cook until it becomes clear. Simmer awhile until the cornstarch is well cooked. Remove from heat and add the vanilla and lemon extract before serving.

Submitted by Mrs. Robert F. DeRevere, Seal Harbor, Maine

Cranberry Duff

2 cups flour
½ teaspoon salt
1 cup milk
½ cup sugar

4 teaspoons baking powder
2 tablespoons shortening
1 cup cranberries (halved)

Sift dry ingredients together and add shortening, milk and cranberries.

Put in well-greased tin (3 lb. shortening can is ideal.) Steam 2 hours.

SAUCE FOR CRANBERRY DUFF

1 cup sugar
4 tablespoons corn starch
½ cup cold water

1½ cups hot water
Vanilla
Nutmeg

Mix sugar and corn starch with ½ cup of cold water then add 1½ cup hot water. Stir in double boiler until thickened. Add vanilla and nutmeg to suit taste.

Submitted by Mrs. Faith Pert, Sedgwick, Maine

Golden Cottage Pudding

½ cup shortening	3 teaspoons baking powder
1½ cups sugar	1 teaspoon salt
2 eggs, separated	¼ cup milk
1½ cups grated carrots	1 teaspoon lemon extract
1½ cups flour	

Cream shortening, add sugar and mix well. Add the unbeaten egg yolks, one at a time, then add the grated carrots. Sift the flour, baking powder and salt; add to the creamed mixture, alternately, with the milk. Add the lemon extract. Fold in the stiffly beaten egg whites.

Pour into greased and floured pan. Bake 55 to 60 minutes in a 350 degree oven. Serve with the following sauce.

SAUCE

1 cup sugar	3 tablespoons grated carrots
4 tablespoons flour	2 teaspoons orange juice
¼ teaspon salt	3 tablespoons butter
1½ cups boiling water	

Mix together sugar, flour, salt and boiling water. Cook until thick and clear. Place over hot water and add grated carrots, orange juice and butter. Serve hot over the golden cottage pudding.

Mrs. Agenard Bourret, Rumford, Maine

Favorite Apple Dessert

3 cups sifted flour	¾ cup sweet milk
2 tablespoons granulated sugar	3 cups sliced apples
3 teaspoons baking powder	1½ cups granulated sugar
1 teaspoon salt	1½ cups water
6 tablespoons shortening	1 teaspoon cinnamon

Mix a stiff dough with the 3 cups of flour, 2 tablespoons sugar, baking powder, salt, shortening and milk.

Add to this the sliced apples and place in a 3 quart casserole and cover with a syrup made of 1½ cups sugar, 1½ cups water, 1 teaspoon cinnamon, boiled together for 5 minutes.

Place in 400° oven for 20 to 25 minutes (or until apples are done.) Serve warm with whipped cream or ice cream.

Submitted by Mrs. Dwight Wallace, Franklin, Me.

Apple Trifle

Twelve apples sliced
Sugar
1 lemon
4 eggs

1½ pints of rich milk
1 large cupful sugar
½ pint of cream

Stew apples to a pulp, beat fine and sweeten well. Add the juice of 1 lemon and a part of the grated rind. (The lemon can be omitted). Beat the whites of the eggs to a stiff froth and whip in with the apples. Refrigerate.

To make the custard part, combine the milk, sugar and egg yolks. Stir and cook until it thickens. When perfectly cold pour over the apples. They must be stiff to prevent rising in the custard.

Lastly whip the cream perfectly light and lay over all. Can be made without the cream. Delicious either way.

Submitted by Mrs. R. W. Richmond, Camden, Maine

Apple Pan Dowdy

1½ cups sugar
½ cup unsulphured molasses
½ teaspoon cinnamon
¼ teaspoon salt
1 quart of sliced cooking
   apples

2 cups hot water
2 cups flour
½ teaspoon salt
2 teaspoons baking powder
2/3 cup of Spry
Milk to mix dough

In a medium sized covered roaster mix sugar, molasses, cinnamon, salt and hot water. Let set while you prepare 1 qt. of sliced cooking apples. Prepare dough using flour, salt, baking powder, and Spry. Mix with enough milk to roll out (about ¾ cup). Roll not quite as thin as pie crust and spread over this the apples. Roll up like a jelly roll, cut in 5 or 6 pieces and stand each on end in the roaster. Add several pieces of butter around and on top. Cover and bake 1½ to 2 hours at 350° temperature.

Serve warm with thin cream, top milk or just plain canned milk.

This has been a favorite in our family for 50 years.

Submitted by Mrs. Bessie Rogers, Hampden Highlands, Maine

Old Fashioned Apple Pan Dowdy

5 tart apples, sliced	½ cup hot water
¼ cup sugar	1 cup flour
¼ cup molasses	2 teaspoons baking powder
½ teaspoon cinnamon	¼ teaspoon salt
½ teaspoon salt	2 tablespoons shortening
½ teaspoon nutmeg	¾ cup milk or water

Wash, pare, core and slice apples. Add sugar, molasses, spices, salt and hot water. Place in a pudding dish on the back of the range and let simmer until soft.

Prepare dough with flour, baking powder, salt sifted. Put in shortening, add milk. Put on top of apple mixture and bake in a moderate oven for 35 minutes. Serve with hard sauce.

Submitted by Gladys Mooers, Milo, Maine

Apple Pan Dowdy

2 quarts sliced tart apples	¼ teaspoon nutmeg
½ cup light brown sugar	¼ cup cold water
½ cup molasses	Butter
¼ teaspoon salt	Pastry
¼ teaspoon cinnamon	

Mix sugar and spices together, add molasses and water. Arrange apples in a large baking dish and pour the mixture of molasses, water and spices over them. Dot with butter and cover with pastry.

Bake in hot oven 425° for about 30 minutes. Then cut slits in the crust and bake for at least 1 hour at 350°. Serve hot with heavy cream or ice cream.

Submitted by Mrs. Arnold Bishop Sr., Wilmington, Mass.
(Formerly from Hancock, Maine)

Texas Pudding

2 tablespoons melted butter	½ cup milk
½ teaspoon each of nutmeg	½ teaspoon salt
and cinnamon	1 cup flour
½ cup sugar	1 teaspoon baking powder

Cream the above ingredients. Put 2 cups of fruit, apples or rhubarb or cherries or any fruit in a 9 x 9 pan. Sprinkle with sugar and cover with the creamed mixture. Sprinkle brown sugar over the top. Add 2 cups boiling water. Bake at 350° for 45 minutes to 1 hour.

Submitted by Lota Ireland, Skowhegan, Maine

Island Apple Cobbler

FILLING:

5 cups peeled, sliced tart apples

¾ cup sugar, more or less, depending on tartness

2 tablespoons all-purpose flour

½ teaspoon cinnamon

¼ teaspoon salt

1 teaspoon vanilla extract

¼ cup water

1 tablespoon butter

BATTER:

½ cup sifted all-purpose flour

½ cup sugar

½ teaspoon baking powder

¼ teaspoon salt

2 tablespoons soft margarine

1 egg, slightly beaten

In medium bowl, combine apples, sugar, flour, cinnamon, salt, vanilla and ¼ cup water. Turn into a 9 x 9 x 1¾ inch baking dish. Dot apples with butter.

Combine all batter ingredients; beat with spoon until smooth. Drop batter in 7 or 8 dollops on apples, spacing evenly. Batter will spread during baking.

Bake 35 to 40 minutes, or until apples are fork-tender and crust is golden brown, in 375 oven. Serve warm with cream.

Submitted by Mrs. Stanley Clifford, Deer Isle, Maine

Apple Dumplings (makes 6)

2 cups sugar

2 cups water

¼ teaspoon cinnamon

¼ teaspoon nutmeg

¼ cup butter

6 apples

3 cups enriched flour

1½ teaspoon salt

3 teaspoons baking powder

1 1/3 cups shortening

¾ cup milk

To make sauce: Combine sugar, water, cinnamon, and nutmeg; cook 5 minutes; add butter. Pare and core apples. Leave apple whole, or dice up. Then sift flour, salt and baking powder; cut in shortening. Add milk all at once. Stir just until flour is moistened. Roll ¼ inch thick. Cut six squares. Place apples on each square; sprinkle with additional sugar and spices; dot with butter; fold corners to enclose apples; pinch edges together. Place 1 inch apart in greased baking pan. Pour over sauce. Bake in moderately hot oven (375°) 35 minutes. Serve hot or cold with cream or ice cream.

For weight watchers: Reduce sugar to 1 cup and eliminate butter. These dumplings are just as tasty prepared this way.

Submitted by Mrs. Forrest Rahrig, Madawaska, Maine

Lemon Party Pie

4 egg whites
1/2 teaspoon cream of tartar
1/4 teaspoon salt
1/2 teaspoon vanilla
1 cup sugar
4 egg yolks
2 teaspoons grated lemon rind

1/4 cup lemon juice
1/2 cup sugar
Dash salt
1 cup heavy cream
2 tablespoons sugar
1/2 teaspoon vanilla
1/2 cup shredded coconut

Day before: Heat oven to 275°. Make meringue. In large bowl combine egg whites, cream of tartar, 1/2 teaspoon salt, 1/2 teaspoon vanilla. Beat with hand beater or electric mixer until stiff enough to hold a peak, but not dry. Gradually add about 2/3 cup sugar, beating constantly — then, with spoon or wire whip, fold in 1/3 cup sugar. Do not beat.

Heap in well buttered 9" glass plate (we use aluminum, sometimes). Bake at 275° for 1 hour until dry and firm to touch, but not browned. Let cool in plate. (It sinks as it cools.)

While meringue bakes make this lemon filling in top of double boiler. Combine: egg yolks, lemon rind, lemon juice, 1/2 cup sugar, dash of salt. Cook over hot water, stirring constantly, until thick and smooth. Cool — then spread over center of cold meringue, chill in refrigerator several hours, or overnight.

About an hour before serving, whip cream, fold in 2 tablespoons sugar, 1/2 teaspoon vanilla and 1/4 cup coconut. Spread over lemon filling, sprinkle with remaining coconut. Chill until served.

Submitted by Mrs. Rita Ridgway, Lewiston, Maine

Lemon Crumb Pie
(Over 85 Years Old)

1 cup sugar
1 cup cold water
1 cup fine bread crumbs
1 lemon (juice and rind)
2 eggs, separated

Salt
2 tablespoons butter
4 tablespoons sugar (for meringue)

Cover bread with water and let set about 1/2 hour. Beat egg yolks. Add lemon juice and rind, butter, sugar and salt. Mix thoroughly. Pour into pastry lined pie tin. Bake about 1/2 hour in hot oven, 400 degrees. Make meringue by beating egg whites until nearly stiff, then add sugar gradually, beating good. Bake in slow oven, 325 degrees until light brown.

Submitted by Mrs. Sally Cross, Rockland, Maine

Quick Mince Pie

½ cup hamburger
1½ cups chopped apples
½ cup seedless raisins
2 tablespoons butter
½ teaspoon salt
½ teaspoon cinnamon

¼ teaspoon cloves
1 tablespoon molasses
2/3 cup sugar
2 tablespoons water
2 tablespoons vinegar

Mix together the ingredients as listed and spread in a pastry lined tin. Place a crust on the top and bake in 425 degree oven for 15 minutes; then turn down to 350 degrees and bake until center of pie is well cooked, about 45 minutes.

Submitted by Miss Mary C. Taylor, Lubec, Maine

Mock Mince Pie

3 old fashioned Boston crackers
1 cup cold water
1 cup molasses
½ cup sugar
½ cup vinegar

1 egg
1 cup chopped raisins
1 teaspoon cloves
1 teaspoon cinnamon
1 teaspoon salt

Roll the crackers very fine and add the cold water and the other ingredients. Pour into pie crust and bake like any mince pie.

Submitted by Mrs. Etta Beverage, North Haven, Maine

Green Tomato Pie

This pie recipe was handed down from my grandmother, Mrs. L. M. Graves, 1866-1954, to my mother and in turn given to my wife. It does not have the exact amount of ingredients, but think anyone can follow the method, as given below.

Line pie plate with your favorite pastry; sprinkle with a small amount of sugar and flour, slice green tomatoes thin in the crust, sprinkle top generously with sugar, butter and nutmeg. Put on top crust and bake in a 400 degree oven, about the same way as you would bake an apple pie; after 20 minutes, turn oven down to moderate, about 350 degrees, until center is tender.

Submitted by Thomas L. Richards, University of Maine, Orono, Me.

Mock Cherry Pie Filling
(About 5 Pints)

1 quart cranberries
1 pound seedless raisins
4 quarts apples (measured after peeled and quartered)

3 cups sugar
1 tablespoon vanilla
Water

Grind the cranberries, raisins and apples together. Put into a kettle and add enough water to make it about the thickness of mince-meat. Add the sugar. Cook slowly, stirring often; when nearly done add the vanilla and finish cooking. Fill sterile jars and seal hot. This makes about 5 pints.

Submitted by Mrs. Arthur J. Cummings, Bethel, Maine

100 Year Old Pumpkin Pie

1½ cups sugar	3 cups pumpkin
½ cup maple syrup	4 eggs
½ teaspoon salt	1 teaspoon cinnamon
1 teaspoon ginger	1 quart milk

Beat separately the whites of eggs, then yolks. Add salt, cinnamon, ginger, syrup and milk. Bake with one crust. When cold spread with tart plum jam and whipped cream. You can use canned pumpkin.

Submitted by Mrs. Charles Tobin, St. Petersburg, Fla.

Spicy Pumpkin Pie

Pastry for 9" pie shell	2 tablespoons flour
2 tablespoons butter	½ cup dark brown sugar
1½ cups cooked pumpkin	(packed)
1 teaspoon ginger	½ cup white sugar
1 teaspoon cinnamon	½ teaspoon salt
¼ teaspoon mace	1 cup milk
¼ teaspoon cloves	1 teaspoon vanilla
2 eggs	

Line a 9" pie plate with pastry and keep it cool in the refrigerator while you make up the pumpkin filling. Start your oven at 450 degrees or hot. Now melt the butter or margarine and stir it into the pumpkin along with ginger, cinnamon, mace and cloves.

In a separate bowl beat the eggs until they look frothy. Stir flour, both types of sugar, salt, vanilla and milk into the beaten eggs. Then mix the egg mixture and pumpkin mixture together with a gentle hand. Pour filling into the unbaked pie shell and bake 15 minutes. At the end of this time reduce the oven temperature to 375 degrees or moderate and bake 45 minutes longer or until the tip of a knife inserted in center of the pie comes out clean.

This is a recipe I have been making during the pumpkin season for 35 or 40 years. Squash may be substituted for pumpkin.

Submitted by Mrs. Albert J. Austin, So. Brooksville, Maine

Vinegar Pie

1 cup sugar	2 teaspoons lemon extract
1 cup boiling water	2 tablespoons cornstarch
5 teaspoons vinegar	2 eggs (separated)

Mix sugar, cornstarch, vinegar and flavoring; slowly add the hot water, stirring constantly, cook until it thickens.

When the mixture is cold, stir in the yolks of the two eggs and pour into a pan lined with pastry, take the whites and make a meringue.

Meringue: Beat the two egg whites until they are stiff; then add gradually 4 tablespoons of sugar until the sugar is well mixed and soft peaks are formed. Brown in a moderate oven, 350 degrees until they are golden brown.

Submitted by Mrs. Isabelle Barbour, Stonington, Maine

Squash Pie

2 cups squash cooked and mashed well	1 teaspoon cinnamon
1½ cups milk	½ teaspoon nutmeg
½ cup sugar	¼ teaspoon ginger
2 eggs	Pinch of salt

Combine squash, sugar, eggs, salt and spices and beat well with mixer. Add milk, turn into uncooked pie shell. Bake at 425° about 1 hour or until cooked. If brown too quickly, finish cooking at a lower temperature, about 350 degrees or cover top with foil. Pumpkin may be used as well as squash.

Submitted by Ruby MacDonald, Carmel, Maine

"Gram Nash" Sliced Pumpkin Pie

1 quart pumpkin (peeled and sliced thin)	1 large cup sugar
	Pinch of salt
1 teaspoon cinnamon (or to taste)	4 tablespoons water
	2 tablespoons butter (about)
½ teaspoon nutmeg (or to taste)	Few drops vanilla (optional)

Prepare pie crust; dust the bottom crust with flour. Add the sliced pumpkin, sugar, salt, spices and water. Sift a small amount of flour over this. Dot with butter; cover with a top crust and bake in the oven at 350 degrees for one hour.

This is wonderful. Many of my friends and neighbors have eaten mine and have asked for the recipe. They had never heard of it.

Submitted by Mrs. Wallace McPheters, West Enfield, Maine

Creamy Custard Pie

(With Caramel Flavor)

1 cup dark brown sugar packed in cup	1 teaspoon vanilla
	1 tablespoon butter
1/3 cup flour	2 cups milk
⅛ teaspoon salt	½ cup cocoanut
2 eggs, separated	1 baked 9" pie shell

Blend sugar, flour and salt, add egg yolks and milk. Cook in bouble boiler stirring frequently till thick. Add vanilla, butter and cocoanut. Beat egg whites stiff with 3 tablespoons sugar. Add ½ to egg yolk mixture, mix in lightly, cover with remaining meringue. Bake 12 minutes at 350 degrees until brown.

Submitted by Ruth Howe, Wells, Maine

Custard Pie

4 large eggs	½ teaspoon salt
1 cup sugar	1 quart milk
1 teaspoon nutmeg	11 inch unbaked pie shell

Beat the eggs, slightly, but not foamy, then add the sugar, nutmeg and salt mixing well. Add the milk to the egg mixture; stir. Pour into an 11 inch unbaked pie shell.

Bake in a 425 degree oven until the crust starts to brown, then reduce heat to 350 degrees and bake until firm.

Submitted by Calla Scribner, Athens, Maine

Mother's Fluffy Pie Crust

4 cups flour	1 teaspoon salt
1 cup lard	1 egg, slightly beaten
3 tablespoons lemon juice	1/3 cup water

Mix the flour, salt and lard together to the consistency of coarse meal. Combine the beaten egg with the lemon juice and cold water; then add a little at a time until mixture clings together. This is enough pastry to make two double crust pies and at least one pie shell.

Submitted by Lillian Elliot, Hanson, Mass.

Potato Pie

Boil either Irish or sweet potatoes until well done, wash and put through a sieve.

To one pint potato pulp add three pints sweet milk, one tablespoon of melted butter, two eggs, two-thirds cup of sugar, half a teaspoon of salt, nutmeg or lemon to flavor. Bake in one rich crust until set.

Submitted by Amy Hanscom, Newry, Maine

Raisin Pie

1½ cups raisins
½ cup sugar
4 tablespoons cornstarch
½ teaspoon salt
1 tablespoon butter
2 cups boiling water

1 teaspoon grated lemon rind
4 tablespoons lemon juice
3 eggs, separated
6 tablespoons sugar (for meringue)

Rinse raisins and put through food chopper, using a medium chopper. Combine sugar, cornstarch, salt and butter, mixing well. Add hot water, stirring to prevent lumping and boil 3 to 4 minutes. Add lemon juice, lemon rind, raisins and bring to boil. Mix small amount of custard with beaten egg yolks, add to hot mixture and boil 3 or 4 minutes longer. Pour into baked pastry shell. Cover shell with meringue. Bake meringue in a moderate oven 350 degrees about 10 minutes.

Submitted by Mrs. Myrtle MacLauchlan, Ripley, Maine

Sour Cream Pie

1 cup sour cream
1 cup sugar
½ cup seedless raisins, chopped
¾ cup walnuts

2 egg yolks
Salt to taste
1 teaspoon vanilla

MERINGUE

2 egg whites   4 tablespoons sugar (powdered)

Mix the ingredients together for the pie filling in the order given and put in an uncooked pie shell.

Bake in a 425 degree oven for 10 minutes. Lower to 325 for about 25 minutes.

Make meringue of egg whites by beating whites until they become stiff and add slowly the powdered sugar while beating continually. Brown in slow oven, about 325 degrees.

Submitted by Mrs. Gladys R. Babb, Farmington, Maine

Oatmeal Pie

¾ cup quick oatmeal
¾ cup dark corn syrup
1 cup white sugar
½ cup coconut

½ cup butter (melted)
¾ cup milk
2 eggs (beaten)

Mix all ingredients together and pour into unbaked pie shell. Bake at 350° oven until brown.

Submitted by Marilyn Wiers, St. Albans, Maine

Chocolate Sundae Pie

1 baked pie shell
1 envelope plain gelatin
3 tablespoons cold water
1½ cups scalded milk
½ cup sugar
3 egg yolks

Salt to taste
Nutmeg to taste
3 egg whites
1 square of chocolate
Whipped cream for topping

Soften the gelatin in the cold water. Let set while you make the following thin custard.

Blend together the egg yolks, sugar, salt, nutmeg and scalded milk; Cook slowly over hot water until the custard just coats a silver spoon (this is very thin). Do not overcook as it will curdle.

Add to this custard, the softened gelatin, stir until it is dissolved. Chill until slightly thick.

Whip the egg whites until stiff, then fold in the custard and gelatin mixture. Pour into the cooked crust. Chill until set. When ready to serve, top with whipped cream and sprinkle top with the square of grated chocolate. Serve cold.

Submitted by Mrs. Athleen Damon, Waldoboro, Maine

Surprise Pie

1 package strawberry jello
(3 oz.)
1 cup boiling water
1 pint vanilla ice cream,
softened

1 jar applesauce (15 oz.)
⅛ teaspoon salt
¼ cup shredded coconut
1 9" baked pie shell

Dissolve jello in water; add the ice cream and blend until it is melted and smooth. Stir in the applesauce and salt. Pour into the 9" pie shell. Sprinkle with the coconut and chill until firm.

Submitted by Mrs. Velma Parker, Westbrook, Maine

Cranberry Pie

1 quart cranberries (chopped)
½ cup molasses
1—1/3 cups sugar
Salt to taste

1 teaspoon cornstarch
(rounding)
1 tablespoon butter

Mix sugar, salt and cornstarch and add to chopped cranberries and molasses. Pour into pastry lined pan. Dot with butter and cover with top crust. Bake at 425 degrees for about 35 minutes. This has been passed down in the family for several generations.

Submitted by Mrs. Kent Stanley, Rockland, Maine

Strawberry Pie

1 quart of strawberries	¾ cup sugar
¼ cup sugar	1 tablespoon butter
2½ tablespoons cornstarch	Few drops of red food coloring
¼ teaspoon salt	Whipped cream topping
½ cup cold water	1 baked pie shell

Arrange the full quart of strawberries in the baked pie shell, which will be heaping. Mix together the ¼ cup sugar, cornstarch, salt and cold water and cook until thick; then add the remaining sugar and butter and cool. Add a few drops of coloring and pour over the pie. Set in the refrigerator until ready to serve. Cover with whipped cream. This is very good.

Submitted by Miss Mary C. Taylor, Lubec, Maine

Peach Pie

9 inch pie shell (unbaked)	2/3 cup sugar
Fresh peaches halved to cover	4 tablespoons flour
bottom of pie shell	½ teaspoon cinnamon
1 cup heavy cream	¼ teaspoon salt

Peel and half enough fresh peaches to cover the bottom of a 9" pie shell. Place peaches, with the cut side down in the shell.

Mix together the cream, sugar, flour, cinnamon and salt. Pour over the peaches. Bake about 35 to 45 minutes; about 15 minutes at 450 degrees and about 25 minutes at 350 degrees.

Submitted by Mrs. Guy Kimball, Bangor, Maine

Mock Cherry Pie

1 cup cranberries	Pinch salt (¼ teaspoon)
1 cup sugar	2 tablespoons vanilla
½ cup raisins	Dabs of butter
1 tablespoon flour	

Cut cranberries in half (crosswise) and soak in cold water ½ hour to remove seeds. Rinse seeds out several times.

Pour hot water over raisins and let stand a few minutes to soften, then drain off water.

Mix flour, sugar and salt and add drained cranberries and raisins, and vanilla — and ½ cup boiling water.

Pour into lower crust and add dabs of butter to filling.

Add top crust and bake at 450 degrees for 10 minutes, then lower oven heat to 325 and cook another 30 to 35 minutes.

The vanilla gives the pie a very distinctive flavor.

Submitted by Mrs. Eloise W. Tribolet, Bangor, Maine

Fresh Strawberry Pie

Use 9 inch baked pie shell
1 quart fresh strawberries
1 (12-oz.) package frozen
sliced strawberries
½ cup water

1 cup sugar
¼ teaspoon salt
3 tablespoons cornstarch
1 tablespoon butter

Wash and hull 1 quart strawberries. Drain. Place in pie shell. Cook 1 (12-oz.) package frozen sliced strawberries with ½ cup water, 1 cup sugar, ¼ teaspoon salt and 3 tablespoons cornstarch. Stir and cook until thickened. Add 1 tablespoon butter. Cool slightly and pour over fresh strawberries in baked pie shell. Set in refrigerator. Top with whipped cream before serving.

Submitted by Mrs. Ernest Ross, Augusta Road, Waterville

Meringue Pie

6 egg whites
2 cups granulated sugar
¼ teaspoon salt

1 tablespoon vinegar
1 teaspoon vanilla

Butter and flour a 9-inch pie plate. Beat the 6 egg whites, but not too stiff. Add 1 cup sugar gradually. Add salt. Add the second cup of sugar, gradually but alternately with the 1 tablespoon vinegar. Add vanilla. Turn into prepared pie plate. Bring meringue to edge, but mound it up in the center. Bake 1 hour in all at 275 degrees for 30 minutes. Then at 300 degrees for 30 minutes. This pie should never be refrigerated. When it is cool spread it with 1 cup cream, whipped. Serve each piece topped with frozen raspberries, strawberries or peaches.

Submitted by Mrs. Lewis Sheaffer, Gardiner, Maine

Ritz Cracker Pie
(No Pastry)

3 egg whites (beaten stiff)
½ cup brown sugar
½ cup granulated sugar
22 Ritz crackers (crushed, but
not fine)

1 teaspoon baking powder
¾ cup nuts, ground
1 teaspoon vanilla
9" pie plate

Mix together the above ingredients in the order given, and pour into a greased pie plate (greased with butter).

Bake in a 325 degree oven for 30 minutes. Cool and cover with whipped cream and nuts. This is very rich, but delicious.

Submitted by Mrs. Raymond Doughty, Howland, Maine

Sweet Crust Apple Pie

Pie Crust (deep dish 9")
2¾ cups flour
1 cup shortening
1 teaspoon salt

1 teaspoon baking powder
2 tablespoons sugar
1 egg
⅛ cup milk

FILLING

10 apples (McIntosh)
½ cup seedless raisins
½ cup sugar

1 tablespoon cinnamon (less if desired)
2 tablespoons cornstarch

Combine flour, salt, baking powder and sugar with shortening. Add slightly beaten egg and milk. Roll out on wax paper sprinkled with sugar. Place one crust in pie baking dish; then pour in combined filling. Cover with top crust, flute edges and brush with a milk and egg mixture (one egg and 3 tablespoons milk beaten). Bake at 400 degrees for 10 minutes and finish baking at 350 degrees for 35 or 40 minutes. Cover with foil, once desired golden brown color is achieved on crust (after about 15 minutes in oven).

Submitted by Mrs. Andrew Demkowicy, Waterville, Maine

Blueberry Pie
CRUST

1½ cups flour
1 teaspoon salt

2/3 cup Crisco
5 tablespoons ice water

FILLING

1 quart blueberries
1¼ cups sugar
1 tablespoon flour, rounded

¼ teaspoon nutmeg
¼ teaspoon cinnamon

Do not refrigerate crust; roll out immediately. Place blueberries in a large bowl and sprinkle sugar-flour mixture, nutmeg and cinnamon over the berries and toss lightly with tined fork so as not to crush the berries. Place mixture in bottom crust and squeeze the juice of ½ lemon over it topping with at least 6 small pats of butter. Wet edge of bottom crust before placing the top crust on and sealing it with a tined fork or edge roller. Top crust must be perforated in center with three or four cuts, allowing steam to escape. Wet bandage around edge of crust prevents leakage on oven and should be removed immediately after pie is baked. Start baking at 425 for 10 minutes, reducing to 375 about 50 minutes. Lightly brush top of pie with a teaspoon of cream.

Submitted by Mrs. Clemice Pease, Rockland, Maine

Apple Pie
THE CRUST

2 cups flour, sifted
2/3 cup lard*
1 egg yolk
1 teaspoon vinegar

Ice water added to yolk and
vinegar to make ½ cup
½ teaspoon salt .

PIE FILLING

8 to 10 green apples (sliced)
2 tablespoons flour
1 cup sugar plus 2 tablespoons
¼ teaspoon cinnamon

Pinch of salt
2 tablespoons butter or oleo
¼ teaspoon nutmeg

Mix the flour and lard together to the consistency of coarse meal. Add the yolk-water mixture a little at a time until mixture clings together. Chill dough for an hour. Divide dough in half and roll out very thin on floured board. Handle as little as possible.

Line plate with half of pastry, add apple filling and cover with remainder. Dot top with butter. Seal, trim pastry rim and flute edge. Slash top to allow steam to escape.

Bake at 425 degrees for 40 to 50 minutes.

*Use lard as pastry will be flaky and crusty, as in no other shortening.

*Use ice water and chilling methods as the dough will be much easier to handle and will require less flour, therefore will make a more tender crust.

Submitted by Miss Mertie Cahoon, Madawaska, Maine

Pork Apple Pie

Apples - peeled and sliced to
fill pan
½ pound salt pork - cut off
rind and slice pork in
small pieces
½ cup molasses

2/3 cup sugar
1 teaspoon cinnamon
½ teaspoon cloves
Pie crust for an 8"x8"x2"
square pan

Line pan with crust, then add all ingredients by layers: apples-salt pork-molasses-sugar-spices, then apples, etc. again until pan is full. Moisten edges of bottom crust around top, put on top crust and roll both edges under. Bake at 300 degrees for 2½ hours or until pie is done. Serve warm. This was handed down from my great grandmother.

Submitted by Mrs. Leroy Bartlett, Bangor, Main

120

Apple Cream Pie

2/3 cup sugar
2 tablespoons flour
⅛ teaspoon salt
1 cup sour cream

1 egg, slightly beaten
1 teaspoon vanilla
*2 cups chopped apples
1 9-inch unbaked pie shell

TOPPING

1/3 cup flour
1/3 cup sugar
1 teaspoon cinnamon

¼ teaspoon nutmeg
¼ cup butter or oleo

Combine sugar, flour, salt. Add cream, egg, vanilla and beat until smooth. Add chopped apples. Pour into unbaked pie shell.

For topping combine flour, sugar, cinnamon and nutmeg. Cut in butter or oleo. Sprinkle over top of pie. Bake at 425 degrees 25-30 minutes.

*I usually use 3 cups apples for 9 inch pie and 4 cups apples for 10 inch pie.

Submitted by Gloria C. Oliver, Dover-Foxcroft, Maine

Butter Pie

1¾ cups sugar
¼ pound butter
2 tablespoons flour

2 eggs
2 cups milk
9 inch pie shell (uncooked)

Cream together the sugar, butter and flour. Add the eggs, continue beating. Lower the beater speed and add the milk. Pour into an uncooked pie shell. Bake for 10 minutes in a 450 degree oven, then lower temperature to 325 degrees. Finish baking until set as custard.

Submitted by Mrs. Eaino Heikkinen, South Paris, Maine

Lottie's Own Apple Pie

Apples to fill a 9" pie shell
1 cup sugar
1 teaspoon apple-pie-spice

Salt to taste
2 tablespoons melted butter

Line a 9" pie plate with the pie crust. Pare and slice several apples. Place one half the amount in the pie plate lined with pastry; sprinkle evenly with ½ cup sugar. Add the remaining apples plus another ½ cup of sugar (that amount depending on the kind of apples used). Sprinkle with apple-pie-spice and a little salt. Last of all add 2 tablespoons of the melted butter. Fix the top crust as follows:

Roll out top crust, place over apples. Spread with melted butter, sift a little flour lightly over top and then brush entire crust with a little milk to make a flaky crust. Bake at 350 degrees until done.

Submitted by Mrs. Lottie E. Leavitt, Winn, Maine

Lottie's Own Pie Crust Mix

7 cups sifted flour   3 tablespoons sugar
1 pound lard   1 teaspoon salt

Place in large mixing bowl and mix thoroughly and store in a 3 pound shortening can and place in refrigerator. This is enough for several pies.

Grapenut Pie

½ cup grapenuts   ⅛ teaspoon salt
½ cup water   1 teaspoon vanilla
3 eggs, beaten   3 tablespoons melted butter or
1 cup dark karo   oleo
¾ cup sugar   One 8" pie shell (unbaked)

Soak together the grapenuts and water, then add the rest of the ingredients as listed. Pour into the unbaked pie shell and bake in a 400 degree oven for the first 10 minutes, then lower temperature to 350 for about 25 minutes longer. Top with whipped cream if desired.

Submitted by Marie Flewelling, Easton, Maine

Brambles

Rind of 1 lemon   1 tablespoon butter
1 cup raisins   ½ teaspoon cinnamon
Juice of one lemon   ½ teaspoon nutmeg
1 egg   ¼ teaspoon cloves
1 cup sugar

Put through a food-grinder the rind of the lemon and the raisins. Add the lemon juice, egg, sugar, butter and spices. Mix all together.

Cut pastry in rounds the size of a small saucer, put on a tablespoon of the filling, fold over, and bake at 400 degrees, until they are well brown.

Submitted by Mrs. Malcolm H. Carman, Deer Isle, Maine

Tarts

½ cup butter   ½ teaspoon soda
½ cup lard   ¼ teaspoon salt
3 cups sifted pastry flour   Milk (given below)
1 teaspoon cream of tartar   White of 1 egg

Mix and sift dry ingredients together and cut in shortening. Beat the egg white stiff, put in a cup and add milk or water to bring the white even with the top of the cup. Combine with dry ingredients. Roll, cut and bake. Fill with jelly just before serving.

Submitted by Mildred Brown Schrumpf, Orono, Maine

Pastry Squares
CRUST

2½ cups flour (sifted)	1 cup lard
1 tablespoon sugar	1 egg, separated
1 teaspoon salt	Milk (given below)

FILLING

1½ pints of mincemeat or   Any favorite filling

Sift flour, sugar, salt and cut in the lard. Beat egg yolk, add milk to make ½ cup. Add to mix. Mix this to form ball. Roll half to 15" x 11". Put on baking sheet. Spread with filling. Roll top crust, seal edges. Beat egg white and spread on top.

Bake in a 400 degree oven for 25 minutes. Mix 1 cup confectionery sugar and 2 tablespoons milk. Spread on top of pastry while hot.

Submitted by Marlene L. Frith, Athens, Maine

Danish Pastry
PASTRY

6 ounce package cream cheese   2 cups flour
2 sticks margarine
Line tiny cup-cake pan with pastry.

FILLING

¾ cup chopped dates   ¾ cup chopped cherries
¾ cup chopped nuts

Drop 1 teaspoon in pastry then top with 1 teaspoon of topping.

TOPPING

2 cups brown sugar   3 tablespoons butter or mar-
3 eggs (beaten slightly)   garine

Bake at 350 for 20 minutes.

This is a recipe which I like to make for weddings and showers.
Submitted by Mrs. Irene Yerxa, Bridgewater, Maine

Chess Pies

½ cup sugar	½ cup walnuts (ground)
2 eggs	1 package dates (cut fine)
½ cup butter (melted)	

Beat eggs, add sugar, melted butter, walnuts and dates. Fill cup cake pans which have been lined with pie crust.

Bake in 400 degree oven. When crust is done the filling will puff up. Serve with whipped cream. Garnish with cherries.

Submitted by Mrs. Raymond Doughty, Howland, Maine

Freezing Ice Cream Using Hand Freezer

According to the old 1894 Practical Housekeeping cook book, the best ice cream is made by first scalding the cream and dissolving the sugar in it while hot. When raw cream is frozen, the flavoring is not so prominent, and the cream has a frozen, snowy taste, and is never perfectly smooth and velvety. Cheaper ice creams are usually made in this way, as they swell to double their original bulk. A good hard or long beating will help dissolve the sugar and improve the texture.

Pound the ice fine in a coarse bag, and get the salt, which should be coarse or rock. A four quart freezer will require ten pounds of ice and 1½ pints to 2 quarts of salt. Less salt is used in today's electrical ice cream freezers; do not use over 1½ pints of salt or go by your freezer directions. In the old-fashioned freezer, use a layer of ice about 3 inches deep then layer of salt one inch deep, and continue this to the top of the can. Turn crank slowly and steadily until it goes pretty hard, about 20 to 25 minutes.

When frozen, remove the crank, wipe the lid of the can, and take it off, being careful not to allow any salt to fall into the can; remove the dasher, and scrape it off; take a large wooden spatula and scrape the cream from the sides of the can, and beat and work steadily for ten minutes; this makes the cream smooth. Now put the lid on the can, put a stopper in the hole where the dasher was taken out, drain off the water from the tub, repack with salt and ice, cover the tub with a piece of carpet, and stand away in a cold place for one or two hours to ripen. After standing for one or two hours the ingredients blend and form a more pleasant flavor.

Best-ever Chocolate Sauce For Ice Cream

1 ounce Baker's chocolate	1/3 cup boiling water
1 tablespoon butter	1 cup sugar
Dash of salt	½ teaspoon vanilla

Melt chocolate in top of double boiler, add butter, then boiling water slowly, stirring constantly, then add sugar. Bring to boil, then put over double boiler and cook 15 minutes. Add vanilla and serve hot. If you so desire, let boil about 5 minutes, stirring constantly; cool and it should be more like a fudge sauce when used. This can be made by two quarts at a time, then put in refrigerator; heat and use as desired. Also good on cottage pudding.

Submitted by Etta Beverage, North Haven, Maine

Vanilla Ice Cream

1½ quarts milk	6 eggs, separated
2 cups sugar	1 quart cream, whipped
1 tablespoon flour (rounding)	2 tablespoons vanilla
½ teaspoon salt	

Mix sugar, flour and salt and add gradually, to hot milk in top of double boiler. Cook five minutes stirring constantly, then add some of the hot mixture to the egg yolks. Return to double boiler mixture, stirring until smooth. Cool and add whipped cream, folding in mixture and then fold in the beaten egg whites. Flavor to taste.

Refrigerator Ice Cream

25 marshmallows	2 teaspoons vanilla
1 cup hot milk	1 pint cream

Melt 25 marshmallows in the hot milk, cool. Add vanilla and whipped cream. Freeze in refrigerator trays. Variation: A large banana, mashed, may be added.

Submitted by Miss Etta Beverage, North Haven, Maine

Vanilla Ice Cream

2 eggs	1 pint milk
1 cup sugar	2 tablespoons vanilla
2 tablespoons flour	1 quart cream
½ teaspoon salt	1 quart milk

Scald milk in top of double boiler. Beat eggs well, add sugar, flour and salt. Stir into hot milk and cook until thickened. Cool, add vanilla. Add cream and milk, stir well and strain into freezer to desired amount. Fill freezer about 2/3. This makes a real smooth ice cream that holds its shape well after frozen. I use this amount for a 6 quart freezer. Variation: Lemon may be used instead of the vanilla. Also cocoa as desired may be added to the custard before cooking. See direction at the first of this section for freezing ice cream.

Submitted by Mrs. Carrie S. Libby, Easton, Maine

Butterscotch Sauce

1 cup brown sugar, packed	2 tablespoons flour
4 tablespoons butter	½ teaspoon vanilla
½ cup boiling water	

Mix sugar and flour; add to melted butter, then to boiling water. Cook about 8 minutes and add vanilla. Good for ice cream or cottage pudding.

Submitted by Etta Beverage, North Haven, Maine

Mrs. Thurslow's Ice (Vanilla)

As Given to Margie Ingraham Thorndike at the Turn of the
20th Century

2 cups sugar, beaten with egg yolks	12 eggs (separated)
	1 quart cream
2 cups sugar, beaten with egg whites	3 quarts top rich milk
	Vanilla to taste
	Pinch of salt

These were put together and beaten about forty minutes; then hand frozen and later packed in cracked ice and rock salt and allowed to stand several hours.

Llewella Thorndike Mills can vouch for the above recipe. She used to be allowed to "lap the dasher."

Submitted by Mrs. Clemice B. Pease, Rockland, Maine

Home-Made Ice Cream

1 quart milk	1¾ cups sugar
2 cans of evaporated milk	½ teaspoon salt
6 eggs	3 tablespoons vanilla

Cook all together over hot water until thick. Chill, beat and freeze. Use 4 quart freezer.

Submitted by Mrs. J. R. Farrell Jr., Deer Isle, Maine

Winter Snow Cream

1 pint sweet cream	Lemon or vanilla
Sugar	New fallen snow

Sweeten 1 pint of cream very sweet; flavor with lemon or vanilla, let stand until very cold.

When ready for dessert beat clean new snow into the cream until it is stiff enough to stand alone.

Serve immediately.

Submitted by Mrs. R. W. Richmond, Camden, Maine

Pineapple Sherbet

1¼ cup pineapple juice	1 teaspoon gelatine
¼ cup lemon juice	1 tablespoon hot water
¾ cup sugar	1 cup cream, whipped

Heat pineapple juice; add lemon juice and sugar. Dissolve gelatine in hot water and add to hot mixture. Cool and freeze to a mush; then whip and fold in the whipped cream and freeze again.

Makes 8 small or 6 large servings.

Submitted by Etta Beverage, North Haven, Maine

Lemon Milk Sherbet

2 lemons, rind and juice   2 cups milk
1¼ cups sugar

Mix together well lemon juice, grated rind and sugar. Stir in the milk (this will curdle but it does not matter as it smooths out during the freezing). Pour into refrigerator tray. Stir outside edges toward the middle every ½ hour, taking about 2 hours before ready to serve. Serve in chilled sherbet glasses. This is very easy to make and a favorite with our family.

Submitted by Mrs. Dorothy Fisher, Rothesay, N. B.
(Formerly of Fort Fairfield, Maine)

Lemon Sherbet
(One Gallon Freezer)

Juice of 3 lemons   1 quart cream
3 cups sugar   1 quart milk
1 can crushed pineapple   ½ teaspoon salt

Let lemon juice and sugar set until sugar is partially dissolved. Combine ingredients, freeze in hand freezer.

Submitted by Mrs. George Cogswell, Fort Fairfield, Maine

Ice Cream Variations
(For 1 gallon freezer—do not fill can over 2/3 full)

Chocolate: Melt 3 squares unsweetened chocolate over hot water, add 1 1/3 cups hot milk or cream gradually; beat until smooth, and add to your regular vanilla ice cream recipe.

Chocolate, using cocoa: Use ½ cup cocoa plus ½ cup sugar; add to a small amount of hot milk or cream to dissolve, then add to regular ice cream.

Caramel: Caramelize ½ of the sugar called for in your vanilla ice cream recipe; add ½ cup of hot water to the caramelized sugar, stirring until sugar is well dissolved. Add to your ice cream mixture and flavor.

Strawberry or raspberry: 1 quart of strawberries, mashed. Sprinkle with sugar and let stand 2 hours in warm place; add to ice cream mix; add ½ teaspoon of strawberry extract, if desired. Taste for sweetness. If preserved fruit is used, do not add sugar.

Peaches: 1 pound of peaches, crushed and add extra sugar to taste.

Candy: 3 to 4 ounces of peppermint or other candy sticks, crushed; also peanut brittle or butter crunch crushed.

Banana: Skin bananas, scrape and force through sieve. Add to any vanilla ice cream mixture.

Lill's Delicious Gingerbread
(With Blueberries)

½ cup shortening
1 cup sugar
1 egg or 2 egg yolks
2 cups all-purpose flour
½ teaspoon ginger
1 teaspoon cinnamon

½ teaspoon salt
1 cup sour milk or buttermilk
1 teaspoon soda
3 tablespoons molasses
1 cup blueberries

Cream shortening with sugar, add egg or egg yolks. Beat well. Mix and sift flour, ginger, cinnamon, salt and add alternately to the creamed mixture with the sour milk, in which the soda has been dissolved. Then add molasses; stir in blueberries which have been sprinkled with a spoonful of the sifted dry ingredients. Pour into a greased 9 x 9 pan. Sprinkle the top of the batter with 3 or 4 tablespoons of sugar. Bake in a moderate oven, 350 degrees, for about 50 minutes. The sugar makes a crusty top on the cake after it is baked. The blueberries may be replaced with 1 cup of raisins. This cake is good hot or cold and even 3 days old.

This recipe is over 90 years old, and came from my family.

Submitted by Mrs. Mildred Brown Schrumpf, Orono, Maine

Soft Gingerbread

1 cup molasses
1 cup sugar
½ cup shortening
1 egg
1 teaspoon soda

1 teaspoon salt
1 teaspoon cassia
2½ cups flour
1 cup boiling water

Cream together the first four ingredients. Sift flour, soda, salt and cassia together and add to creamed ingredients, then add the boiling water. Beat all together and bake in a greased tin at 350 degrees for 30 to 35 minutes. This is my mother's recipe.

Submitted by Mrs. Mahlor E. Williamson, Stratton, Maine

Hard Gingerbread

1 cup butter
1 cup sugar
1 cup molasses
2 eggs
1 teaspoon ginger

2 teaspoons vinegar
2 teaspoons soda
6 cups flour (reserving 1 cup
   to "knead'n" with)
1 teaspoon salt or to taste

Cream butter and sugar, add beaten eggs, molasses, vinegar, sifted dry ingredients, reserving the 1 cup of flour, to knead till smooth and glossy. Divide in 4 equal parts; put 2 parts in each baking sheet and roll by hand in long rolls (½ inch thickness) to length of pan, then transfer to pan. Score with back of fork. Bake at 350 degrees until done, about 15 minutes. Cut while warm in squares or bars. Pack in tins. This keeps well, indefinitely, and seems to improve, after the first day.

This is a very old New England recipe handed down through generations, from the "Early Settlers" and given to me in 1916, when I came here as a bride. It is very quick, simple and nutritious.

Submitted by Mrs. Nell J. Chadwick, Houlton, Maine

Mother Ranger's Molasses Cake

1 cup sugar	2/3 cup shortening
2½ cups flour (unsifted, all purpose)	2 eggs
	1 rounding teaspoon soda
1 cup milk	1 teaspoon cinnamon
1 cup molasses	½ teaspoon cloves

Mix sugar, melted shortening and eggs then add the molasses and stir well.

Sift all dry ingredients and add alternately with the milk to the first mixture.

Bake in a 11 x 16 inch pan, (2 smaller ones if you wish.) at 375° for about 20 minutes. This is delicious served warm with whipped cream.

For the gingerbread, you use the same recipe only leave out the 2 eggs, and add 1 teaspoon ginger, plus 2 cups flour.

Stir as before, turn this quite stiff batter onto a well floured board and roll with the hands into a round mound. Roll out to about ¾ inch thickness and cut into squares, or any shape you wish. Lay these squares close to each other on a cookie sheet. Bake at 325° for about 30 minutes. Turn bottom side up onto a cookie cloth. When cooled a little, break apart into the squares.

Note: I roll out just once so I do have some odd shaped pieces which I place into the pan as closely as I can. These make lovely gingerbread men, or round cookies.

Submitted by Mae Ranger, Farmington, Maine

Heidelburg Cake

1 cup seedless raisins

1½ cups cold water

1½ teaspoons soda

2 cups sugar

3 eggs

1 cup cooking oil

1 teaspoon vanilla

½ teaspoon salt

1 cup chopped walnuts

3 cups all-purpose flour

Bring water and raisins to boil and add the soda and cool. Mix together the sugar, eggs, cooking oil and vanilla. Beat well.

Add the all-purpose flour and salt, then add raisin mixture and walnuts. Bake 1 hour at 375 degrees in a 10" greased angel cake pan (tube pan).

Submitted by Mrs. Charles F. Miller, Bangor, Maine

Eggless Spice Cake

½ cup melted shortening

1 cup sugar

½ teaspoon salt

1 cup sour milk

1—2/3 cups flour

1 teaspoon cinnamon

¼ teaspoon cloves

¼ teaspoon nutmeg

1 teaspoon soda

Nuts and raisins (optional)

Mix together fat, sugar and salt. Add the sour milk. Sift together the flour, cinnamon, cloves, nutmeg and soda and add to the creamed mixture. Bake at 350 degrees in a pan 8 x 8 for one hour.

Submitted by Mrs. Eveline Snow Gross, Guilford, Maine

Nutmeg Cake

1 cup sugar

½ cup shortening

1 egg yolk

1 cup sour milk

2 cups flour

1 teaspoon soda

½ teaspoon salt

1 teaspoon nutmeg

1 cup seedless raisins

Cream shortening and sugar, add egg yolk and beat until light. Add sifted dry ingredients alternately with sour milk. Blend thoroughly and add raisins. Bake in 9 x 13 pan. Bake in a 350 degree oven 35 to 40 minutes. When cool, frost with brown sugar boiled frosting.

FROSTING

1 cup brown sugar

¼ cup water

1 egg white beaten stiff

Cook the brown sugar and water together until it spins a thread, remove from heat and add slowly to the stiffly beaten egg white. Stir until it begins to harden then spread on cake.

Submitted by Mrs. Harold Bonney, West Paris, Maine

Apple Sauce Spice Ring

½ cup oleo
1½ cups sugar
2 teaspoons cinnamon
½ teaspoon nutmeg
1 teaspoon cloves
½ cup milk
¾ cup apple sauce
¼ teaspoon salt

3 eggs
1 cup flour
½ cup chopped dates
½ cup raisins
1 cup chopped nuts
1 cup uncooked rolled oats
2 teaspoons baking powder

Cream oleo and sugar. Add eggs, one at a time, beat after each. Sift dry ingredients, add to oleo mixture with milk. Stir in remaining ingredients. Pour into well greased ring mold or angel tin. Bake 350 degrees for 50 to 55 minutes.

This cake may be iced with a thin orange glaze. Very good cake.

Submitted by Mrs. Burt Hazelton, Winslow, Maine

Dutch Apple Cake

2 cups flour
½ teaspoon salt
½ teaspoon soda
1 teaspoon cream of tartar
3 tablespoons sugar
¼ cup butter

1 egg
1 cup milk (scant)
4 sour apples
Sugar (about ½ cup)
¼ teaspoon cinnamon

Mix and sift together the dry ingredients; rub in the butter or cut in with a pastry blender. Beat the egg and mix it with the milk, then stir into the dry ingredients. The dough should be soft enough to spread ½ inch thick in a shallow baking pan.

Core, pare and cut the apples (it may take 5) in eighths and lay slices in parallel rows on the dough, sharp edges down; press to make the edges penetrate slightly. Sprinkle sugar on the apples and then the cinnamon to suit your taste.

Bake in a hot oven 400 degrees for 20 to 30 minutes. Serve warm with lemon sauce or whipped cream; also very good with ice cream.

LEMON SAUCE

2 cups hot water
1 cup sugar
1 tablespoon cornstarch

1 lemon (rind and juice)
1 tablespoon butter

Boil the sugar and water for 5 minutes. Add the cornstarch which has been mixed well with 2 tablespoons of cold water. Cook for 8 to 10 minutes, stirring often. Add the lemon juice, rind and butter. Stir until the butter is melted. Serve over cake while hot. Freshly grated nutmeg can be added and this sauce used on puddings or gingerbread.

Submitted by Edith Herman, Athens, Maine

Apple Sauce Cake

1 cup apple sauce (hot)	½ teaspoon cinnamon
1 teaspoon soda	½ teaspoon salt
1 cup sugar	½ teaspoon nutmeg
1 egg	½ teaspoon lemon
½ cup shortening	1¾ cups flour
½ teaspoon allspice	1 cup chopped raisins

Add soda to the hot apple sauce. Cream sugar, shortening and egg well; sift and measure the flour, salt and spices and add to the creamed mixture with the hot apple sauce. Add the lemon flavoring and the chopped raisins.

Bake at 350 for 40 minutes.

Submitted by Mrs. Helena K. Norton, W. Jonesport, Maine

Boiled Raisin and Fruit Cake

1½ cups seeded raisins, chopped if desired	2 teaspoons cinnamon
	1 teaspoon cloves
1½ cups dates, cut up	1 teaspoon salt
2 cups sugar	1 cup chopped nuts
2 cups boiling water	1 cup mixed candied fruits
5 tablespoons shortening	(optional)
3 cups all-purpose flour	Candied Cherries (for
1 teaspoon soda	decoration, optional)

Place the raisins, dates, sugar, water and the shortening in large saucepan and simmer gently for 20 minutes after it comes to a boil.

Sift flour once before measuring, then sift flour, soda, cinnamon, cloves and salt together into the cooled mixture, adding the nuts last mixed with a little of the flour.

Pour into well greased and floured pans. Bake 1½ hours at 325 degrees. Use 2 loaf pans 3¾" x 7¾" across the bottom and 2¾" in depth.

Add the candied fruits to this batter and it makes a delicious fruit cake; decorate top with candied cherries and halves of walnuts before putting into oven. This keeps very well.

Submitted by Mrs. Mary W. Sibo, Old Town, Maine

Old Fashioned Pork Cake
(Over 200 Years Old)

1 pound salt pork	1 teaspoon mace
2 cups boiling water	1 teaspoon allspice
2 cups molasses	½ teaspoon cloves
1 cup sugar	1 pound raisins
2 teaspoons soda	1 cup dates
8 cups sifted flour	1 cup currants
2 teaspoons cinnamon	1 cup walnut meats
1 teaspoon nutmeg	¼ pound ground citron

Grind salt pork; pour boiling water over it and let cool. Add molasses and sugar. Sift flour with dry ingredients and add; then the fruits and nuts. Bake in loaf pans for 1 hour, 325 degrees or until it tests done. Makes 3 large loaves.

Submitted by Mrs. Katherine G. Rumill, Seal Harbor, Maine

Grandma's Canadian Cake
(With Raisin Filling)

1¾ cups sifted cake flour	1 cup firmly packed brown sugar
1 teaspoon baking soda	
½ cup butter	¾ cup buttermilk
3 tablespoons molasses	3 large egg whites

Sift together the flour and soda, cream butter and sugar; beat in molasses. Beat in just until smooth the flour (in 4 additions) alternately with buttermilk. Beat whites until stiff; fold in. Pour into two 8-inch round layer cake pans that have been greased and lined with wax paper also greased. Bake in moderate 350 degree oven 25 to 30 minutes, cool in pans on wire racks 10 minutes, turn out on racks; remove paper; turn layers right side up. When cold put together with Raisin Filling. Sift confectioners' sugar over top.

RAISIN FILLING

3 egg yolks	1 cup raisins (rinsed in hot water and drained)
¾ cup milk	
¾ cup firmly packed light brown sugar	1 tablespoon butter
	1 tablespoon vanilla

In a heavy saucepan beat egg yolks slightly; add milk; beat to combine. Add sugar, raisins and butter. Cook and stir constantly over medium low heat until visibly thickened; stir in vanilla. Allow to stand until cold, then spread over cake.

Submitted by Mrs. Pearl M. Smith, Presque Isle, Maine

My Fruit Cake

(Light)

1 cup salad oil	2 teaspoons cinnamon
1½ cups firmly packed brown sugar	2 teaspoons allspice
	1 cup pineapple juice
4 eggs	1 cup raisins
3 cups flour (divided)	1 cup dates
1 teaspoon baking powder	1½ cups walnuts
2 teaspoons salt	1 jar mixed fruit

Beat together well the oil, brown sugar and eggs. Mix one cup of flour with fruits and nuts, and add this to the sugar mixture. Beat vigorously for 2 minutes.

Sift the remainder of the flour with the baking powder, salt and spices; stir alternately with the pineapple juice, then add the fruit mix. Pour in greased loaf tins and bake in a slow oven 275 degrees for about 2½ hours.

Submitted by Mrs. Eleanor Hall, Rockport, Maine

The Best Fruit Cake Of ALL

2 cups of oleo	1 tablespoon cinnamon
3 cups dark brown sugar	1 teaspoon cloves
1 pound box seedless raisins	1 teaspoon mace
1 box currants (1 lb.)	6 egg yolks
½ pound citron cut in strips	6 egg whites
½ cup molasses	Wine glass of brandy
½ cup sour milk	4 cups all-purpose flour
1 teaspoon nutmeg	1 teaspoon soda

Cream the butter and sugar well and add the nutmeg, cinnamon, cloves, mace and the molasses and sour milk. Beat well. Beat the egg yolks and add the brandy and stir again. Add the flour with the stiffly beaten egg whites; then add a level teaspoon of soda and stir thoroughly.

Mix fruit together with 2 heaping tablespoons of flour and stir floured fruit in the cake.

Grease two common sized baking tins lined with paper. Bake 2 hours at 325 degrees. Remove from oven and let cool in the pans. Place cakes in a tight can or let it remain in the pans and cover tightly.

A month or more is recommended for the waiting period.

Submitted by Mrs. Helen Gray, Newport, Maine

Salt Pork Cake

1 pound fat salt pork
2 cups strong coffee, boiling hot
2 cups brown sugar
3 eggs, beaten
1 cup molasses
1½ teaspoons soda
3 teaspoons cinnamon
1 teaspoon cloves
1½ teaspoons nutmeg
6 cups flour
1 pound raisins
1 pound currants
½ pound citron, thinly sliced
2 cups walnut meat
1 teaspoon almond flavoring

Put pork through fine blade of grinder. Pour boiling coffee over pork. Add brown sugar and eggs. Add soda to molasses and stir into pork mixture. Mix flour, spices in another bowl, add raisins, currants and citron. Add pork mixture to dry ingredients. Bake at 325° for 2 hours.

Submitted by Yensie M. Moore, Saponac, Maine

Canadian War Cake

2 cups brown sugar
2 cups hot water
4 tablespoons lard
1 cup raisins
1 teaspoon salt
1 teaspoon cinnamon
1 teaspoon cloves
3 cups sifted flour
1 teaspoon soda

Boil together the brown sugar, hot water, lard, raisins, cinnamon, cloves and salt for five minutes. Let them get cold.

Sift together the flour and soda and add to the cold boiled mixture.

Bake in a loaf pan for 1¼ hours or in half loaves for 45 minutes. Use a slow oven about 325°.

Submitted by Mrs. Gladys Dunning, Madison, Maine

Fruit Cake
(Over 100 Years Old)

1 cup white sugar
1 cup grape juice
1 cup seeded raisins
1 package (large) mixed fruit
1/3 cup butter
¼ teaspoon nutmeg
½ teaspoon ground cloves
¼ teaspoon salt
1 teaspoon cinnamon
2 cups all-purpose flour
½ teaspoon baking powder
1 teaspoon soda

Put in a saucepan the sugar, grape juice, raisins, mixed fruit, butter, nutmeg, cloves, salt and cinnamon and boil three minutes.

When cool sift together and add the flour and baking powder.

Dissolve the soda in a little warm water (about 2 tablespoons) and add to cake mixture.

Bake either in loaf pan (bread pan size or in a tube pan) for one hour in 300 oven. Cake can be tested by inserting a toothpick, which should come out clean. Be sure cake pan is well greased and floured before adding cake mixture.

Submitted by Mrs. Lenora Cusson, Rockland, Maine

Dried Apple Cake

2 cups dried apples or 4½ to
    5 cups fresh apples, sliced
2 cups molasses
1 cup hot water
1 cup sugar
2/3 cup shortening
1 teaspoon cinnamon
½ teaspoon nutmeg
½ teaspoon cloves
1 teaspoon salt
1 cup sour milk
1 teaspoon soda
1 cup raisins (heaping)
3 cups flour
1 egg

Cook the apples in the molasses and hot water until thick; cream the sugar, shortening and egg together well, and add the cooled molasses-apple mixture. Sift dry ingredients together and add to the creamed mixture with the sour milk and soda. Fold in raisins.

Bake in a slow oven 325 degrees for more than an hour. Test with a toothpick or cake tester before removing from oven. This keeps well. This recipe makes 2 loaves.

Submitted by Mrs. Ruth Bowden, Blue Hill, Maine

Banana Cake

½ cup butter or oil
½ cup white sugar
½ cup brown sugar
2 eggs, beaten separately
¼ cup milk
½ teaspoon vanilla
¼ cup boiling water
½ teaspoon soda
2 cups flour
1½ teaspoons baking powder
½ teaspoon salt
1 cup mashed (very ripe)
    banana pulp
½ cup chopped walnuts

Beat together well the butter, white and brown sugars. Add eggs separately, beating well. Add milk and vanilla, then add the soda to the boiling water and add. At last, add the sifted flour which has been mixed with the baking powder and salt; fold in the mashed banana pulp and walnuts.

Bake in a moderate 350 oven for 30 to 40 minutes.

Submitted by Dorothy Dill Flagg, Strong, Maine

Brown Sugar Loaf Cake With Dates

1¼ cups brown sugar
1 teaspoon vanilla
1/3 cup shortening
1 egg
1 cup sweet milk
2 cups all-purpose flour
2½ teaspoons baking powder
½ teaspoon salt
1 teaspoon cinnamon
½ teaspoon nutmeg
½ teaspoon cloves
½ cup dates, cut up
½ cup chopped nuts (optional)

Cream together brown sugar, vanilla, shortening, egg and milk until smooth.

Measure and sift together all of the dry ingredients, sifting flour before you measure it. Fold in the dates and nuts last.

Pour into a greased 8 x 8 x 2 inch or 9 x 9 x 2 inch pan. Sprinkle granulated sugar over the top and bake at 375 degrees for 35 minutes.

Submitted by Mrs. Lois M. Carlow, Waterville, Maine

Date Cake

1 cup dates, cut fine
1 teaspoon soda
1 cup hot water
1 cup sugar
1 egg
½ cup melted butter
1¾ cups flour
¼ teaspoon salt
1 teaspoon vanilla

Pour hot water over dates and soda and let cool. Add the sugar, egg and melted butter. Measure sifted flour, then sift together flour and salt; add to creamy mixture.

Bake in a moderate oven, 350 degrees, in a greased cake tin for 30 to 40 minutes.

Submitted by Emily Sadler, West Jonesport, Maine

Loaf Spice Cake

1 cup sugar
1 egg
1 cup raisins (ground)
½ cup shortening
2 cups flour
2 teaspoons cinnamon
1 teaspoon ginger
½ teaspoon cloves
½ teaspoon salt
2 teaspoons vanilla
1 cup sour milk
1 teaspoon soda

Cream together the sugar, egg and shortening. Sift the dry ingredients together and add alternately to the creamed mixture with the sour milk. Add the vanilla.

Bake in a moderate oven 350 degrees for 30 to 40 minutes.

Submitted by Mrs. N. H. Brown, Augusta, Maine

Fresh Apple Cake

1¾ cups chopped apples
1 cup sugar
1 egg, beaten
½ cup salad oil
1½ cups flour
1 teaspoon soda
½ teaspoon salt

1 teaspoon cinnamon
½ teaspoon nutmeg
½ teaspoon allspice
½ cup seedless raisins
(optional)
½ cup chopped nuts
(optional)

Add the sugar to the chopped apples and let stand 10 minutes.
Sift together all dry ingredients.

Add the well beaten egg and salad oil to the apple and sugar mixture; then add flour and spices all at once and mix together until well moistened.

If desired add the raisins and nuts. Bake in a 375 degree oven for 40 minutes, using an 8 x 8 x 2 pan. This is a family favorite with the men.

Submitted by Mrs. Dorothy Soule, Freeport, Maine

Cranberry Cake

2 sticks oleo
1 cup sugar
2 eggs
1 teaspoon almond extract
2 cups cake flour
1 teaspoon baking powder
1 teaspoon baking soda

½ teaspoon salt
½ pint commercial sour cream
6 ounces whole cranberry
sauce
¼ cup finely chopped nuts
(floured slightly)

Cream together the oleo and sugar, add the eggs and almond extract. Beat well.

Sift the flour, baking powder, soda, and salt. Add alternately with the sour cream.

Add the cranberry sauce between the layers of batter and swirl in. Sprinkle the floured nuts on top of the batter.

Bake 55 minutes at 350 degrees in greased and floured angel tin. Cool 30 minutes.

ICING

1 cup confectionary sugar
½ teaspoon almond extract

Hot water to make thin icing

Drizzle over top of cake and let run down the sides of cake.

Submitted by Mrs. Paul Plourde, Dover Foxcroft

138

Queen Elizabeth Cake

1 cup boiling water	¼ teaspoon salt
1 cup chopped dates	1 teaspoon vanilla
1 teaspoon soda	½ cup walnut meats
¼ cup butter or shortening	1½ cups sifted all purpose
1 cup sugar	flour
1 egg	1 teaspoon baking powder

Add the soda to the dates and pour the boiling water over them. Cool. Cream the shortening. Add the sugar and blend well. Beat in the egg and vanilla. Mix and sift the flour, baking powder and salt and add alternately to the creamed ingredients, with the cooled date mixture and nuts. Bake in greased 8 x 12 pan at 350° — (about 30-35 min.—test). Prepare icing. When cake is done remove from oven and spread icing over cake. Return to oven until icing is golden brown. (Just few minutes).

ICING

5 tablespoons brown sugar	3 tablespoons butter
2 tablespoons cream	½ cup cocoanut

Mix in pan. Boil for 3 minutes. Pour over cake. Return to oven.

Submitted by Mrs. Kenneth M. Curtis, Augusta, Maine

Bertha's Cake

(Old Flagstaff, Maine recipe)

2 cups cold water	1 tablespoon drippings
2 cups sugar	3 cups flour
1 pound raisins (seeded)	1 teaspoon soda
1 teaspoon cinnamon (or other	1 teaspoon salt
spices)	Nuts or other fruits (optional)
1 tablespoon butter	

Mix together the cold water, sugar, raisins, cinnamon, butter and drippings and boil for 5 minutes. Let cool and then add flour sifted with salt and soda. Pour into greased baking pan and bake for about one hour in a moderate oven, 350 degrees.

Submitted by Faye M. Taylor, Lexington, Maine

Coffee Flavored Cake

(Economical Moist Cake)

1½ cups flour
1 cup sugar
1 teaspoon salt
1 teaspoon baking powder
1 cup milk (minus 3 tablespoons)

½ cup vegetable oil
1 egg
1 teaspoon vanilla
3 tablespoons hot water
6 teaspoons instant coffee

Mix flour, sugar, salt and baking powder together in a large bowl. On top of this add milk, oil, egg and vanilla. Mix all of these together until smooth (mixes together by hand in a few minutes). Put instant coffee into the hot water and stir until blended into a paste. Then pour in bowl of cake batter and mix until well blended. Pour into greased 11½" x 7½" cake pan. Bake in 350 degree oven for 30 minutes or until it tests done. When cool, top with chocolate frosting.

CHOCOLATE FROSTING

½ box confectionary sugar
3 tablespoons cocoa

1 teaspoon vanilla
3 full tablespoons soft oleo

Put sugar, cocoa, vanilla and soft oleo in a bowl and add enough canned milk until mixture is of spreading consistency. Mix until smooth.

Submitted by Mrs. Cecilia Henderson, Madison, Maine

Norwegian Coconut Cake

2 cups plus 2 tablespoons flour
4 teaspoons baking powder
1 teaspoon soda
½ teaspoon salt
1¼ cups sugar
½ cup shortening

1 cup milk
1 teaspoon almond flavoring
2 eggs (large)
1 package coconut (8 oz.)
4 tablespoons sugar
5 tablespoons oleo

Sift together into bowl the flour, baking powder, soda, salt, and sugar. Add the shortening, milk and almond flavoring. Beat, then add 2 large eggs and beat two minutes longer.

Grease and flour baking pan and bake at 350 degrees for 15 minutes, then open oven door and spread on top of cake a mixture of coconut, sugar and oleo and bake 30 minutes longer.

Submitted by Mrs. Julia Lanpher, Staten Island, N. Y.

Party Pecan Nut Cake With Seafoam Icing

½ cup shortening	2/3 cup milk
1 cup sugar	4 egg whites
1 teaspoon vanilla	1/3 cup sugar
2 cups sifted cake flour	1 cup chopped nuts
2 teaspoons baking powder	Chopped nuts to decorate
½ teaspoon salt	

Cream shortening well; add 1 cup sugar gradually. Beat until light and fluffy. Add vanilla, then sift in dry ingredients alternately with milk, until smooth. Beat egg whites until foamy; add the 1/3 cup sugar gradually and continue beating until stiff, but not dry. Fold into batter and add 1 cup nuts. Pour into 2 (8" x 8") cake pans lined on the bottom with paper, then greased. Bake at 375 degrees, about 25 minutes. While cakes are cooling on cake racks, make the icing.

SEAFOAM ICING

1½ cups brown sugar	2 egg whites
1/3 cup water	1 teaspoon vanilla
¼ teaspoon salt	

Combine all ingredients, except vanilla, in top of double boiler. Beat with rotary beater until mixed. Place over rapidly boiling water, beat constantly for 7 minutes or until frosting forms peaks. Add vanilla, beat until cool. Spread between layers and on top and sides of cake. Sprinkle ground nuts on the top.

Submitted by Mrs. Willie Templeton, Rockland, Maine

An Excellent Chocolate Cake

1 cup boiling water	2½ cups flour
2 squares unsweetened choc.	½ teaspoon salt
1 teaspoon soda	1 teaspoon baking powder
1 stick butter	2/3 cup sour cream (butter-
2 cups sugar	milk may be substituted)
3 eggs, separated	1 teaspoon vanilla

Pour boiling water over chocolate, add soda and stir in a small pan until thick. Cream butter and sugar until creamy; add yolks of eggs, beat well and add chocolate mixture. Sift flour, measure, then add salt and baking powder and sift together with the flour. Add flour mixture and sour cream, alternately, to the creamed mixture, mixing lightly until well mixed. Fold in stiffly beaten egg whites with a spatula, add vanilla; pour in a greased 9" x 9" deep pan or 9" x 13" pan. Bake at 325 degrees for 45 to 50 minutes.

Creamy Chocolate Frosting

2 cups powdered sugar
2 tablespoons cream
2 squares chocolate
2 tablespoons butter

2 tablespoons white karo syrup
1 teaspoon vanilla
Few grains salt

Add cream to powdered sugar and cream together until thick and smooth, using a little more cream, if necessary. In a small sauce pan, melt the chocolate, butter and karo together until the mixture is creamy. Combine the mixtures and beat to a spreading consistency. Frost top and sides of cake.

Submitted by Harold Goss, Thomaston, Maine

Copper Kettle Fudge Cake

Kindness of Patricia Allen Huntley, Granddaughter of Ava Smith Lawry of The Copper Kettle.

2 cups light brown sugar
½ cup butter and lard
2 eggs (well beaten)
½ cup milk
2 cups flour

Few grains salt
1 teaspoon cream of tartar
½ teaspoon soda
2 squares melted chocolate
1 teaspoon vanilla

Cream sugar, butter and lard together until light; add well beaten eggs and beat until fluffy. Add milk, then the dry ingredients that have been sifted together three times. Add melted chocolate and vanilla last. Bake in two 9 inch cake pans (oblong). Bake at 350 degrees for about 35 minutes or until it tests done. Use the following fudge filling between the two cakes and as a frosting.

FILLING AND FROSTING

¼ pound butter
4 squares chocolate
3 cups light brown sugar

1½ cups sour cream
2 teaspoons vanilla
½ pound quartered walnuts

Cook the first four ingredients together, stirring continually until the brown sugar is dissolved and the mixture begins to boil. Cook, without stirring, until a small amount, when dropped in water, forms a soft ball that keeps its form well. Because of the brown sugar and cream the ball should not be too soft. Remove from heat, cool slightly and beat until creamy and ready to use for filling. Spread filling between cakes with the quartered walnuts laid edge to edge upon the filling. Frost top and sides; nuts were not used in the top and sides of cake frosting. This kept for weeks refrigerated as fruit cake.

Submitted by Mrs. Clemice B. Pease, Rockland, Maine

Never-Fail Cake

½ cup milk	1 teaspoon baking powder
1 tablespoon butter	1 teaspoon salt
2 eggs, beaten light	1 teaspoon vanilla or lemon
1 cup sugar	extract
1 cup flour	

Put milk and butter in a small sauce pan and heat until hot.

Beat together until smooth the sugar and the well beaten eggs. Add the flour, baking powder, salt, and the flavoring. Add the hot milk and stir well.

Bake in a greased cake pan 9" x 9", for 35 to 40 minutes in a 350 degree oven.

Submitted by Mrs. Maurice Glidden, Coopers Mills, Maine

Companion Yellow Cake

1 cup sugar	2 cups flour
½ cup butter	½ teaspoon cinnamon,
1 cup raisins	nutmeg, etc.
1 cup sour milk	3 egg yolks
1 teaspoon soda	½ teaspoon salt

Soak raisins in warm water, then drain before adding to cake.

Cream sugar and butter well. Add milk in which the soda has been dissolved. Add the well beaten egg yolks and then the flour that has been sifted with the salt and spices. At last add the soft raisins.

Bake in a moderate oven, 350 degrees for about 40 minutes.

Companion Moist White Cake

1 cup sugar	¾ cup milk
1½ cups flour (all-purpose)	3 egg whites
2 teaspoons baking powder	1 teaspoon vanilla
½ cup butter	¼ teaspoon salt

Cream sugar and butter well. Sift together the flour, baking powder and salt. Add flour mixture and milk alternately to the creamed mixture. Add the stiffly beaten egg whites lastly, folding in until well mixed.

When I double this recipe, I use 4 eggs and 2 level teaspoons cornstarch.

Bake in a moderate oven 350 degrees for about 40 minutes.

Submitted by Mrs. Ralph C. Waye, Skowhegan, Maine

Coffee Cream Cake

(Two Layer Hot Milk Sponge Cake)

2 eggs

1 cup sugar

1 cup flour

1/4 teaspoon salt

3 teaspoons baking powder

1/2 cup milk

1 teaspoon butter

1 teaspoon vanilla

Beat eggs well, add sugar and beat. Sift flour, baking powder and salt 3 times and add to the creamed mixture.

Heat the milk and butter until it is hot and add the last thing with the vanilla.

Bake in a moderate oven about 375 degrees until it tests done. When cool, put the following cream filling between layers and on top of the cake.

COFFEE CREAM FILLING

1 cup sugar

1 cup coffee (liquid)

Pinch of salt

2 tablespoons corn starch (heaping)

Heat coffee, sugar and salt and thicken with cornstarch which has been mixed with cold water to smooth. When cold add to a cup of cream whipped. Put between layers and on top of the cake.

Submitted by Hazel G. Monroe, Milo, Maine

Saucy Surprise Cake

1 1/2 cups sifted flour

2 teaspoons baking powder

1 teaspoon salt

1/4 cup butter

2/3 cup sugar

1 cup milk

1/2 cup seedless raisins

1 lemon (grated peel)

SAUCE

Juice of one lemon

1/2 cup molasses

1 1/4 cups water

1/4 cup butter

Sift flour, baking powder and salt. Cream the butter, gradually add the sugar, cream until light and fluffy. Add milk, alternately with flour mixture, beating until smooth after each addition. Stir in raisins and lemon peel. Spoon into well greased 8-inch square baking pan.

Combine lemon juice, the butter, molasses and water in a saucepan. Bring to a boil. Remove from heat, pour gently and evenly over the batter. Bake at 350 degrees for 45 to 50 minutes. Serve warm. Makes 9 servings.

Submitted by Carrie C. Libby, Easton, Maine

Mystery Cake

1 cup sugar	1 teaspoon soda
1½ cups flour	½ teaspoon salt
2 tablespoons butter (melted)	½ teaspoon cloves
1 teaspoon cinnamon	1 can tomato soup
1 teaspoon nutmeg	½ cup nuts

Sift together the dry ingredients, add the tomato soup, butter and the nuts. Bake in a moderate oven 350 degrees for about 40 minutes. Test. Frost when cool with cream cheese frosting.

FROSTING

1 package cream cheese	Pinch of salt
1½ cups confectionary sugar	½ teaspoon vanilla

Beat softened cream cheese with the other ingredients until they are smooth and fluffy. Flavor to taste.

Submitted by Mrs. Elsie Pennell, Machias, Maine

"Wowie" Cake (Chocolate)

1 cup sugar	1/3 cup oil
1½ cups flour	1 teaspoon vanilla
½ teaspoon salt	1 cup cold water
¼ cup cocoa	1 tablespoon vinegar
1 teaspoon soda	

Sift first 5 ingredients into bowl. Add rest of ingredients and stir until smooth, then beat for 2 minutes, pour into ungreased pan, 8" x 8", and bake for 35 minutes at 350 degrees.

Submitted by Mrs. Sidney L. Cullen, Rockland, Maine

and

Mrs. Glen Feeney, Machias, Maine

Mother's Molasses Angel Cake

1 egg	1 cup flour
½ cup sugar	1 teaspoon soda
1/3 cup molasses	½ cup boiling water
¼ cup melted shortening	1 teaspoon vanilla

Mix together egg, sugar, molasses and shortening. Sift flour and soda together and add to creamed mixture. Fold in vanilla. Add boiling water gradually. Bake at 350 degrees about 35 to 45 minutes in an 8" x 8" pan.

Left over coffee may be used in place of boiling water. Ginger may be used and vanilla omitted.

Submitted by Eveline Snow Gross, Guilford, Maine

Honey-Molasses Sponge Cake

1¼ cups flour
1 teaspoon soda
Pinch of salt
¼ teaspoon nutmeg
1 egg
¼ cup lard (scant)

¼ teaspoon cinnamon
¼ teaspoon cloves
¼ teaspoon allspice
¼ cup honey
½ cup molasses
½ cup boiling water

Sift into a mixing bowl the sifted flour, soda, salt, cinnamon, cloves, allspice and nutmeg. Add the egg, lard, honey and molasses and stir thoroughly. Add the boiling water and beat well. Bake at 350° about 35 to 45 minutes in a greased 8" x 8" pan.

Submitted by Mrs. Bertha Hoyt, North Anson, Maine

Persuasion Cake

(Real Old Recipe)

1½ cups flour
1 cup sugar
1 teaspoon cream of tartar
½ teaspoon soda
½ teaspoon salt

½ teaspoon vanilla or lemon
    flavoring
2 eggs broken into cup, add
    1/3 cup melted butter, fill
    cup with milk

Add the dry ingredients to the egg, butter and milk mixture. Add the vanilla or lemon flavoring. Beat until smooth. Bake at 350 degrees for 25 minutes. Frost with your favorite butter frosting.

Submitted by Mrs. Clement Barter, Bath, Maine

Mincemeat Cake

1 cup sugar
½ cup shortening
1 egg
1½ cups flour
½ cup sour milk

1 teaspoon soda
1 cup drained mincemeat
½ teaspoon vanilla or lemon
    extract

Cream together well the sugar and shortening, then add the egg and beat well. Add soda to the sour milk and add alternately to the creamed mixture with the flour. Add the flavoring desired. Fold in the mincemeat.

Bake at 350 degrees about 45 minutes.

This cake is better if canned milk is soured by adding vinegar.

Submitted by Mrs. Norman Calder, Penobscot, Maine

Four-Egg Sponge Cake

4 eggs
1 cup sugar
4 tablespoons cold water
1 cup flour

1 teaspoon baking powder
½ teaspoon vanilla or
lemon extract

Beat yolks of eggs, add the sugar, then the cold water and beat well. Add the sifted flour, baking powder and extract. Fold in the beaten whites of eggs.

Bake in moderate oven, 350°F., for 45 minutes. Makes a delicious sponge cake.

Submitted by Mrs. Francis J. Cyr, Old Town, Maine

Mock Angel Cake

2 egg yolks
½ cup cold water
1 cup sugar
1 teaspoon vanilla

¼ teaspoon salt
1 cup flour
1 teaspoon baking powder
2 egg whites

Beat egg yolks and add the cold water and beat 3 minutes. Add the sugar and beat 1 minute. Stir in vanilla and salt.

Sift together flour and baking powder and add to creamed mixture. Fold in stiffly beaten egg whites.

Pour into ungreased angel food cake pan. Bake 60 minutes in a 350 degree oven.

Submitted by Mrs. Gwendolyn Philbrick, Anson, Maine

Minikin Jelly Roll

1 cup sifted flour
1 teaspoon baking powder
¼ teaspoon salt
4 eggs (room temperature)

1 cup sugar
1 teaspoon vanilla
¾ to 1 cup tart red jelly

Sift the flour once and measure. Combine the baking powder, salt and eggs in a bowl. Beat, adding sugar gradually until mixture becomes thick and light colored. Gradually fold in flour and then the vanilla.

Turn into 15 x 10 inch pan, which has been lined with waxed paper, then greased. Bake in hot oven at 400 degrees for 10 minutes or until it tests done by finger test.

Turn cake out on cloth dusted with powdered sugar. Quickly remove paper and cut off crisp edges of cake.

Spread with jelly and roll while hot. This never fails.

Submitted by Mrs. Marilyn Sawtelle, Dexter, Maine

Blueberry Cake

1/3 cup butter
1 cup sugar
2 eggs
½ cup sour milk
1 teaspoon soda

2 cups flour (scant)
1 teaspoon nutmeg
1 teaspoon salt
1½ cups blueberries (floured)

Cream butter and sugar together. Add eggs and beat well. Add sour milk. Then add flour, soda, nutmeg and salt sifted together. Blend at low speed until well mixed. Then add floured blueberries.

Bake in a 9 x 9 cake pan at 350 degrees about 50 minutes or until done.

Submitted by Mrs. Ernest Mitchell, Sangerville, Maine

Melt In Your Mouth Blueberry Cake

2 eggs separated
½ cup Spry
1 teaspoon vanilla
1½ cups sifted flour (all-purpose)

1 teaspoon baking powder
1 cup sugar
¼ teaspoon salt
1/3 cup sweet milk
1½ cups blueberries

Beat egg whites until stiff, add ¼ cup of the sugar to these and set aside. Cream shortening, add salt and vanilla to this; add remainder of sugar, then the egg yolks. Beat until light and creamy. Sift flour and baking powder together, add alternately to creamed mixture with the 1/3 cup milk. Fold in the egg whites then the blueberries that have been dusted with flour. Turn the batter into an 8 x 8 inch pan. Sprinkle batter with a little sugar. Bake in 350 degree oven for 50 minutes. Serve warm or cold. It will freeze well. Wrap in aluminum foil. Serves 8.

Submitted by Mrs. Alice M. Holbrook, Lexington, Mass.
(From Marjorie Standish's "As Maine Cooks")

Cocoa Fudge Cake

1½ cups sifted flour
1¼ cups sugar
1 teaspoon soda
1 teaspoon baking powder
½ teaspoon salt

½ cup cocoa
½ cup shortening
1¼ cups sour milk
1 teaspoon vanilla
2 eggs

Sift dry ingredients into bowl. Add shortening, milk and vanilla. Beat 2 minutes in the electric mixer. Add eggs and beat 2 minutes more. Pour into two wax paper lined layer cake pans. Bake at 350 degrees for 35 to 40 minutes.

Submitted by Mrs. Beverly Oliver, Farmington, Maine

Cinnamon Swirl Coffee Cake

1/4 pound margarine
1 cup sugar
2 eggs
1 teaspoon vanilla
1 cup sour cream (commercial)
2 cups flour, sifted
1 teaspoon baking powder
1 teaspoon baking soda
1/2 teaspoon salt

TOPPING

1/2 cup chopped walnuts
1 teaspoon cinnamon
1/4 cup sugar

Cream together the margarine, sugar, eggs, vanilla and sour cream. Sift together the flour, baking powder, soda and salt; add to the creamed mixture.

Pour half of the batter into a greased 10" tube pan. Mix together the chopped nuts, cinnamon and sugar and sprinkle half this nut mixture over the batter in the pan. Add rest of the batter, spread evenly, and sprinkle rest of cinnamon, nut mixture on top. Bake in 350 degree oven for 45 minutes.

This makes a moist cake which will retain its freshness for days.

Submitted by Mrs. Stanley Clifford, Deer Isle, Maine

Jewish Coffee Cake

1 cup sugar
2 eggs
1/2 cup butter
1 teaspoon vanilla
1 teaspoon salt
1 teaspoon baking powder
1 teaspoon soda
1 cup buttermilk
2 cups flour
1 cup raisins
1 cup dates
1 small bottle cherries
1/2 cup walnut meats
1/3 cup sugar
1 teaspoon cinnamon

Cream together the sugar, eggs, butter and vanilla. Sift dry ingredients flour, baking powder, soda and salt together; mix alternately with buttermilk to the creamed mixture, beginning and ending with dry ingredients.

Pour half of the batter in an angel food pan. Cover batter with the fruit mixture, raisins, dates, cherries and half of the walnuts. Sprinkle half of the sugar, cinnamon mixture over the fruit in the middle. Pour rest of the batter over the fruit and sprinkle the remainder of sugar, cinnamon and nuts on top.

Bake in a 350 degree oven for 45 minutes or until done when tested with cake tester.

Submitted by Mrs. Hazel A. Firth, Rockland, Maine

Fruity Frosting

4½ oz. can strained fruit   1½ cups sugar
2 egg whites   1 tablespoon lemon juice

A fruity variation of seven minute frosting can be made this way. Combine a jar of strained fruit from the baby food shelf, egg whites, sugar and lemon juice in a double boiler. Beat seven minutes with a rotary beater over boiling water. Remove and continue to beat until it is a good consistency to spread. Try strained apricots for a white cake, prunes for spicy cupcakes or applesauce for chocolate cake.

Taken from a cook book of the late Mrs. Elmer E. Barde
Rockland, Maine

Cake Frosting
(not too sweet)

2½ tablespoons flour   ½ cup shortening
½ cup milk   Pinch of salt
½ cup sugar   1 teaspoon vanilla

Mix flour and milk in a sauce pan and boil together until thick, stirring constantly; cool.

Place sugar and shortening in a small mixing bowl and add cooled flour-milk mixture, mix well and beat with beater for 5 minutes on highest speed if you have a mixer. Flavor with vanilla.

Submitted by Marie Gilman, Newport, Maine

Double Frosting

1½ cups sugar   Few grains salt
½ cup milk   1 teaspoon vanilla

Boil hard for 7 minutes the sugar and milk. Let this mixture cool without stirring. When cool beat until creamy, flavoring with vanilla. Spread on cake.

Melt 2 squares of baking chocolate and spread over the top of the vanilla fudge frosting.

Submitted by Mrs. Davis Burrill, New Vineyard, Maine

Brown Sugar Frosting

1½ cups brown sugar   1 egg white
4 tablespoons hot water   1 teaspoon vanilla (optional)
Pinch of cream of tartar

Boil together the brown sugar, water and cream of tartar until it threads. Remove from stove and add very slowly to a well beaten egg white. Flavor with vanilla, if desired. Beat until frosting is creamy and will stand up by itself. Spread on cooled cakes.

Submitted by Mary Schoppee, Machias, Maine

Soft Molasses Cookies

Won $50 Prize In 1896

½ cup molasses
½ cup sugar
1/3 cup butter
1/3 cup lard
1 egg (beaten)
2 tablespoons cold water
1 tablespoon vinegar

1 heaping teaspoon ginger
1 teaspoon cinnamon
   (optional)
1 teaspoon salt
2 teaspoons soda
3 cups flour (after sifting)

Add soda to molasses and let foam for five minutes. Cream sugar and shortening with the salt and spices, then add to molasses and soda mixture. Add the beaten egg, water and vinegar and beat well.

Stir in the three cups of flour.

Roll cookies quite thick on a floured board. Cut with large cookie cutter.

Stripe the top with a fork or rolling pin and sprinkle with a sugar and cinnamon mixture.

Bake at 350 degrees until done (10 to 12 minutes).

Submitted by Mrs. Frieda H. Matheson, Castine, Maine

Blethen House Cookies

Molasses Lace Cookie

(1845 old secret recipe)

¾ cup melted shortening
1 cup granulated sugar
¼ cup molasses
1 egg
2 cups flour

3 level teaspoons soda
½ teaspoon salt
1 teaspoon cloves
1 teaspoon cinnamon
½ teaspoon ginger

Cream together shortening, sugar, molasses and egg. Sift together the dry ingredients and add to creamed mixture. Cool in refrigerator about ½ hour before rolling in a ball, especially if shortening is warm.

Roll by level tablespoons in small ball. Roll ball in granulated sugar. Place 2 inches apart on greased pan. Bake about 12 minutes at 350° or until cookies become flat. Cool 5 minutes before removing from pan.

Submitted by Paul and Val Plourde, Dover-Foxcroft, Maine

Rolled Snap Cookies

1 cup sugar

1 cup molasses

1 cup melted shortening

2 eggs

2 tablespoons vinegar

1 tablespoon soda

1 tablespoon ginger

½ teaspoon salt

Flour to make soft dough

(about 6 cups)

Mix sugar, molasses, shortening and eggs. Dissolve soda in vinegar and add to molasses mixture while still foaming.

Sift salt and ginger with flour and add to above mixture. Roll very thin, cut with floured cutter and bake in 350° oven about 10 minutes. Makes over 100 cookies.

Submitted by Mrs. Robert Harris, Newport, Maine

Down East Molasses Cookies

1 cup molasses

2 teaspoons soda

1 cup sugar (white)

1 cup shortening (melted)

1 egg (unbeaten)

2 teaspoons ginger

1 teaspoon cinnamon

¼ teaspoon cloves

¼ teaspoon allspice

⅛ teaspoon nutmeg

1 teaspoon salt

2 teaspoons baking powder

½ cup strong coffee (can use 2 teaspoons instant coffee mixed with warm water)

5 cups flour (about) pre-sifted takes ½ cup more

Bring molasses to a boil, remove from heat and stir in soda until foamy. Add sugar, egg and cooled shortening, mix well. Add spices, salt and baking powder. Mix well. Add the coffee. Add about 3 cups of the flour, beat until smooth. Add flour gradually until you can pick up the dough and roll it in a ball.

This is a very versatile cookie dough. It can be left in the bowl and chilled. It can be rolled into balls and flattened with a wet cloth, wrapped around a glass. It can be rolled on a lightly floured board and cut with cookie cutter. If one likes a soft cookie they can be dropped on a greased cookie sheet. Sometimes I pat the dough quite thin into a 9 inch square pan or a cookie sheet and when done cut in squares. Bake 10-12 minutes at 375°.

Original recipe from watching my mother, when I was a child.

Submitted by Mrs. Corris Preble, East Sullivan, Maine

152

Molasses Cookies

(Recipe came from Salem more than 100 years ago)

1 cup molasses
½ cup sugar
2/3 cup butter and lard
   mixed
1 egg

1 tablespoon ginger
1 tablespoon vinegar
1 tablespoon soda
2 tablespoons cold water
4½ cups flour

Mix in order given and roll thin. Cut out size desired. Bake 350° about 12 minutes or until done.

Submitted by Mrs. Isabelle Barbour, Stonington, Maine

Sour Milk Cookie (Sugar)

1 cup shortening
2 cups sugar
2 eggs
1 cup sour milk (can use
   sweet milk with 1½ teaspoons vinegar added)

4 cups flour
1 teaspoon salt
1½ teaspoons soda
2 teaspoons cream tartar
2 teaspoons vanilla

Cream sugar and shortening. Add eggs. Sift flour with salt, soda and cream tartar, add alternately with milk. Chill. Roll and cut to desired size. Bake 400° for 10 to 12 minutes.

If preferred these can be filled with date or raisin filling as follows:

1 cup dates or raisins
¾ cup cold water
1 teaspoon oleo

½ cup sugar
2½ teaspoons flour
¼ teaspoon salt

Combine above and cook slowly until thickened. Cool and place between 2 uncooked cookies and bake as above.

Submitted by Mrs. Marie Flewelling, Easton, Maine

Grandma's Hermits

1 cup softened butter or oleo
1½ cups sugar
3 eggs
3 cups flour
½ teaspoon soda
1 teaspoon nutmeg

1 teaspoon cinnamon
½ teaspoon cloves
½ teaspoon salt
1½ cups chopped raisins
1 cup chopped nut meats

Cream well together butter, sugar and eggs. Sift dry ingredients and add to creamed mixture. Mix well. Add raisins and nuts. Drop by teaspoon on greased baking sheet. Bake in 350° oven about 12 minutes.

Submitted by Mrs. Elsie C. Pratt, Winthrop, Maine

Date Dropped Cookies (Swirled)

1 package dates	2/3 cup shortening
½ cup hot water	2 cups all-purpose flour
2 cups brown sugar	1 teaspoon soda
2 eggs	½ teaspoon salt

Cut dates in half in a saucepan. Pour hot water over dates. Place over low heat and let set while mixing cookies.

Cream shortening and sugar. Add eggs and beat with electric mixer until light and fluffy. Sift dry ingredients. Add slowly to creamed mixture.

Swirl and fold in the dates to the creamed mixture. Drop by teaspoon on greased cookie sheet. Bake at 350° for 12-15 minutes.

Submitted by Mildred Thomas, Winter Park, Fla.

Chocolate Filled Cookies

½ cup melted butter and lard (mixed)	1 egg, well beaten
	1 teaspoon cream tartar
6 tablespoons cocoa	½ teaspoon soda
1 cup sugar	¼ teaspoon salt
2¼ cups flour	¼ cup milk

Combine all ingredients and mix well. Chill. Roll thin. Cut size desired. Bake 375° for 6-8 minutes.

BUTTER CREAM FILLING

½ cup butter	½ teaspoon vanilla
4 cups confectionery sugar	¼ teaspoon almond
¼ cup evaporated milk	¼ teaspoon salt

Mix ingredients and blend well. Use to fill chocolate cookies above. (Two cookies with filling between.)

Submitted by Mrs. Harold D. Miller, Bangor, Maine

Icebox Oatmeal Cookies
(No Eggs)

3 cups quick cooking oats	¼ cup boiling water
1 cup brown sugar	1 teaspoon soda
1 cup flour	1 teaspoon salt
1 cup shortening	

Combine oats, sugar and flour. Add the shortening and mix well. Add boiling water in which is dissolved 1 teaspoon soda and 1 teaspoon salt.

Form in rolls, chill, slice and bake at 375° until done (about 10 minutes).

Submitted by Nancy Williams, Orr's Island, Maine

Orange-sugared Cranberry Drops

½ cup butter or margarine
1 cup sugar
1 egg
1 cup whole cranberry sauce
  (Maine cranberries!)
2 tablespoons powdered orange
  drink (I use Tang)
1½ cups flour
½ teaspoon salt
1 teaspoon baking powder

Use powdered orange and 1 tablespoon of the sugar to make a sprinkle for top of cookies.

Mix sugar, egg and softened butter. Stir in the cranberry sauce, and the other tablespoon of powdered orange. Let stand a minute or 2. Then add flour, salt and baking powder. Mix well. Drop by tablespoon on greased cookie sheet. Leave room between as cookies will spread. Sprinkle tops with sugar and orange sprinkle.

Bake at 370° about 10 minutes. Makes 40-50 cookies.

Submitted by Mrs. Julian Howell, Whitefield, Maine

Quick Mix Lumber Jack Molasses Cookies

1 cup white sugar
2 cups molasses
1 cup soft lard or shortening
  (not melted)
½ teaspoon black pepper
½ teaspoon nutmeg
½ teaspoon ginger
1½ teaspoons salt
1 teaspoon cream of tartar
1 cup cold water
2 teaspoons soda
8 cups flour (approximately)

Cream the sugar, molasses and soft shortening together; then add the pepper, nutmeg, ginger, salt and cream of tartar. Add 2 teaspoons of soda to the cup of cold water; then add to the creamed mixture with the flour. Roll out on floured board to thickness desired. Cut with cookie cutter.

If desired this mixture can be left in cool place (not refrigerator) over night and baked off next morning. Use less flour if you let them stand over night as they seem to thicken and are much better with less flour.

Use flour enough to handle dough easily.

Mrs. Pine says that she made these cookies in her father's lumber camp in 1921. The recipe was her mother's for many years. Do not leave out any ingredients or add to them as there is a special reason for the pepper, ginger and nutmeg and it has been a secret for years.

Bake cookies at 350 degrees, 10 minutes for thin cookies and 15 minutes for thick cookies.

Submitted by Mrs. Ada Pine, South Lincoln, Maine

Ginger Snaps

2 cups flour
1 tablespoon ginger
2 teaspoons soda
1 teaspoon cinnamon
½ teaspoon salt

¾ cup shortening
1 cup sugar
1 egg
¼ cup molasses

Sift flour, ginger, soda, cinnamon and salt. Combine shortening, sugar, egg and molasses. Add the flour mixture to the creamed mixture. Mix thoroughly.

Roll into small balls. Refrigerate 1 hour. Bake 12 to 15 minutes in 350° oven.

For chewy cookies underbake slightly.

Submitted by Marguerite Haskell, Rockland, Maine

Grapenut Cookies

1¾ cups flour
½ teaspoon baking powder
1 teaspoon baking soda
1 teaspoon cinnamon
½ teaspoon cloves
½ teaspoon nutmeg
½ teaspoon salt

¾ cup shortening
1 cup sugar
1 egg
1 cup thick unsweetened
applesauce
½ cup raisins
1 cup grapenuts

Sift ingredients. Cream shortening, sugar, blend well; add the egg and beat well. Add applesauce and flour mixture; mix well. Then add grapenuts and raisins. Drop by teaspoon on greased cookie sheet 2 inches apart. Sprinkle with sugar or chopped nuts if desired. Bake 350° for 10 minutes.

Submitted by Mrs. Dorothy Young, Camden, Maine

Carlton County Jumbo Cookies

1 cup water
2 cups raisins (or dates)
1 cup shortening
2 cups white sugar
3 eggs (well beaten)
4 cups flour

1 teaspoon baking powder
1 teaspoon soda
1 teaspoon salt
¼ teaspoon nutmeg
1 teaspoon cinnamon

Boil raisins and water together for 5 minutes. Cream shortening and sugar and add well beaten eggs. Sift together flour and all dry ingredients. Combine raisins, creamed mixture and flour mixture. Mix well. Drop by teaspoon on greased cookie pan. Bake at 400° for 10 minutes. Makes 6 or 7 dozen.

Submitted by Mrs. Erla Kierstead, Caribou, Maine

Peanut Cookies

Almost Like Peanut Brittle

½ cup butter or margarine
1 cup brown sugar
1 egg
1 cup flour
½ teaspoon baking powder

½ teaspoon soda
1 cup quick cooking rolled oats
2 cups peanuts (any kind)

Cream together butter and brown sugar. Add the egg and mix well. Sift flour, soda and baking powder. Add to creamed mixture. Stir in rolled oats and peanuts. Drop by teaspoon on cookie sheet. Flatten with glass (covered with wet cloth). Bake 350° 10 to 12 minutes.

Submitted by Mrs. Ralph MacLean, Brunswick, Maine

Peanut Butter Cookies

1 egg
1 cup sugar (white or brown or ½ cup of each)
½ cup shortening
2 tablespoons molasses
½ cup cold coffee

¼ to 1/3 cup peanut butter
1 teaspoon vanilla
2 cups flour
½ teaspoon salt
1 teaspoon soda

Combine egg, sugar and shortening and blend well. Mix in molasses, coffee, peanut butter and vanilla. Sift flour, salt and soda and add to above mixture. Drop by teaspoon on greased tin.

Bake at 350° about 12 minutes.

Submitted by Alice W. Amazeen, Skowhegan, Maine

Spice Cookies

2¼ cups all-purpose flour
1½ teaspoons baking soda
½ teaspoon cloves
1½ teaspoons cinnamon
1 teaspoon ginger
½ teaspoon salt

¾ cup cooking oil
1 cup white sugar
1 egg
4 tablespoons molasses
½ cup chopped nuts
Granulated sugar

Sift, then measure flour. Sift again with baking soda, spices and salt.

Cream cooking oil and sugar together. Blend in egg and molasses. Add flour mixture, blend well. Add nuts.

Chill for 1 hour or longer. Form into balls about the size of walnuts. Dip in granulated sugar. Place on ungreased baking sheet about 1½ inches apart. Bake 350° for 10-15 minutes.

Submitted by Mrs. Paul F. Byard, Franklin, Maine

Economical Toll House Cookies

1 package brown sugar
1 cup shortening
2 unbeaten eggs
1 teaspoon vanilla
3 cups sifted flour

1 teaspoon soda
2 teaspoons cream of tartar
1 package chocolate bits
Salt

Beat together the brown sugar, shortening, eggs and the vanilla. Add flour sifted with the soda, cream of tartar and salt. Mix in the chocolate bits and let stand ½ hour before baking. Drop onto baking sheet.

Bake in a 350 degree oven for 10 to 15 minutes.

Submitted by Mrs. Maxine Andrus, Rockland, Maine

Chocolate Chip Bars

½ cup shortening
½ cup sugar
½ cup brown sugar
3 eggs (yolks and whites separate)
1 tablespoon cold water
¼ teaspoon salt

2 teaspoons vanilla
2 cups flour
1 teaspoon soda
1 package chocolate bits
1 cup brown sugar
½ cup nuts (chopped)

Cream shortening, salt, sugars and beat well. Add 3 egg yolks and mix until light and creamy. Mix vanilla and water. Add to first mixture alternately with flour and soda. Spread mixture in a jelly roll pan or an 8" by 13". Cover with chocolate bits. Beat egg whites until stiff and add brown sugar. Spread over chocolate bits.

Top with chopped nuts. Bake 350 degrees for 30 minutes or until done. Cool. Cut in squares.

Submitted by Mrs. Harriet Grover, Rockland, Maine

Nutty Fingers

1½ sticks butter or margarine
2 cups flour
4 tablespoons sugar
2 tablespoons cold water

4 tablespoons confectionery sugar
1 cup pecans (chopped fine)
1 teaspoon vanilla

Mix ingredients in order given. Roll, in your hands, finger size lengths of dough. Bake on a cookie sheet 375° for about 20 minutes. When cold roll in confectionery sugar.

"If you don't double the recipe, you'll wish you had."

Submitted by Mrs. Edith R. Richards, New Vineyard, Maine

Molasses Fruit Bars

¼ cup shortening	½ teaspoon salt
½ cup sugar	¼ cup milk
1 egg	1 cup chopped (in meat
½ cup dark molasses	grinder) dates, raisins and
1 teaspoon vanilla	nuts mixed
2 cups sifted flour	1 cup confectioner's sugar
¼ teaspoon soda	1 teaspoon butter
½ teaspoon baking powder	1 tablespoon milk

Cream shortening and sugar, add egg and mix well. Blend in vanilla and molasses. Sift together flour, soda, baking powder and salt, and add to creamed mixture alternately with milk.

Dust the fruit lightly with flour and add to dough.

Spread batter thin in a greased 10" x 12" pan and bake 15 minutes at 350°.

While bars are baking, mix together confectioner's sugar, butter and milk. Brush this mixture on bars immediately after they are removed from oven. Cool in pans and cut in squares or bars.

Submitted by Mrs. Elwin B. Farnham, Dexter, Maine

Graham Cracker Squares

31 single graham crackers rolled fine	2 tablespoons sugar
	1 cup coconut
2/3 cup of butter or margarine (soft)	1 teaspoon vanilla
	1 cup mixed candied fruit
1 15 ounce can of sweet Eagle brand condensed milk	½ cup walnuts

Mix graham cracker crumbs, sugar and shortening as for pie crust. Pack in a pan and bake 10 minutes at 350°.

Mix together milk, coconut, vanilla, fruit and walnuts. Put on top of above crust, sprinkle a few crumbs on top and bake about 20 minutes 350°.

Submitted by Mrs. Harry Morris, Fort Fairfield, Maine

Marilda's Peanut Squares

1½ cups flour	¾ cup shortening
1½ cups oatmeal	1 cup brown sugar
1 teaspoon soda	2/3 cup milk
1 teaspoon cream tartar	

Mix all ingredients except milk in order given until crumbly. Add 2/3 cup milk. Mix well. Spread in pan 9 x 13 or 8 x 12. Cook

20 minutes (until golden brown) at 375 degrees. After removing from oven spread a thin layer of peanut butter over squares. Cool and then frost with a white or chocolate confectionary frosting and top with crushed peanuts. The frosting I use is ¼ cup shortening, 1½ cups confectionary sugar, 1 teaspoon vanilla. Milk to give right consistency to spread. These squares freeze very well.

Submitted by Mrs. Joan Caron, Old Town, Maine

Gillie Whoopers

¾ cup sifted flour	½ cup brown sugar
¼ teaspoon baking powder	¼ cup water
¼ teaspoon salt	2 squares baking chocolate
2 tablespoons cocoa	3 tablespoons butter
¾ cup sugar	2 tablespoons vanilla
½ cup shortening	1½ cups powdered sugar
2 eggs	1 package miniature
1 teaspoon vanilla	marshmallows
½ cup walnuts	

Combine flour, baking powder, salt, cocoa and sugar. Blend in shortening, eggs, and teaspoon vanilla. Add walnuts. Spread in baking pan and bake at 350° for 20 minutes. Take from oven; sprinkle miniature marshmallows over the top keeping away from sides. Put back into oven for 3 minutes.

Make frosting by combining ½ cup brown sugar, water, chocolate. Boil for three minutes; take from burner and add butter, vanilla and powdered sugar (enough to make smooth icing). Spread over marshmallows and let cool. Cut in squares.

Submitted by Mrs. Thurle Gray, Brewer, Maine

Chocolate Coconut Bars

½ cup margarine (1 stick)	1 egg
1/3 cup granulated sugar	1 teaspoon vanilla
1/3 cup brown sugar	½ cup nut meats (chopped)
2 tablespoons water	½ cup shredded coconut
1 cup sifted flour	1 6-oz. package chocolate bits
1¼ teaspoon baking powder	

Melt margarine, add sugars and water, blend well. Stir in flour sifted with baking powder. Beat in egg and vanilla. Lightly combine nuts, coconut and chocolate bits with above mixture. Pour into greased 9" pan. Bake 350° for 30 minutes. Cool in pan. Cut in bars. Makes 18.

Submitted by Mrs. Louise M. Grindle, Brooksville, Maine

Mincemeat Squares

1 cup softened butter
(or shortening)
1½ cups sugar
3 eggs
1 teaspoon vanilla

4 cups flour
1 teaspoon salt
1 teaspoon soda
2 cups mincemeat

Cream butter and sugar, till you get it good and fluffy. Add eggs and vanilla. Beat well. Sift together flour, salt and soda. Add mincemeat to the creamed mixture. Blend in the sifted flour mixture. Spread out on two greased cookie sheets (one will not be enough). Bake 15-20 minutes at 375°. Cool and cut into squares.

Submitted by Mrs. Edward Chambers, Grand Lake Stream, Me.

Hawaiian Brownies

1½ cups flour
1 teaspoon baking powder
½ teaspoon salt
¼ teaspoon cinnamon
¼ cup butter
½ cup shortening
1½ cups sugar

2 squares chocolate (melted)
3 eggs
1¼ teaspoons vanilla
1 cup crushed pineapple
(drained)
2/3 cup nuts

Mix and sift dry ingredients. Cream butter and shortening and sugar until fluffy. Mix in eggs, one at a time, beating well after each addition. Add vanilla. Add dry ingredients and mix well. Remove 1 cup of batter and add pineapple. Set aside.

To remaining batter add chocolate and nuts.

Spread half of the chocolate mixture in a greased pan, well floured. (9 x 13) pan). Cover this layer with pineapple mixture; then spoon on remaining chocolate batter. Bake 350° 35 minutes.

Submitted by Mrs. Carl White, Jonesport, Maine

Apple Squares

1 egg, beaten
¾ cup sugar
¼ cup evaporated milk
1 teaspoon vanilla
¾ cup flour
1 teaspoon baking powder

½ teaspoon cinnamon
½ teaspoon salt
½ cup chopped nuts
1 cup chopped apple
1 tablespoon sugar
½ teaspoon cinnamon

Combine all ingredients and mix well. Bake in 9 x 9 pan at 350° for 35 minutes. Sprinkle top with sugar and cinnamon mixture before baking. Cool and cut in squares.

Submitted by Marion Edgerly, Sangerville, Maine

Diabetic Section

The recipes in this section have been planned for the diabetic using the seven exchange lists based upon the recommendation of the American Diabetes Association and the American Dietetic Association, in co-operation with the Diabetes Branch of the Public Health Service, Department of Health, Education, and Welfare.

A few luncheons and dinners, including these recipes, have been listed for persons restricted to 1200, 1500 and 2500 daily calories.

In another section there are sugar-substitute recipes that may be used by people who have to restrict their sweets, but are not recommended for the diabetics who are on a calorie diet, unless approved by their doctors.

Many requests have been made for pies, and other sweet food using sugar substitutes, so these are included for your convenience. We hope they will save you time and waste, as these have all been tested by people on restricted diets. Sugar substitutes vary so read directions included with the kind you purchase.

Lunch
(For 1200 Calorie Daily Diet)

½ cup tomato juice
*Welsh rarebit
Dill pickle

½ cup skim milk
Coffee or tea

Fresh fruit dessert (¼ small orange, ¼ small pear, ¼ small banana, lettuce and 2 tablespoons whipped cream.)

Calories: 458; exchanges: 2 meat exchanges, 1½ bread exchanges, 1 fruit exchange, 1 skimmed milk exchange and 2 fat exchanges.

*Recipe given. Use 7½ saltines in place of 5 for 1½ bread exchanges; also change recipe by substituting skim milk in place of whole milk

Dinner
(For a Person On a 1200 Calorie Daily Diet)

*Hamburg vegetable soup
Celery sticks
2½ saltine crackers

1 large tangerine
Coffee or tea

Calories: 369; exchanges: 2 meat exchanges, 1½ bread exchanges, 1 B vegetable exchange, 1 fruit exchange and 1 fat exchange.

*Recipe given. To change the recipe to 2 meat exchanges, use 3 ounces of raw hamburg in place of 4 ounces. If you prefer crackers to macaroni, use ½ as much macaroni and then you can have 5 crackers in place of 2½.

Lunch

(For 1200 Calorie Daily Diet)

*Beef shish-kabobs (beef, mushrooms, green peppers, tomatoes)

Baked potato, small	Baked apple
½ slice cracked wheat bread	1 cup skimmed milk
2 teaspoons butter	Tea or coffee

Calories: 458; exchanges: 2 meat exchanges, A vegetables, 1½ bread exchanges, 2 fat exchanges and 1 fruit exchange.

*Recipe given. In recipe, substitute mushrooms for onions. This meal may be all cooked on the grill out doors. Wrap potato in foil; also place apple in center of a piece of foil (with a drop or two of liquid sweetener, if you desire) making a double fold and cook over coals. Both may be started at the same time, but remove apple from coals when done and let cool. When potato tests almost done, start cooking shish-kabobs.

Dinner

(For a Person on a 1200 Daily Calorie Diet)

*Baked red flannel hash	and sugar-free gelatin dessert)
½ slice rye bread	
¼ cup green peas	½ teaspoon butter
Peach gelatin dessert (1 peach	Coffee or tea

Calories: 369; exchanges: 2 meat exchanges, 1½ bread exchanges, 1 B vegetable exchange, 1 A vegetable, 1 fruit exchange, and 1 fat exchange.

*Recipe given.

Dinner

(For 1500 Calorie Daily Diet)

½ cup tomato juice	Green salad (Tossed with
Broiled haddock fillet, 3 ounces raw	vinegar, teaspoon diced onion and seasonings)
Baked potato, small	½ cup applesauce
½ cup squash	½ cup milk
½ slice whole wheat bread	Tea or coffee
1 teaspoon butter	

Calories: 454; exchanges: 2 meat exchanges, 1½ bread exchanges, 1 B vegetable exchange, A vegetables, as desired, 1 fruit exchange, ½ milk exchange, and 1 fat exchange.

Lunch

(For 1500 Calorie Diet)

*Cheese custard   2 graham crackers
Dill pickle   ½ cup pineapple
Lettuce, celery, tomato salad   Coffee or tea
*Tomato juice dressing

Calories: 537; exchanges. 2 meat exchanges, 2 bread exchanges, 1 milk exchange, 1 fat exchange and 1 fruit exchange.
    *Recipes given.

Dinner

(For 1500 Calorie Daily Diet)

*Beef vegetable soup   2 tablespoons light cream
¼ cup sliced sour beets   ½ cup milk
½ banana, sliced   Coffee or tea
1 tablespoon cream or

Calories: 527; exchanges: 3 meat exchanges, 1½ bread exchanges, 1 B vegetable exchange, 1 fruit exchange, ½ milk exchange and 1 fat exchange.
    *Recipe given. Give up one meat exchange from lunch or use 1 ounce less of meat in recipe given. Omit rice in soup if you prefer ½ slice of bread or 2½ saltines with the soup.

Dinner

(For a Person on a 2500 Calorie Daily Diet)

½ cup grapefruit juice   French dressing (1 tbsp.)
2 slices ham   ½ cup squash
*Oven hashed brown potatoes   1 teaspoon butter
    (double recipe)   1 cup milk
1 piece cornbread (1½" cube)   1 medium peach
Tossed salad: lettuce, tomato,   Coffee or tea
    green pepper, celery,
    cucumber with

Calories: 816; exchanges; 2 meat exchanges, 3 bread exchanges, 1 B vegetable exchange, 4 fat exchanges, 2 fruit exchanges and 1 milk exchange.
    *Recipe given. If you like more dressing, dilute the French dressing with vinegar, lemon juice or tomato juice. You may also add a few drops of liquid sweetener.

Lunch
(For 2500 Calorie Daily Diet)

*Chicken salad in tomato cup
2 biscuits
2 teaspoons butter
2 graham crackers

*Apricot whip
1 cup milk
Coffee or tea

Calories: 808; exchanges: 2 meat exchanges, 4 bread exchanges, 1 fruit exchange, 1 milk exchange and 4 fat exchanges.

*Recipes given.

Lunch
(For 2500 Calorie Diet)

*Individual meat loaf
1 large baked potato (4" diameter)
*Cole slaw
1½ graham muffins

2½ teaspoons butter
½ cup applesauce
1 cup milk
Coffee or tea

Calories: 917; exchanges: 3 meat exchanges, 4 bread exchanges, 1 fruit exchange, and 4 fat exchanges.

* Recipes given. Omit one meat exchange at breakfast to make up for the 3 meat exchanges at noon or make meat loaf with less meat.

Dinner
(For 2500 Calorie Daily Diet)

½ cup fresh fruit
*Baked fish with stuffing
½ cup mashed potato
1 cup cooked spinach
½ cup carrots
1 dark yeast roll

2 teaspoons butter
1 cup milk
* Grape frozen ice (serve ¼ of recipe for 1 fruit exchange)
Coffee or tea

Calories: 816; exchanges: 2 meat exchanges, 3 bread exchanges, 1 A vegetable exchange, 1 B vegetable exchange, 4 fat exchanges, 2 fruit exchanges, and 1 milk exchange.

* Recipes given. Use milk for mashed potato from the milk allowed for your meal.

Baked Fish With Stuffing

Haddock fillet (3 oz. raw)
Salt and pepper to taste
1 slice dry bread, crumbled
Onion flakes to taste

1 tablespoon chopped celery
⅛ teaspoon poultry seasoning
2 teaspoons butter
⅛ teaspoon parsley flakes

Sprinkle fish fillet with salt and pepper. Combine bread crumbs, onion flakes, celery, salt, pepper and poultry seasoning, 1 teaspoonful melted butter and a little warm water to moisten the dressing and hold together; spread stuffing over top of fillet. Roll up and hold together with skewers. Wrap up in foil; place in small shallow pan. Bake at 350 degrees for 20 minutes. Unwrap and bake for 15 minutes longer. Test for flakiness. Brush with the other teaspoonful of butter and sprinkle with parsley flakes.

Calories: 304; exchanges: 2 meat exchanges, 1 bread exchange and 2 fat exchanges.

Welsh Rarebit

1 teaspoon butter	Drop of prepared mustard
Dash Worcestershire sauce	½ cup milk
Few grains salt	1 ounce sharp cheese, cut up
Few grains pepper	1 egg
Speck of red pepper	5 saltine crackers

Melt the butter in a small sauce pan and add the seasonings; then add milk and cook over boiling water. Add cheese, stirring until melted. Beat egg and add a little of the hot mixture to beaten egg; add to rest of hot mixture and cook just until heated and starts to thicken slightly. Serve immediately on crackers.

Calories: 344; exchanges: 2 meat exchanges, 1 bread exchange, ½ milk exchange, 1 fat exchange.

Baked Red Flannel Hash

1 small cooked potato	1 tablespoon chopped onion
¼ cup cooked beets	Salt and pepper to taste
¼ cup cooked corn beef	1 tablespoon milk
½ cup cooked cabbage	½ teaspoon butter

Use milk from your cup allowed at your meal. Finely chop meat and measure ¼ cup (solid pack); add chopped vegetables and mix together all ingredients, except butter. Heat butter in a small heavy fry pan, add hash mixture, pressing into an even layer. Cook over low heat until a brown crust is formed on bottom, then place in oven to brown on top under broiler. If your diet calls for more fat, more butter may be used and then turn hash over and cook other side on top of stove.

Calories: 254; exchanges: 1 bread exchange, ½ B vegetable exchange, 2 meat exchanges, 1 A vegetable exchange and ½ fat exchange.

Beef Vegetable Soup

4 ounces cubed beef (fat removed)
1½ cups water
¼ teaspoon salt
Few grains pepper
Few grains Accent
Onion flakes to taste
1 stalk of celery, cut up
1 small tomato, cut up
½ cup potatoes, cut up (1 small)
¼ cup carrots, cut up
1 tablespoon uncooked rice (¼ cup cooked)

Add water and seasonings to cubed beef, which has been fat trimmed. Simmer slowly until meat is almost tender. Then add rice and all of the vegetables and cook until vegetables are tender. Add more water during cooking, if necessary. Season to taste.

Calories: 357; exchanges: 3 meat exchanges, ½ B vegetable exchange, 2 A vegetables exchanges, 1½ bread exchanges.

Beef Shish-Kabobs

3 ounces raw cubed beef (1½" cubes)
2 small tomatoes (optional)
½ green pepper, quartered
½ cup small white onions (about 3)
*Tomato juice dressing

Marinate the beef cubes in some of the dressing for 4 or 5 hours. Using barbecue skewers or metal sticks, alternate beef cubes with onions, green peppers and tomatoes. Brush dressing over all and cook over hot coals, turning frequently until beef is cooked as you desire. Canned or partially cooked onions may be used, if you like your beef rare. Brush dressing over as you cook your shish-kabobs.

Calories: 182; exchanges; 2 meat exchanges, 1 B vegetable exchange, A vegetables, *Recipe given.

Individual Meat Loaf

4 ounces ground beef (3 oz. cooked)
¼ medium onion, chopped
3 saltine crackers, crumbled
¼ teaspoon salt
Dash pepper
½ cup tomato juice (pure)

Combine all ingredients, except tomato juice. Measure out 2 tablespoonfuls of the tomato juice and mix in with the other ingredients. Mix well. Pat into a loaf; place in a small individual baking dish. Pour remaining tomato juice over loaf. Bake at 400 degrees for 20 minutes or until it is done. It would be easy to make four of these loaves and freeze the extra ones for future use.

Calories: 278; exchanges: 3 meat exchanges, ½ group B vegetable exchange, ½ bread exchange.

Chicken Salad In Tomato Cup

2 ounces chicken, cut up	2 teaspoons mayonnaise
2 tablespoons chopped celery	2 tablespoons milk (use from
1 teaspoon onion	milk allowed)
½ cup cooked potato, diced	1 large tomato
Salt and pepper to taste	Lettuce leaves

Combine first four ingredients and season to taste with salt, pepper and Accent. Beat the mayonnaise and milk together to stretch the dressing. Add to the salad. Make a cup out of a tomato by cutting tomato in 8 sides from top almost to the bottom. Open up, fill with chicken salad. Place on lettuce leaves.

Calories: 304; exchanges: 2 meat exchanges, 1 bread exchange, 2 fat exchanges.

Cheese Custard

1 slice bread	1 egg
1 teaspoon butter	1 cup milk
1 slice cheddar cheese, diced	Salt and pepper
(1 oz.)	

Butter the bread using only 1 teaspoon butter. Place in a small casserole and top with the diced cheese. Beat egg, add milk and seasonings; pour over bread and cheese. Place casserole in a pan of hot water. Bake in a moderate oven, 350 degrees, for 20 minutes or until a silver knife comes out clean when tested in the center.

Calories: 429; exchanges: 2 meat exchanges, 1 bread exchange, 1 milk exchange, 1 fat exchange.

Submitted by S. Marjorie Hatch, Bar Harbor, Maine

Hamburg Vegetable Soup

4 ounces lean hamburg (3 oz. cooked)	¼ cup carrots, cut up
	¼ cup turnips, cut up
Onion flakes to taste	¼ cup uncooked macaroni (½
1 teaspoon butter	cup cooked)
1 small can tomatoes	Salt and pepper to taste
1 small can water	

In a small frying pan, melt the butter; add onion and hamburg and cook until just browned. Put tomatoes, water, carrots, turnip and macaroni in a small sauce pan, add hamburg mixture and cook together until vegetables are tender.

Calories: 368; exchanges: 3 meat exchanges, 1 fat exchange, 1 B vegetable exchange, 1 bread exchange, and 1 A vegetable exchange.

Oven Hashed Brown Potatoes

1 small potato, cooked   1 tablespoon onion, chopped
1 teaspoon butter

Brown onion slightly in butter and add chopped potato and mix together firmly. Brown on bottom using just one teaspoon of butter; after bottom of hash is brown, place in oven, under broiler and brown top.

Calories: 113; exchanges: 1 bread exchange, 1 fat exchange.

Cole Slaw

¼ cup vinegar	¼ teaspoon dry mustard
1½ teaspoons butter	⅛ teaspoon celery seeds
Noncaloric sweetener, as	Few grains pepper
desired	Few grains paprika
¼ teaspoon salt	¼ head cabbage, shredded

Bring the vinegar and butter to a boil. Remove from heat and add all ingredients, except cabbage. Cool and pour over freshly shredded cabbage.

Calories: 68; exchanges: 1½ fat exchanges.

Tomato Juice Dressing

½ cup tomato juice	1 teaspoon grated onion
2 tablespoons lemon juice	½ teaspoon Worcestershire
1 teaspoon salt	sauce
½ teaspoon paprika	½ clove garlic, cut up
½ teaspoon mustard	

Mix all ingredients together in a jar and shake well. This will make ¾ cup of dressing. This is the dressing often used by the women in the weight control classes and excellent for diabetics. This counts as zero calories for the diabetic.

Diabetic Jelly

1 package Kool Aid	½ cup cold water
(artificially sweetened)	1½ cups hot water
2 teaspoons plain gelatin	

Soften the plain gelatin in the cold water; then add the boiling water stirring until gelatin is dissolved, and next the Kool Aid. This should be kept in refrigerator and only one batch made at a time. In place of 1½ cups of hot water, part of this could be mashed fruit, using just enough water to dissolve Kool Aid and gelatine or bring fruit to a boil.

Submitted by Ernestine Ingraham, Warren, Maine

Apricot Whip

1 envelope orange dietetic gelatin

½ cup boiling water

4 dried apricots (cooked and
mashed)

Add gelatin to boiling water, stirring until dissolved. Chill in refrigerator until it starts to thicken; beat until it looks like stiff egg whites, then fold in mashed apricots. Pour into individual dishes to set. Calories 40: exchanges; 1 fruit exchange.

Grape Frozen Ice

1 cup grape sugar-free soda

1 cup grape juice, unsweetened

Few drops lemon juice

Mix together and pour into freezer tray or divide into four parts. Use ¼ of this recipe as one fruit exchange.

Total calories: 160; One-fourth of this recipe equals 40 calories and 1 fruit exchange.

Pumpkin Custard

2 cups canned or mashed cooked pumpkin

½ teaspoon salt and ginger

1 teaspoon cinnamon

¼ teaspoon nutmeg and cloves

3 slightly beaten eggs

2 cups non-fat reliquefied dry
milk

Non-caloric sweetener equivalent to 8 tablespoons sugar (see label on your bottle for this).

Combine pumpkin, salt, spices. Add remaining ingredients. Pour into nine five-ounce custard cups and set in shallow pan with one inch of hot water. Bake in moderate oven, 350, about 40 minutes or until mixture doesn't adhere to a knife. Serve warm or chilled. This can be topped with whipped dry milk sweetened with non-caloric sweetener if desired.

Calories: 523 for 9 custard sups; one custard cup: 57 calories.

Submitted by Mrs. Hazel Hills, Warren, Maine

Fresca Orange Salad

1 large package dietetic
orange jello

1 small can dietetic crushed
pineapple

2 cups Fresca

1 apple, chopped

2 stalks of celery, cut up

1½ cups boiling water plus
Pineapple juice to make 2 cups

Dissolve the jello in boiling water, to which the pineapple juice has been added. When it is half jelled add the drained crushed pineapple and other ingredients. Pour into mold and set in the refrigerator until ready for use. Calories 40; 1 fruit exchange.

Submitted by Mrs. Ruth Carlson, Rockland, Maine

Diabetic Cucumber Pickles

1 cup dry mustard	1 gallon vinegar
1 cup salt	Cucumbers
32 (½ grain) saccharin tablets	

Pack cucumbers in jar and fill jar with the vinegar mixture and a small amount of pickling spice. These are ready to eat in three weeks.

Submitted by Hazel Hills, Warren, Maine

Vegetable Salad For Diabetics

1 tablespoon unflavored gelatin	¼ teaspoon favorite food coloring
¼ cup cold water	½ cup sliced radishes
2 cups hot water	1½ cups cucumber slices
¼ cup lemon or orange juice	¼ cup raw cabbage (cut very fine)
¼ teaspoon salt	
2 teaspoons sweetener	

Dissolve the gelatin in the cold water, then add to the hot water, stirring until well dissolved. Add fruit juice, salt, sweetener and food coloring. Set in the refrigerator until partly jelled, then add other ingredients. Pour into mold and refrigerate.

This makes 6 servings of 14 calories each.

Submitted by Mrs. Leon Beal, Waterboro, Maine

Crisp Cucumber Chips

1 quart thinly sliced cucumbers	2 tablespoons sweetener (more if wanted)
¾ cup sliced onions	¼ cup golden brown prepared mustard
1 cup chopped green peppers	½ teaspoon turmeric
1 cup chopped celery	¾ cup water
¼ cup salt	1 cup vinegar

Place vegetables in a bowl, sprinkle with salt, add water to cover. Let stand two or three hours. Drain well. Combine sweetener, mustard and turmeric, add water and vinegar. Bring to a boil; add vegetables, bring to a boil and simmer three minutes. Turn into hot sterilized jars and seal. This makes two pints.

Submitted by Mrs. Hazel Hills, Warren, Maine

The following recipes have been submitted by Mrs. Edna Moore of Warren, Maine. These have all been tested and used many times. Mrs. Moore used Sweetco, but any sweetener, you prefer, may be used. Test your sweetener for the correct amount to use.

Applesauce Cupcakes

1 cup all-purpose flour
1½ teaspoons cinnamon
¼ teaspoon each nutmeg, ginger, cloves, salt and soda
½ cup raisins
½ cup unsweetened applesauce

1 egg
1 teaspoon vanilla
2 teaspoons sweetening solution
¼ cup melted oleo

Sift together in a bowl, flour, spices and soda. Stir in raisins. In a separate bowl combine applesauce, egg, vanilla, sweetening solution and oleo or cooking oil. Add all at once to dry ingredients, stirring only until all is moistened. This makes 12 medum cup cakes. Bake 20 to 25 minutes in a 350 degree oven.

Total calories: 1161; one cupcake equals 97 calories; exchanges for one of 12 cupcakes; ½ bread exchange, 1 fat exchange.

Chocolate Chiffon Pie

2 (8-gram) envelopes diatetic chocolate pudding
1/3 cup cocoa
2 envelopes unflavored gelatine

1¾ cups skim milk
3 egg whites
½ cup whipping cream
*Thin pastry shell

Mix in sauce pan, pudding mix, cocoa and gelatine, slowly stir in enough milk to form a smooth paste. Add remaining milk and sweetening; let stand five minutes. Heat, stirring constantly, until mixture boils. Cool slightly, then cover the surface of pudding with wax paper. Refrigerate until pudding reaches room temperature or is slightly cooled. Beat with hand beater or electric mixer, until consistency of soft whipped cream. Beat egg whites stiff, but not dry. Whip cream and fold both into mixture. Pour into baked or prepared crumb shell. Refrigerate 2 or 3 hours before serving. *For a thin pastry shell, calories have been estimated for using ½ cup flour and 2 tablespoons plus 2 teaspoons of shortening, made the same as regular pie crust, but rolled very thin.

Total calories for filling: 584; total calories for thin pie crust: 534; calories for ⅛ of pie: 140.

Custard Pie

2 2/3 cups skim milk	¼ teaspoon salt
1 tablespoon sweetening solu-• tion	¼ teaspoon nutmeg
	5 eggs

Mix ingredients together and pour in unbaked pie shell. Bake in hot oven 450 degrees for 5 minutes, reduce heat to 350 degrees and bake 15 minutes longer. This can also be baked as a plain custard.

Calories: 552 for custard; thin pie crust: 534; ⅛ piece of pie: 136.

Pumpkin Pie

1½ cups pumpkin	1½ teaspoons cinnamon
1 2/3 cups evaporated milk	½ teaspoon each of ginger,
1 tablespoon sweetening solution (Sweetco)	nutmeg, allspice and cloves
	2 eggs

Bake at 425 degrees for 15 minutes, then reduce to 350 degrees; bake about 30 minutes longer or until a silver knife tests clean.

Calories, filling: 821; thin pie crust: 534; ⅛ piece of pie: 169; if made with skim milk ⅛ piece will have 115 calories.

Muffins

½ cup soy bean flour	2 eggs
1 teaspoon baking powder	½ teaspoon salt
1/3 cup water	

Mix dry ingredients. Beat egg yolks and water; add to dry ingredients. Fold in stiffly beaten egg whites. Bake at 375 degrees, about 20 minutes.

Total calories: 315; one muffin of six equals 53 calories.

Bread

1 cup soy bean flour	2/3 cup water
1 teaspoon salt	4 egg yolks
2 teaspoons baking powder	4 egg whites
1 tablespoon shortening	

Combine flour, salt and baking powder. Add water, shortening and egg yolks and mix well; fold in the egg whites, beaten stiff. Bake in a loaf pan in a 350 degree oven 30 to 40 minutes.

Total calories: 764; One of 12 slices equals 64 calories.

Raisin Bread Pudding

2 cups bread cubes
3 cups skim milk
1 tablespoon sweetening solution
½ teaspoon cinnamon
1 teaspoon vanilla
2 eggs, lightly beaten
½ cup raisins

Soak bread cubes and milk together 5 minutes; add sweetening solution, cinnamon, vanilla, lightly beaten eggs and raisins. Bake at 400 degrees for 15 minutes, reduce heat to 325 degrees and bake 40 minutes or until firm.

Calories: 818; ⅛ portion: 102.

Cream Tapioca Pudding

1 tablespoon tapioca (minute)
1 cup milk
1 egg yolk
Few grains salt
½ tablespoon sweetening
1 egg white
1 teaspoon vanilla

Cook tapioca, milk and salt in double boiler until tapioca is clear. Add beaten egg yolk and sweetening, cook 5 minutes; remove from heat, fold in egg white beaten stiff and vanilla. This is nice served over fruits of all kinds.

Calories: 279; using skim milk: 189.

Pear Tapioca

5 or 6 pears, sliced
1 cup hot water
¼ cup tapioca (minute)
1 tablespoon sweetening solution
¼ teaspoon salt
Few drops of lemon extract

Slice pears into a double boiler; add hot water and tapioca. Cook until pears are tender and tapioca is clear, stirring often. Remove from heat, add sweetening solution, salt and a few drops of lemon extract. Cool. Calories: 384.

Coffee Pudding

1½ cups coffee
1 cup milk
3 tablespoons tapioca (minute)
2 beaten egg yolks
1 tablespoon sweetening solution
¼ teaspoon salt
2 egg whites, beaten
1 teaspoon vanilla

Cook coffee, milk and tapioca together in a double boiler 15 minutes. Add the egg yolks, beaten, sweetening and salt and cook 5 minutes longer. Remove from heat and fold in stiffly beaten egg whites and vanilla.

Calories: 424; ⅛ portion: 53.

Weight Watchers Brown Derby Pie
CRUST

1 cup cornflakes, crushed

2 tablespoons melted butter

1 tablespoon nonfat dry milk

1 teaspoon Sucaryl solution

FILLING

1 tablespoon cornstarch

1 tablespoon Sucaryl solution

½ teaspoon salt

2 cups skim milk

2 eggs, separated

1 teaspoon vanilla

2 teaspoons Sucaryl solution

2 tablespoons cocoa

1 envelope gelatin

¼ cup cold water

2 teaspoons rum flavoring

Crust: Combine all ingredients. Press into 9" pie plate. Bake in hot oven, 375 degrees, about 12 minutes. Save a few crumbs for the top.

Filling: Combine cornstarch, Sucaryl, salt, in top of double boiler. Gradually add milk mixed with egg yolks. Cook over hot water until thick, stirring constantly. Remove from heat. Add vanilla. To 1 cup custard mixture, add 2 teaspoons Sucaryl and cocoa, blending well. Pour into crust. Chill until firm. Soften gelatin in cold water and blend into remaining custard. Stir until dissolved; add rum flavoring, cool. Beat egg whites stiff and fold into custard. Spoon over chocolate layer and chill until set. (6 servings).

Total calories: 754; 1/6 piece of pie: 126 calories.

Submitted by Mrs. Hazel Hills, Warren, Maine

Apple Muffins
(Using Sugar Substitute)

1 2/3 cups all-purpose flour

2 teaspoons Adolph's sugar
  substitute

2½ teaspoons baking powder

½ teaspoon salt

1 teaspoon cinnamon

¼ teaspoon nutmeg

1 egg, lightly beaten

2/3 cup skim milk

¼ cup melted shortening

1 cup minced apples (2
  medium)

Sift flour, sugar substitute, baking powder, salt and spices into mixing bowl. Combine egg, milk and shortening; add to dry ingredients, blend until flour is moistened. Do not over-mix, batter should be lumpy; fold in minced apples. Bake in greased muffin pans in 400 degree over for 20 to 25 minutes.

Total calories: 1478; one of 12 muffins: 123 calories.

Submitted by Mrs. Mary Holmes, Tenants Harbor, Maine

Never Fail Divinity Fudge

3 cups sugar
¾ cup light corn syrup
¾ cup cold water
2 egg whites

1 package orange jello (dry)
1 teaspoon vanilla
½ cup fine coconut
Nut meats

Combine sugar, corn syrup and cold water in a sauce pan and cook to 252 degrees.

Beat the egg whites and orange jello together until stiff peaks are formed. Slowly add the cooked syrup to this stiff egg white mixture. Add the vanilla and beat for five minutes.

Fold in the coconut and drop by teaspoon on to wax paper. Top each piece with a nut meat.

Submitted by Gertrude Moulton, Newport, Maine

Divinity Fudge
(Without egg whites)

3 cups sugar
1 cup milk
⅛ pound butter
Few grains salt

1 jar marshmallow fluff
1 cup walnuts, cut up
1 teaspoon vanilla

Mix together sugar, milk, salt and butter and cook until a hard ball is formed when tested in cold water. Add marshmallow fluff, nuts and vanilla. Beat until it starts to set. Pour into greased pan.

Submitted by Dorothy Flagg, Strong, Maine

Gertrude Smith's Divinity Fudge

3 cups sugar
½ cup red label karo syrup
2/3 cup warm water
¼ teaspoon salt

2 egg whites
½ cup nut meats
1 teaspoon vanilla

Mix together the sugar, karo syrup, water and salt and cook, without stirring after it has dissolved and started to boil. Cook to 250 degrees on a candy thermometer.

Beat the egg whites until stiff and pour the cooked hot syrup over the stiffly beaten whites slowly, beating with the mixer at a high speed until thoroughly mixed.

Add nut meats and the vanilla and beat by hand until the fudge will keep shape when dropped by teaspoon on the buttered pan. Pour into buttered 8½ x 8½ inch tin. Chopped candied cherries may be added for a christmas touch with chopped angelica, or chopped candied cherries in green color. Pistachio nuts may also be used for the green.

Submitted by Mildred Brown Schrumpf, Orono, Maine

Magic Candy
(Basic recipe)

¼ cup butter ¾ cup sugar
½ cup white corn syrup

Combine ingredients together in a heavy one quart sauce pan. Cook, stirring occasionally until mixture boils. Reduce heat slightly and continue cooking to 270 degrees (soft crack stage). Remove from heat. Follow directions, given below, for the kind of candy you want to make. You can make any amount of magic candy by following these simple proportions: 1 part butter—2 parts corn syrup—3 parts sugar.

Butter Toffee

1 cup chopped pecans 1 magic candy recipe
½ cup chocolate chips

Sprinkle the chopped pecans on the bottom of a buttered 9 x 9 x 1¾" pan. Follow basic magic candy recipe. Pour the hot candy over nuts. Cool until set, but still hot. Sprinkle with the chocolate chips; allow chips to soften then spread on top. This may be refrigerated to set the chocolate. This makes 36 one-half inch squares.

I use my electric fry pan for the heat regulator, as I do not have a candy thermometer, and it works fine.

Butter Brittle

¼ teaspoon soda 1 cup salted Spanish peanuts
1 magic candy recipe

Follow recipe for magic candy recipe, except add the salted Spanish peanuts to the butter, corn syrup, sugar mixture after the sugar is melted; then continue to boil with the added peanuts until it reaches 270 degrees (soft crack stage). Remove from heat, add the soda and stir to blend. Pour out on a warm buttered cookie sheet. Spread to desired thickness. When cold crack into pieces.

Submitted by Mrs. Helen Smith, York, Maine

Pop Corn Balls

1 cup molasses ½ teaspoon salt
1 tablespoon vinegar 4 quarts popped corn
1 teaspoon soda ½ cup peanuts (optional)

Boil molasses, vinegar, soda and salt until it tests brittle in cold water. Pour the molasses mixture over the popped corn and mix. Grease hands and form into balls. Peanuts may be added if desired.

Submitted by Mrs. Evelyn Shorey, Bangor, Maine

Toasted Almond Crunch

1 cup margarine (2 sticks)
1 cup sugar
3 tablespoons water
1 tablespoon light corn syrup
½ cup chopped nuts
3 squares semi-sweet chocolate
½ cup ground nuts

Melt the margarine over heat, add the sugar, stirring constantly until sugar dissolves. Remove from heat. Slowly stir in the water and corn syrup. Heat, stirring constantly to boiling; then cook over medium heat, stirring occasionally, wiping sugar crystals from side of pan. Cook to 300 degrees. Remove from heat at once. Stir in the chopped nuts (any kind) and pour into buttered pan. Cool.

Melt the semi-sweet chocolate in double boiler. Spread over the cooled candy. Sprinkle top of candy with the ground nuts. Chill until chocolate is firm. Break into bite-size pieces. This keeps well.

Submitted by Mrs. Evelyn Ware, Skowhegan, Maine

Scotch Toffee
(Baked)

¼ pound melted oleo
2 cups quick cooking oatmeal
½ cup brown sugar
¼ cup dark corn syrup
½ teaspoon salt
2 teaspoons vanilla

TOPPING

1 package chocolate bits
¼ cup finely cut nuts

Mix together above ingredients (except topping) and pour into greased pan. Bake in a 400 degree oven 15 to 20 minutes. Cool slightly, then spread top with one package melted chocolate bits and ¼ cup finely cut nuts.

Submitted by Dorothy Flagg, Strong, Maine

Pop Corn Brittle

1 cup sugar
½ cup water
1 teaspoon vinegar
2 tablespoons molasses
2 tablespoons butter
½ teaspoon salt
Popped corn (3 to 4 quarts)

Boil sugar, water and vinegar together for 5 minutes. Add molasses, butter and salt and boil until it becomes hard and brittle in cold water. Pour over the popped corn, mixing well. Press in greased cookie sheet and when cold break up into pieces.

The lady who gave me this recipe added, "This is the exact recipe, but I use more molasses and add a pinch of soda just before pouring over corn."

Submitted by Mrs. Evelyn Ware, Skowhegan, Maine

178

Date Roll

2½ cups sugar
1 cup milk
1 tablespoon butter

1 package of dates, pitted
1 cup walnuts, cut up
1 teaspoon vanilla

Boil together the sugar, milk, butter and a few grains of salt until it forms a soft ball in cold water. Remove from the fire and add dates and stir until creamy, then add the walnuts. Pour into a wet cloth; shape into a roll; hang on a line to dry; cut as it is needed.

Pecan Roll

2 cups dark brown sugar
1 cup white sugar
1 cup canned milk, not diluted

⅛ teaspoon salt
1 teaspoon vanilla
2 cups pecan nuts, finely cut

Mix together in a sauce pan the brown sugar, white sugar, canned milk and salt, bringing to a boil stirring continually until the mixture begins to boil; if it curdles, it will become smooth when beaten. Cook until it forms a soft ball in cold water. Remove from stove and cool. Add vanilla and beat till creamy; when it begins to stiffen form into rolls with your hands and then roll in chopped pecan nuts. Moisten hands slightly in warm water if mixture gets too stiff. This makes one large or several small rolls.

Submitted by Mrs. Alice N. Pike, Springvale, Maine

Three Minute Fudge

2 cups sugar
2 teaspoons cornstarch
1 tablespoon cocoa

½ cup milk
2 tablespoons butter
1 teaspoon vanilla

Boil mixture for three minutes and beat in a pan of cold water. Pour into greased pan and let cool. This is not too thick, so cut fudge after it cools.

Submitted by Miss Dorothy Perkins, Hampden Highlands, Maine

Chocolate Fudge

4 cups sugar
2 squares chocolate
2 tablespoons butter
1 tall can evaporated milk

1 small jar marshmallow fluff
1 teaspoon vanilla,
1 cup chopped nuts

Cook together, stirring constantly until a medium firm ball is formed, when tested in cold water (234 degrees).

Cool slightly, then add small jar of marshmallow fluff (or 1/3 large jar fluff) and 1 teaspoon vanilla. Beat until cool and creamy. Add 1 cup nuts chopped fine. Pour into buttered pan and cool.

Submitted by Mrs. Doris Hiscock, Livermore, Maine

Sour Cream Candy

2 cups sugar

1 cup sour cream

1 cup chopped walnuts

½ cup chopped raisins

Cook the sugar and sour cream together until it forms a soft ball when dropped in cold water; cool slightly. Add nuts and raisins. Beat until it commences to sugar the same as fudge. Pour into buttered pan.

Submitted by Muriel Polley, Machias, Maine

Never Fail Fudge

1 package confectionary sugar

2 squares baking chocolate

2 tablespoons butter

2/3 cup or small can evaporated milk

1 teaspoon vanilla

Put sugar, chocolate and milk into a sauce pan and bring to boil. Using a timer, boil for 5 minutes.

Remove from heat. Add vanilla, butter and beat for five minutes; use timer. I sometimes add a spoonful peanut butter, nuts or marshmallows, etc. Pour into buttered tin.

Submitted by Evelyn Comey, Shapleigh, Maine

Chocolate Peanut Butter Fudge

2 cups sugar

2 squares chocolate

½ cup milk

2 tablespoons peanut butter

2 tablespoons marshmallow fluff

½ teaspoon vanilla

½ cup walnuts

Boil the sugar, chocolate and milk together until it forms a soft ball in cold water. Remove from fire; add the peanut butter, marshmallow fluff, vanilla and walnuts (if desired). Beat well.

Submitted by Mrs. Evelyn M. Shorey, Bangor, Maine

Peanut Butter Fudge

3 cups white sugar

1 cup milk (or ½ evap. milk and water)

¼ cup oleo

1 tablespoon white karo syrup

Salt to taste

1 pint jar marshmallow fluff

1 12 ounce jar peanut butter (chunk style)

1 cup walnuts, cut up

1 teaspoon vanilla

Cook sugar, milk, oleo, syrup and salt together until mixture forms a firm ball in cold water.

Remove from heat and add the marshmallow fluff, peanut butter, walnuts and vanilla. Beat well until mixture begins to set. Pour quickly into buttered tin.

Submitted by Athena Taft, Rockland, Maine

INDEX

BREADS

CAKES

CANDY

COOKIES AND BARS